Lecture Notes in Computer Scie

Edited by G. Goos, J. Hartmanis and J. van

T0230202

Springer

Berlin
Heidelberg
New York
Barcelona
Hong Kong
London
Milan
Paris
Singapore
Tokyo

Vincenzo Ambriola (Ed.)

Software Process Technology

8th European Workshop, EWSPT 2001
Witten, Germany, June 19-21, 2001
Proceedings

 Springer

Series Editors

Gerhard Goos, Karlsruhe University, Germany
Juris Hartmanis, Cornell University, NY, USA
Jan van Leeuwen, Utrecht University, The Netherlands

Volume Editor

Vincenzo Ambriola
Università di Pisa, Dipartimento di Informatica
Corso Italia, 40, 56125 Pisa, Italy
E-mail: ambriola@di.unipi.it

Cataloging-in-Publication Data applied for

Software process technology : 8th European workshop ; proceedings / EWSPT
2001, Witten, Germany, June 19 - 21, 2001. Vincenzo Ambriola (ed.). - Berlin ;
Heidelberg ; New York ; Barcelona ; Hong Kong ; London ; Milan ; Paris ;
Singapore ; Tokyo : Springer, 2001
    (Lecture notes in computer science ; Vol. 2077)
    ISBN 3-540-42264-1

CR Subject Classification (1998): D.2, K.6, K.4.2

ISSN 0302-9743
ISBN 3-540-42264-1 Springer-Verlag Berlin Heidelberg New York

Springer-Verlag Berlin Heidelberg New York
a member of BertelsmannSpringer Science+Business Media GmbH

http://www.springer.de

© Springer-Verlag Berlin Heidelberg 2001
Printed in Germany

Typesetting: Camera-ready by author, data conversion by PTP Berlin, Stefan Sossna
Printed on acid-free paper   SPIN 10781810   06/3142   5 4 3 2 1 0

Preface

The software process community has developed a wide range of process modeling languages and tools, and methods and techniques to support process management, design, and improvement. The focus of this workshop on software process technology, the eighth in its series, was on the meeting point between software process technology (concepts, languages, tools, methods, techniques) and the practical application of this technology to achieve demonstrable effects on the quality of software products and processes.

During the last workshop, the one held in Kaprun, the participants were engaged in a lively discussion about continuing this series, started in 1990 as an opportunity for the European community to meet and discuss the issues of the emerging discipline of software process. The final decision was to move along this road with an open attitude towards the emerging issues of mobility, distribution, architecture, and new technologies. It was also decided to confirm the attention and the interest on case studies and experiments. Based on these assumptions, the call for papers was prepared and made public.

The response from the scientific community was encouraging: 31 papers were submitted from 13 nations of 4 continents. The program committee selected 18 papers that were formally presented during the workshop in 5 sessions devoted to process evolution, experiences, mobility and distribution, UML process patterns, and process improvement. A keynote speech was given by Frank Leymann on the theme of Web services and their composition.

The preparation of this workshop was successful due to the timely and professional work of the members of the Program Committee: Giovanni A. Cignoni, Reidar Conradi, Pierre-Yves Cunin, Volker Gruhn, Nazim Madhavji, Leon J. Osterweil, Wilhelm Schäfer, and Brian Warboys. Volker Gruhn, as general chair, together with his team made a splendid job of the local organization. Finally, we acknowledge the editorial support from Springer, for the publication of these proceedings.

April 2001   Vincenzo Ambriola

Table of Contents

Web Services and Their Composition

Frank Leymann[1]
IBM Software Group
Schönaicherstr. 220
D-71034 Böblingen
Germany

Web Services gained a lot of attention in the software industry over the last couple of months (e.g. [1, 2, 3, 4, 5, 6]). Roughly, a *web service* is any piece of code that can be interacted with based on Internet technology.

The interface of a web service can be defined via the *Web Services Description Language* (WSDL; see [7]). This language also allows specifying how to bind to a web service, e.g. how to encode the messages to be exchanged, which protocol to use, and the address at which the web service is available.

The most prominent protocol in this area is the XML-based *Simple Object Access Protocol* (SOAP; see [8]). It is a mechanism to describe how to process a message, and it defines a convention for using lower level protocols like HTTP as a remote procedure call (RPC).

Directory facilities that help finding web services that provide particular business functionality are specified in *Universal Discovery Description & Integration* (UDDI; see [9])). These facilities allow providers of web services to publish business aspects as well as technical aspects of their web services. Users that require a particular business function use UDDI query capabilities to find corresponding web services. Finally, users can retrieve the required technical information to appropriately bind to the web service chosen.

Together, WSDL, UDDI and SOAP enable to build software in a *service oriented architecture* (SOA) structure. In this architecture, components are found dynamically by describing functionality needed instead of interfaces required, and components found can be bound and invoked dynamically at runtime.

This enables dynamic electronic business: For example, companies can easily outsource functions offered by other providers as web services. Or functions can be made available as web services for a huge set of potential exploiters very quickly. For this purpose providers describe their software granules via WSDL, wrapper them for SOAP interactions, and publish them in UDDI. And users find appropriate providers in UDDI and invoke their services via SOAP. The relationship between the partners can be just for a single interaction or it can last for a long period of time.

---

[1] LEY1@DE.IBM.COM

V. Ambriola (Ed.): EWSPT 2001, LNCS 2077, pp. 1–2, 2001.
© Springer-Verlag Berlin Heidelberg 2001

The spectrum of granularity of web services reaches from simple functions to complex business processes. Thus, business processes must become web services and must facilitate the interaction with web services. For this purpose, workflow technology (e.g. [10]) is extended towards web services environments.

1.   http://www.ibm.com/developerworks/webservices/
2.   http://www.alphaworks.ibm.com/
3.   http://msdn.microsoft.com/library/techart/websvcs_platform.htm
4.   http://technet.oracle.com/products/dynamic_services/
5.   http://www.sun.com/software/sunone/wp-arch/
6.   http://e-services.hp.com/
7.   http://www.w3.org/TR/WSDL
8.   http://www.w3.org/TR/SOAP
9.   http://www.uddi.org
10. F.Leymann, D.Roller, Production Workflow: Concepts and Techniques, Prentice Hall 2000.

The PIE Methodology – Concept and Application

Pierre-Yves Cunin[1], R. Mark Greenwood[2], Laurent Francou[1],
Ian Robertson[2], and Brian Warboys[2]

[1] LSR-IMAG, University Joseph Fourier, Grenoble, France
{pierre-yves.cunin, laurent.francou}@imag.fr
[2] Informatics Process Group, University of Manchester,
Oxford Road, Manchester M13 9PL, U.K.
{markg, ir, brian}@cs.man.ac.uk

Abstract. This methodology is concerned with technologies for supporting contemporary business processes. In particular, it concerns those that are long-lived, critical to the businesses' success, are distributed and supported on heterogeneous systems. Many of today's organizations fall into this category and, for them to be effective, support technologies must be able to deal with dynamic evolution. This paper describes a methodology offering such a capability.

1   Introduction

There have been a number of methodologies published on the subject of process modelling [1][2][3]. In general, they comprise collections of tools and techniques for structuring the life cycle of a system aimed at developing some process model artefact, be it a descriptive model, a simulation, an analysis model, or an enactable model for workflow or process support environments.

One aspect that these methodologies have in common is that they almost invariably assume that the model, or the behaviour that the model represents or supports, is unchanging or, if it does change, it is of no consequence for the methodology. Where they do consider evolution, it is essentially evolution of the design artefact, not the implemented system. As such, they are of limited use to business in general.

The Process Instance Evolution[1] (PIE) Methodology aims to address this limitation. It is intended to enable the evolution of process instances where these process instances are long-lived, distributed and supported on diverse systems. In other words, to be of real world application. The issues that must be dealt with include: distributed applications, heterogeneous platforms, multiple modelling formalisms and diverse enactment systems.

This paper falls naturally into two parts, Sections 1 to 6 describe the Methodology, Section 7 describes the application with the implementation attached as an Annexe, and Section 8 is the Conclusion.

---

[1]Process Instance Evolution (PIE) is an E.C. Esprit Framework IV LTR project, number 34840.

V. Ambriola (Ed.): EWSPT 2001, LNCS 2077, pp. 3–26

2   The Project

The methodology is one of three major results from the project [4]. The other two are a set of tools to support the definition, execution, monitoring and dynamic modification of ongoing processes; and a platform to federate the heterogeneous tools and components involved in the process, allowing them to interoperate consistently, possibly under various levels of control and automation.

The work is divided into five workpackages, and the Methodology aspect is an amalgam of the results of all workpackages.

3   The Conceptual Domain

The aspect of the world with which this work is concerned is populated by *Process Elements* (PE). A Process Element is a software system that includes some kind of support, to a greater or lesser extent, for human-intensive organizational processes. These processes are characterized by their non-determinism, and their need to undergo dynamic evolution, as a result of real-time re-engineering. The term support is intended in its widest sense and includes, as well as conventional workflow management or process support systems, systems such as Lotus Notes and Microsoft Project. These fall into this category even though they offer no capability for dynamic evolution.

In our approach we consider two kinds of Process Elements: *PIE components* and *PIE applications*. The former are process support systems and tools that provide the specific high-level functionality of the PIE environment, and the latter are usually coordination, process support, or workflow systems in the widest sense that support enacting models capable of evolution. The term also includes systems, that are Commercial Off The Shelf (COTS) applications. These are black boxes which, like the systems referred to above, are not capable of dynamic evolution. They are relevant because they provide essential services to enacting model instances.

A particular system may be categorized differently, deoending on the context. For example a support system such as ProcessWeb ([3] page 199) can be viewed as a PIE component (enacting the Evolution Strategy process model).   It can be viewed as a PIE application, because it is running an enacting process model that can be subject to evolution, and it can also be considered to be a COTS, because part of the system that supports the enacting model is a black box which is not evolvable at run time.

The domain is represented by the *Common Universe* (CU), a repository of, inter alia, references to, and state descriptions of, the systems that participate in the PIE federation. The view of this domain adopted for this explanation of the Methodology is that of a non-specialist manager who is responsible for performance and outcomes of human-intensive processes.

4   Core Rationale

The essence of the methodology emerges from an understanding of the organization, its processes, and how they are controlled. Control in an organization generally uses a mix of two techniques – continuous regulation with respect to a model, and ad hoc decision making in response to situations. Just how they are used is dependent on context. The former involves the continuous detection of events or reading of values, comparison with a plan or template, identifying deviations that are outwith stated bounds, and notifying the user responsible. The corrective action is often well established. An example is monitoring project activity durations with regard to planned durations.

The latter involves the emergence of problem situations to which a responsible user must react, and for which the corrective action is often unclear. Support is needed in assisting users to assess the risks implicit in alternative solutions and to understand the relative importance of different aspects of solutions such as impacts on cost, time and quality. An example of such a situation is the need to revise a product development strategy (possibly initiated by news that a competitor is already doing this).

In both these situations, technology can play a substantial part and this leads to the identification of two key support components: *Monitoring* and *Decision Support* [5]. Both technologies have been under active development for many years. Associated with the use of such technologies, however, is the need to relate one to another in a systematic way. They have dependencies on one another, and they are both factors in the controlling process. This overarching process, referred to as *Evolution Strategy* (ES) [6], has been modelled as the Process for Process Evolution (P2E). This is a meta-process, and it operates on instances of organization processes with the purpose of ensuring that their outputs (in terms of both results and costs) are as close as possible to what is intended. The key control action is that of evolution: the ability to transparently adapt at run-time an instance of an enactable model definition.

Until now, it has only been possible to dynamically evolve model instances within specific environments. The facts of corporate life mean that it must be possible to carry out this evolution across environment boundaries. The organizational, distributed and heterogeneous nature of the Process Elements has certain consequences. Evolutionary change has a time dependency (the state of the enacting process is changing as the evolutionary change is being implemented) and is also dependent on the nature of the PE system. In order to facilitate this change in diverse instances, the *Change Support* (CS) component was conceived. This component, allows specialized change mechanisms to be inserted and thus bridges the gap between identification of desired change and the consistent implementation of that change in a remote heterogeneous environment.

5   Architecture

5.1   Infrastructure

The purpose of the PIE project is the development of tools and techniques to facilitate the management of Process Instance Evolution. In order to address real world issues, it includes the management of multiple, distributed and heterogeneous Process Engines and Process Support Systems or Tools (PSS).

The population of Process Elements is represented in the Common Universe which contains the information about local instances that is required for global processing. This information relates models, meta models, and information about process instances. These are abstract views of the local components. The possible relationships among components are based on a distinctive paradigm that is highly flexible in the spectrum of control behaviour that can exist varying between absolute and lax. This selection of behaviour is defined in *Federation Control* whose rules operate in the Control functions of the *Control and Communication* layer of the *PIE Middleware* [7]. Communication among components is by Message or Service Request. The Common Universe and Federation Control together comprise the *PIE Foundation*. This approach provides for a degree of flexibility that can be responsive to the needs of different organizations and to the need to support evolution in terms of communication behaviour and services. See Section REF6.3 for more information on these aspects of the architecture.

The following figure (Figure 1) describes the global architecture of the PIE federation of components. The upper layer is concerned with the evolution control of the PIE applications, and the lower one is concerned with the PIE applications themselves.

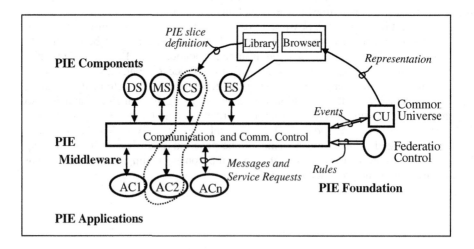

Fig. 1. The PIE Architecture

5.2   Components

Amongst Process Elements, two principal types of components can be distinguished. They are distinguished by their role in the Methodology, and by the federation control mechanisms that they utilize:

- PIE applications. They interact with other members of the federation to achieve the goals of the global cooperative process, and include COTS.
- PIE components. They interact one with another to detect the need for evolution in a PIE Application and then to carry through that evolution. The PIE components are described in Section 6.1.

6   Essential Behaviours

There are of three kinds of essential behaviours from the viewpoint of the users of the Methodology.

- Behaviours associated with particular PIE components.
- Behaviours associated with two (or more) interacting components - either PIE components or PIE applications.
- Behaviours associated with the infrastructure.

6.1   PIE Component Behaviours

The PIE components, together with their associated behaviours are:

Evolution Strategy

Responsible for providing a structure to the federation members identified to the Common Universe, and for providing technologies needed to facilitate the evolution of Process Elements. There are three aspects to Evolution Strategy:

- Structure. Each system in the federation can be represented by a hierarchy of components, and one particularly useful hierarchy, the *PIE tower*, structures the network of components of concern to a particular organization and particular user. The PIE tower is a development of the Peltower described by Greenwood et al [6]. ES provides a browser that allows navigation among nodes, where a node is a package of behaviour related to one (or more) entities in the CU. In effect it provides a browser of the Common Universe.
- Behaviour. Reference was made in REFSection 4 to the behavioural model of ES, the Process for Process Evolution. This remains the driving process model however the need has emerged for additional Decisioning support at the meta-process level that has resulted in the Decisioning for Decision Support (D2P) model [8]. This model is used in association with P2E.
- Resources. ES maintains the *PIE slice* Library. The manager (the user of the PIE tower) invokes operations available in the PIE tower node to apply PIE tools on a selected node, e.g. 'monitoring the instance of hood design with regard to the elapsed time', or 'evolving the instance of hood design from version 11 to version

11a'. The binding of a node to a PIE tool instance (such as CS, DS) is realised by the subscription to events. This is the PIE slice and it is described more fully in the following section.

Monitoring Support

Detecting and measuring imprecise indicators of process performance from the process model instance. The outputs trigger messages notifying the other components of deviations from target performance, or trends that indicate future departures.

MS is invoked by users when they wish to be notified and advised of situations that indicate that process goals might not be achieved. The MS instance is tailored to suit the user, the context, and the particular subject model instance. The conventional monitoring of values is extended to their evaluation with respect to goals and with regard to human perceptions of goal attainment. The entities that are monitored have also been extended to include message patterns. This is the context in which the *Interaction Modelling Language* (IML) was developed [9]. IML defines a valid sequence of messages between components and between components and CU. An implementation of IML in an Interaction Monitoring System (IMS) application will detect an invalid sequence of messages. This can either be reported to the user or prohibited, depending on the configuration of the application, i.e. providing *passive* or *active* control.

Decision Support

There are two key aspects to DS design. One deals with support for alternatives-finding, the other deals with support for process model manipulation. The former provides support to users faced with the need to generate alternative solutions in problem situations. One technique is to identify solutions that were successful in the past, and this is used in an Experience Database. It will be able to hold models of processes that have (successfully and unsuccessfully) been used to address problems in the past, together with outcomes.

The latter aspect of the support provided by DS is the evaluation of the risk associated with multiple outcomes of the enaction of a process model, given the definition, planned outcome and current state of the model instance.

Change Support

Support for making specific changes to an enacting instance. Change is a complex issue and this component is intended to address most aspects of change management - specifying and implementing the change, providing a context for reasoning about change, and preservation of system integrity during change. In order to deal with this complexity, the term CS refers to three interworking sub-components: Change Installer (CI), Change Policy Handler (CPH) and a Constraint Checker (CC).

The primary user interaction is with the Change Installer component and occurs in two distinct phases. The first phase involves choosing the appropriate Change Model for the subject PIE application. This specifies the high-level change modelling language in which the user will define the change, and then the appropriate low-level language for the subject containing primitives from the application. The second phase involves the editing of Change Scripts and their translation into low-level language ready for constraint checking and testing prior to implementation. The Constraint

Checker checks if system integrity is being preserved. This is an important aspect of change as the state of the enacting process instance may be changing as the evolution is actually being implemented.

The Change Policy Handler provides a context for reasoning about the impacts of change. For example, there will be a policies for dealing with integrity violations reported by the CC, or the kind of transactions to be supported.

6.2   System Behaviours

There are only two system behaviours that characterize the PIE methodology, and they referred to as the *PIE slice*, and *PIE evolution*.

PIE slice

This refers to the associating of two Process Elements to achieve some goal. Typically one is a PIE component, such as Decision Support, and the other is a PIE application such as a process model instance running in a workflow system (see Figure 2). This behaviour is under the control of Evolution Strategy. It involves identifying the Process Elements to each other, executing a model (from the model library) that confirms that the elements can respond in a consistent manner to certain messages, and that the responses are in a format that can be understood.

The message pattern is described in Interaction Monitoring Language, stored in the ES Library, and executed by ES.

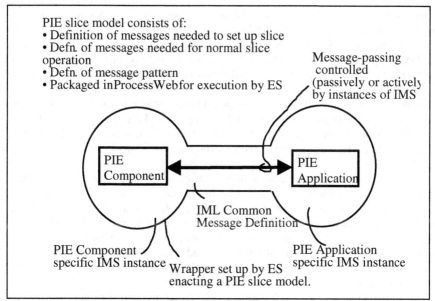

Fig. 2. The PIE slice

PIE Evolution

This involves the evolution of a process model instance at run time on a system alien to that of ES, but one that participates in the PIE federation. It is a combination of a behavioural model and a number of bindings between components, i.e. certain PIE slices.

The model of the evolution process is P2E. It invokes a library model setting up a PIE slice that allows P2E to interact with the target application component (the one that is running the subject process model instance). The user is thus able to determine a new definition for the subject model instance. Once determined, a new PIE slice allows communications with the Change Support component that is responsible for implementing the change. The user then interacts with this component to make the changes to the running instance. The evolution is restricted to PIE applications. The PIE components themselves and components that are COTS are, in general, not subject to evolution however the Middleware has been designed with the utmost flexibility in mind.

6.3   Infrastructure Behaviours

As mentioned in Section REF5.1 the control paradigm over the federation components allows for flexibility, i.e. for communication control to be configurable and for this configuration to be evolvable by a user (control may vary from a 'dictatorial' model to an 'anarchic' one). This can have an effect on the outcome of the process, and is referred to as *PIE customization.*

Which components are used, and the way they are used can affect the achievement of the goals of the global process. Using PIE customization, messages and service requests can be manipulated by the Middleware to best use the federation resources. For example, where Decision Support is needed, a user might wish to interact with any DS component, with a specific DS component, or a combination of services that together offer DS functionality. The Middleware can accommodate such preferences.

It may be appropriate for a service process to be executed concurrently on more than one system, and for the results compared before selecting the best. Alternatively, if time is a constraint, the first result can be accepted, and the others cancelled.

Evolution can be facilitated by PIE customization. If a component API evolves, the original API service can be maintained by introducing a service request mapping in the Middleware.

The middleware controls the communication, either the notifications sent and received by components or the API calls to change the CU. The control is configurable in order to manipulate the communication in a way that is invisible to end users. Thus the notifications or calls can be rerouted or modified according to the model put in place by the Manager (at a strategy level for example). In the same manner, at a lower organisational level, some adaptation can be done dynamically to change and improve the process (modifying the data flow) without impact on the organisational model.

The management of the behaviour of COTS components is performed by the Federation Control of the PIE Middleware. As COTS can be considered as black boxes, the common universe represents an abstract view of some of the knowledge of each COTS and any change in the CU must be propagated in the real world of the components. Being autonomous, each component may also change the CU unexpectedly. The federation designer defines the Operational model to describe how components have to react to CU changes, which components are involved and when. To define this model and compose the link between the federation and the components, the federation support provides to the federation designer some concepts among which *Aspects* and *Roles*:

- An *Aspect* defines an operation in the CU at a high level of abstraction. It defines which component must do what and how to control it.
- A *Role* decouples the Aspects from actual components, and defines the federation behaviour at a logical level. A Role can be considered as a virtual high level component (facilitating reuse and evolution) and can be attached to one or more components.

7   Application and Illustration of the Methodology

This section details concrete process experiences taken from fields that are familiar to the industrial members of the PIE consortium. From this description, we derive typical process-oriented problems that are either not supported, or inadequately supported by current process support technologies (Section 7.1 following). In Section 7.2 the emerging issues are discussed, and we then describe how the scenario would execute if solutions to the described problem were available (in Section 7.3). Finally in Section 7.4 we point out the PIE contribution in terms of such solutions. The implemented scenario is listed as an annexe.

Throughout this section we adopt the point of view of a user, as opposed to a solution provider. Such a user, as mentioned in Section 3, is a manager responsible for performance and outcomes in an organization where processes are human-intensive.

7.1   A Deviation Process in a Design Variant Study

The scenario described below is taken in the context of the automotive industry and deals with the design of a variant of an existing car that causes a 'deviation process' to be put in place. For the purpose of this paper, those processes are simplified and 'depersonalised'.

Step 1- (new hood preliminary design)
The body-in-white[2] department modifies the design of the hood for a given car model. The context is the study of a new sport variant for an existing car platform.
Actors: Body-in-white Department.
Input: Previous hood shape and sketches from the Style Department.
Output: New hood shape.

---

[2] Body-in-white (BIW) designate the subdivision of the design office that designs the external shape of the vehicle from specifications issued by the styling department.

Step 2 - (Integration test)
The packaging department checks the integration of the new hood shape with its environment. A problem appears. Although the specification for the new hood was that the shape of the headlights should not change, digital mock-up shows that this is not the case. The front shape of the headlight fits perfectly with the external shape of the hood, but this is not the case internally: the rear part of the headlights now interferes with the new hood shape.
Actors: Packaging department.
Input: New hood design.
Output: Problem report and associated data.

Step 3 - (Decision to study alternative)
A decision meeting with the product line manager takes place. A decision is made to launch a recovery process (conciliation process, deviation process) consisting of:
• Headlight variant study that would have the same front shape, but be more compact on the rear side. Constraints are that new headlight cannot be more than 20% more expensive than the previous one, and that it should be equipped with new generation bulbs in order to maximise the payback of the study. Results have to be available within one week in order that overall project planning is not put at risk.
• Hood modification study that allows old headlight to fit in, as an alternative solution.
Actors: Product line manager, head of BIW, head of Packaging.
Input: Clash reports from packaging, hood and headlight designs.
Output: Engineering order for equipment design office and BIW office.

Step 4.a - (New headlight design)
Equipment Design office sketches in 3D the envelope for the new headlight.
Actors: Head design office.
Input: Clash reports from packaging.
Output: New envelope for headlights.

Step 4.b - (Hood modification)
BIW studies how new hood can be modified to support existing headlights while still meeting styling requirements.
Input: Current hood design and headlight shape.
Output: Hood design variant.

Procurement Process
The procurement department starts using its general procurement process.

Step 5.a - (RfQ Procurement)
Procurement department prepares a Request for Quotation to send to headlight suppliers.
Actors: Procurement department
Input: New headlight shape and specifications (bulbs) from Headlight Design Office; quantities and durations from project planning; cost constraints; list of approved suppliers.

Step5 .b - (Design tradeoff)
Hood design variant is less compliant to Design Office specifications.
A conciliation meeting is held.
The Hood design has to be reworked until it fits with the specifications, e.g. redoing step 4.b or some other appropriate action.
...

Output: An official request for quotation sent to the suppliers.

Procurement process evolution
The procurement department decides to take this opportunity to try a new procurement process, by replacing its usual Proposals Evaluation Process by an external 'internet-based' auction process. Suppliers are not informed about that change (they have already received the RfQ).

Step 6.a - (RfQ Supplier study)
Suppliers study RfQ and submit bids.
Actors: Suppliers.
Input: RfQ from procurement
Output: Quotations.

Step 7.a - (Auction RfQ Supplier selection)
A supplier selection process through electronic auction, offered by an internet based marketplace, is used in order to select one of the received quotations. The procurement department informs the product manager that new headlights can be obtained under the specified constraints.
Actors: Supplier, procurement department, internet-based auction service.
Input: Quotations.
Output: Confidence about succeeding to get new headlight CAD.

Step 8 - (Design option decision)
As soon as enough confidence is gained in the success of the procurement alternative the product manager (project leader) decides to go with the 'new headlights' option, based on the progress of the two alternatives studied. The hood redesign option is stopped.
Actor: Product manager.
Input: Information from steps 7.a and 5.b.
Output: Decision to pursue with the new headlights option, hood redesign option to be stopped.

Step 9 - (headlight CAD delivery)
A proposal is selected and the headlights CAD are sent to the procurement department by the selected supplier. The procurement department delivers it to the integration process. This step ends the recovery of the clash.
Actor: Selection process (auction service), procurement department, supplier
Input: Specs for new headlights, project leader decision.
Output: Headlight CAD.

7.2   Scenario Analysis: Why Are New Process Management Capabilities Needed?

What can be observed from this process at work?

Processes Are Intricate

Industrial companies are often tightly integrated, and the trend is towards more and more integration. As a result, their processes too have to be integrated and cannot be considered separately one from another. Here the procurement process, which is itself a complex process, is triggered by the design process, one that is an even more complex.

Processes Need to Evolve Independently

Companies' performance relies upon their ability to change their processes in a permanent way. But this has to be done in an insulated manner: if procurement changes its way to select a supplier, this should not affect its client processes, the design and supplier processes.

Processes Are Not All Completely Planned

A static, build-time definition of processes, as commonly found in many commercial offerings today, do not take into account two fundamental situations of the real world: accident and innovation. Accident occurs when something goes 'wrong', that is to say, not as planned. In the plan for this scenario, the old headlight was intended to be usable in the new hood design. But the requirement was, as quite often, somewhat ambiguous, and as a result plans, and hence process, had to be changed 'in real time'. From this fork point on, the process applied was in deviation from that planned, and was designed along with the solution itself. A second factor is innovation. Winning companies always reinvent the way they do things in order to improve. This is the opposite of the 'business as usual' philosophy that lies behind most workflow management systems. In our example, the product manager (project leader) took the opportunity, since a new design study for a headlight was needed, to include in that study a technology change (bulbs). This decision, headed towards innovation, cannot be made if the process management system cannot take into account its implications.

Planned Processes Are However Still Needed

This is not to say that we need very soft process models that almost anybody can change at any moment. All product security related processes, for instance, are of course mandatory, and cannot be shortcut just because the product is 'late in planning'. So both flexibility and control over that flexibility is required.

Federation of Processes Requires Encapsulation

In the negotiation between Procurement and Suppliers in the example, we observe a federation of processes at work. Each supplier has its own process (formal or not) to respond to Request for Quotation. Clearly the global car design process here spans across companies' boundaries, from carmaker to suppliers, each of the supplier's processes being enacted in parallel. From the procurement process perspective, each of those external processes has to be considered in a similar way, despite their differences in implementation. As a consequence, there is a need for making very different processes encapsulate their implementation and present a common neutral interface to other processes that are their clients.

Information May Be Needed or Produced on Demand
Traditional workflow approaches separate the data they manipulate between action flow and data flow. Action flow models the steps of a process, and the current state of a process instance with regard to its model. Data flow models which data is needed or produced by the steps of the process. In the example above, it is difficult to predict which data are needed by each step. Important steps in this process are decision steps, when for instance design alternatives previously studied are compared and one of them is elected as the preferred one. Coding at process 'build time' what information is needed at each step can be a handicap to good decisions, because the decision maker can decide on the fly to add, or even generate a new piece of information to the file in order to justify his decision. For instance, after the headlight decision, the product manager (project leader) could decide to produce a 'Policy Statement' document for the project, saying that further arbitrating decisions should be made in order to privilege style over cost, with a 20% limit. Such a document cannot be forecast as a result of the process at process design time.

Decisions Can Be Made on Partial Information
In step 8 above, a decision is made not to continue with a new hood design because the other alternative being studied, new headlight design, is *likely* to produce a preferable result. This is an example of using information to guide processes that are not in the black-or-white range. The more complex the processes, the more useful this capability. If processes are only deterministic (something that works with today's technology), then all the non deterministic logic that goes along with them will be taken in charge by human brains. Although it works, this solution is not optimal because then control over the process is weaker: different people, or the same people at different moments, can make different decisions. Furthermore, this cannot be captured as an enrichment of the process intelligence. It is part of the 'art' of the product manager (project leader) to know that stopping the new hood design is the better decision at this point. The consequence of having only process management systems that process black-or-white information is that the processes they pilot cannot be somehow intuitive, nor can they 'learn' by themselves while executing.

7.3 Life in a Better World

Now imagine how the innovative process management technologies, developed in PIE, could change the way such a process is handled.

7.3.1 Finding the Problem
Step 1- (new hood preliminary design) and *Step 2 - (integration test)* are conducted in the same way. It is expected that the Process Management System (PMS) manages the list of the people (each person with his tasks) in the departments in charge of the

conducted tasks. This means that this process (the definition of the design for the hood for the sport variant) has to be linked to some more general process (e.g. the sport variant car overall design). Even if different PMS's are used for overall design of the sport variant and the sub process that redesigns the hood, the two processes still communicate with each other.

The association of a PIE component, (such as Decision Support) with a process model instance running in a workflow system can be configured under the control of Evolution Strategy. This is called a 'PIE Slice'. This configuration of what is valid or not in the communication between the two process elements of the associations adds some flexibility in the strategy for the evolution of processes.

7.3.2 Detecting the Need for Process Evolution
While inconsistency is detected during integration test, monitoring support is actually going to report that the operational process cannot progress anymore.

7.3.3 Designing a Deviation Process
As soon as the hood vs. headlight problem is discovered, the Product Manager (project leader) knows that he has to modify the current flow of process so as to solve the problem. To do so, he uses a process editor, and retrieves from the company approved processes database the nominal process he was supposed to execute. For solving such an integration problem, an experience data base can propose alternative solutions, for example :
- A new design of the product parts (e.g. hood redesign), or
- the procurement of a product from a supplier (e.g. new headlights), or
- to implement several solutions in parallel.

Thanks to the impact and risk analysis functionality, the Decision Support tool shows that it could be worth while exploring the redesign of the hood together with the procurement of new headlights. Thus, the decision is made to launch the study for a headlight variant and hood redesign. The Product Manager graphically designs a new version of the process that he calls 'Recovery process: Sport version hood vs. headlight conciliation process'. He designs the additional threads in the process ('study new headlight design', 'study new hood version', etc.) and details for each step the actors, mandatory inputs, expected outputs, etc.

7.3.4 Exploring and Monitoring Alternatives
Now the (recovery) deviation process can start. All the staff and teams that are involved in it are notified that a process in deviation impacts them. They receive the new process description so that they can see where they fit in to the big picture.

The Product Manager should also modify monitoring so that the hood and headlight design activities will produce parts that are consistent one with another. This might involve the way that activities report progress to monitoring which would feed information to the PMS so that it could help in the making of choice.

On the procurement side, the sub-process is monitored by a 'chance of success' variable. It indicates the confidence of the procurement system in succeeding to find a suitable supplier. There will be interactions between new Hood design and Headlight procurement, and these will be monitored. The interaction monitoring system (IMS) is launched and configured with a message pattern indicative of success.

7.3.5 Selecting Design Alternatives

This likelihood of success, attached to the procurement sub-process, indicates to the project leader that procurement is confident that they can succeed. This knowledge is used by the IMS to indicate to the project leader that the BIW office should cease design work on the new shapes for the hood, thus allowing economy of resources. By doing so, time is not only saved in the BIW office, but also in the Styling Department, as the number of loop-back meetings will be reduced.

7.3.6 Selecting the Supplier

Once the Procurement department has sent a Request for Quotation (RfQ) to a set of potential suppliers, it enacts its own supplier selection process. Once again, this process is able to communicate with other processes that may be implemented on different systems, thanks to a process interoperability framework.

This framework enables communication between distributed processes (e.g. suppliers' Quotation Submission processes), yet allows these communicating processes to evolve independently from each other (the supplier can improve its own submission process during a Request for Quotation).

The Procurement department decides to replace the initial selection process on the fly (without informing the suppliers and other participants) by an internet auction based sub-process in order to experiment with it and to assess its potential.

This experiment should have no impact at all on the whole process and should remain 'invisible'. This does not concern the PMS of the upper level management. The Middleware that controls the federation of processes provides the necessary support through redirection and transformations which keep the change hidden.

7.3.7 Resuming the Process

The recovery process ends with:
- the selection of the 'best' proposal by the internet auction process.
- the provision by the selected supplier of the design for new generation headlights that complies with stated constraints (integration, cost, time, etc.)

Then the nominal process can resume and proceed as initially planned.

7.3.8 Managing Process Libraries

Now the deviation process is over and the crisis has been overcome. But the process that has been developed and put in operation can be used the next time such a situation occurs.

So the product manager stores the process in the company's process bank, along with the information necessary to retrieve it the next time that it is needed.

Similarly the proposal selection based on the internet auction process has proved its efficiency and flexibility. The Head of the Procurement department decides to create a new procurement process model and to keep it in his private bank for later experiments (for a more complete assessment before validation at the company level).

7.4   The PIE Contribution

The scenario has been purposely developed without precise references to PIE technologies, in order to focus on the user perspective, and to describe problems with no *a priori* about solutions.

Here is an attempt to position PIE as a potential contributor to solve issues outlined by this sample process.

7.4.1 Evolutive Federation of Processes

PIE will be useful in providing articulation between processes that are not defined nor run by the same PMS. Rather like the Internet web, a company is an endless network of interrelated processes that produce and consume deliverables of all kinds. This is neither limited in time (processes are born, live, and die continuously), nor in space (processes cross company boundaries).

In our example, the design process relates to the procurement process, that itself relates to processes at external suppliers, and so on. Of course, these processes do not necessarily have to be managed by the same PMS but they still need to cooperate.

The Evolutive Federation of Processes has to provide a framework that allows such processes to interact closely and evolve independently.

The Internet based auction mechanism provided by the electronic market place is, in itself, running an auction process that selects the best bid amongst several. This process is not included in the hood/headlight process as defined in the beginning of the scenario, but comes into the play following a decision by one of the actors (the procurement department.). This illustrates the fact that the general hood/headlight process is evolutive: it must operate a new process as a sub process (the auction) within the course of its execution. Those processes have to act as a federation, because it is very likely that they are managed by different PMSs. Lastly, they are distributed, because the auction process is living in some virtual place on the internet, outside of the boundaries of the companies that use it.

This 'on the fly' adaptation is intentionally kept hidden as much as possible and has no impact at all on the rest of the process. The PIE Middleware provides the mechanism to achieve this through the management of the communication layer services between the components (processes, tools, PMS) of the federation. This is PIE customization.

7.4.2 Proactive Monitoring Support

PIE provides tools to detect the need for process change, as in this case when the integration test points out inconsistency between products. A decision has to be made so that the operational process can restart.

When modelling the deviation process, care should be taken to make sure that no clash will occur again during the subsequent integration test. That could be done by monitoring specific parameters published by enacting design activities.

Thus PIE needs to provide tools for gathering the necessary data on running processes so as to feed Decision Support. In our example, for instance, the Product Manager should not have to continuously wait for the progress of the procurement sub process. The process interaction monitoring is proactive, so the Product Manager can propose that a decision might be advisable. Since two sub processes are running in parallel as alternatives, and one of them is likely to be able to achieve its goal, it might be a good idea to decide to abandon the other.

7.4.3 Change and Decision Support
Change and decision support are illustrated in our sample by the tasks conducted by the supervisor. It illustrates the need for impact and risk analysis and shows the difference between the two.

The supervisor could query an Experience Database provided and populated by Decision Support. In our scenario, Decision Support could suggest the exploration of the two design alternatives in parallel when looking for a deviation (recovery) process.

What is expected from PIE are technologies for the efficient in measurment of risks and impacts for a given change. The PIE system can act as a Corporate Knowledge database (process libraries, technological links issued from product definition, etc.) integrator which exploits them for the benefit of process evolution, as well as providing strategies for detecting process-optimisation opportunities.

7.4.4 Evolution Strategy Support
One of the key properties of the defined evolution process is its ability to recurse. This means that the same process model can handle evolution at any level in an organization. Thus, looking at the PIE tower framework, the evolution mechanism operates at each and every node, not simply at the root node, and the same mechanism is available at all nodes.

This means that the processes and process instances to which nodes refer are all capable of independent evolution. However if the evolution of one instance interferes with another, then there has to be a corresponding co-evolution of the second process. The need for this is identified by a 'Verify' operation provided with each node.

This scenario illustrates this point very well. There are two cycles of evolution, one within the other. The first cycle of evolution is the Choice, Design, Implementation and execution of the Recovery process. The second cycle, taking place within the context of the previous cycle, and under the control of another instance of the evolution process, is the adaptation of the Procurement process instance to incorporate an experimental Internet Auction process.

The actual process models used are chosen from a number of available models. There is no single 'best' model for, say, developing the car hood. There is usually a choice and this choice needs to be accessible by the Project Manager (PM), thus the need for the process library. The Model Library is a repository for all models needed by the PIE components. These are not restricted to conventional process models, but include models that are used by ES to set up PIE slices or PIE evolutions. For example, the model that allows the PM to monitor an instance of the Integration process is kept here, and the model of the evolution of the Procurement process (but not of the Internet Auction process) is also kept here.

These process models - the Methods that the PM uses to achieve certain results, can when instantiated themselves be evolvable. For this to be possible, they simply need to be packaged not as a Method but as a Method node. They thereby acquire many of the properties of the Pie tower including the ability to spawn further methods or method nodes and thus be fully evolvable in the fullest sense of the term.

The evolution process model has itself evolved in the conceptual sense. There are two examples: one is P2E, and the other is D2P. The former assumes that no support is needed by the user in choosing appropriate solutions, and the later provides such support when needed. The choice of which model to use is made by the user.

8   Conclusion

The project from which this Methodology has emerged set out to determine what computer-assisted services are needed to support human-intensive processes, i.e. those that are long lived, distributed, assembled of heterogeneous components, mobile, and subject to dynamic evolution. The project is ongoing however a substantive lesson is emerging.

The project was illustrated originally with the notion of a non-specialist manager evolving an instance of an enacting process model, with the manager participating in a meta-process, and the enacting process model being a subject process. This notion has itself evolved, as illustrated in the demonstration application where:

- Multiple levels of control are accommodated.
- Alternative meta-process definitions could be instantiated and enacted.
- User-tailored monitoring can set prescribed bounds to be interaction patterns as well as property values.
- Technology support of the decision process that is integrated into the business process itself.
- The support to the change process can be as simple or as complex as need be.
- Complex transient changes can be supported at the process level and at the communications level as appropriate.

All technological approaches have contributed to the development of the Methodology. Each will contribute to its particular domain, but the current aggregation of results indicates the significance of recursion support. Two of these contexts are illustrated:

- Both the meta process and the subject process mentioned earlier can each be composed of meta-process/process tuples which can recursively contain more tuples at deeper and deeper levels in the organization. In other words if the meta process or the subject process is refined, it will reveal control elements and subject elements within it.
- The need for a process and associated meta-process has emerged in the PIE components other than ES, i.e. MS, DS and CS. This is needed to ensure that the functionality of the component is operating as intended, and that there is provision for evolution if need be. In fact the concept of Change Support can take the dimensions of a project with its own enactable process (the transient change process), together with its own meta-process and support components.

Successful generic methods and tools will need to be capable of supporting recursion to a greater extent than has hitherto seemed necessary.

By realizing Process Instance Evolution, the PIE project will have made a contribution to narrow the gap between the needs of the organization and the capabilities of the machine.

References

[1] Castano S., De Antonellis V., Melchiori M. 1999. *A methodology and tool environment for process analysis and reengineering,* Data and Knowledge Engineering, Vol. 31, pp 253 - 278.

[2] Konsanke, K., Zelm M. 1999. CIMOSA modelling processes. *Computers in Industry.* Vol. 40, pp 141-153.

[3] Warboys, B.C., Kawalek P., Robertson I., and Greenwood R.M. 1999. *Business Information Systems: a Process Approach.* McGraw-Hill, London.

[4] Cunin P.Y. 2000. *The PIE Project: an Introduction,* Proceedings 7th European Workshop on Software Process Technology. Lecture Notes in Computer Science, Vol. 1780, pp 1 - 5, Springer Verlag.

[5] Alloui I., Beydeda S.,Cîmpan S., Gruhn V., Oquendo F., Schneider C. 2000. *Advanced Services for Process Evolution: Monitoring and Decision Support,* Proceedings 7th European Workshop on Software Process Technology. Lecture Notes in Computer Science, Vol. 1780, pp 21 - 37, Springer Verlag.

[6] Greenwood R.M., Robertson I., Warboys B.C. 2000. *A Support Framework for Dynamic Organizations,* Proceedings 7th European Workshop on Software Process Technology. Lecture Notes in Computer Science, Vol. 1780, pp 6 - 20, Springer Verlag.

[7] Gugola G., Cunin P.Y., Dami S., Estublier J., Fuggetta A., Pacull F., Rivière M., Verjus H. 2000. *Support for Software Federations: the PIE Platform,* Proceedings 7th European Workshop on Software Process Technology. Lecture Notes in Computer Science, Vol. 1780, pp 38 - 53, Springer Verlag.

[8] Oquendo F., Robertson I., Papamichail K.N. 2000. *Overcoming Inadequacies in Process Modelling: The need for Decisioning to be a First Class Citizen,* Proceedings 7th European Workshop on Software Process Technology. Lecture Notes in Computer Science, Vol. 1780, pp 84 - 89, Springer Verlag.

[9] Alloui I., Oquendo F. 2001. *Supporting Decentralised Software-Intensive Processes using Zeta Component-Based Architecture Description Language,* 3d. International Conference on Enterprise Information Systems (IECIS 2001), Abal, Portugal, July 7-10 (to appear).

Annexe: The Implemented Scenario

Step	Actor	Action	Tool (s)	Comments
Phase 0: Initialise processes				
1	Project Leader (PL)	Hood Design Process	ES APEL	Assume the hood design process ("HoodDesignProcess") has reached the Integration Test in the Packaging department
2	PL	Start the activity "CADIntegration".	ES APEL	It is up to the PL to start the activity either from ProcessWeb or from his agenda (APEL). The activity is assigned to a performer who is involved in the packaging process (let's say the head of the Packaging Dept = HPD) with "hoodCAD" as input.
3	PL	Launch the Monitoring of the progress of the activity "CADIntegration".	ES, MS APEL	Create the PieSlice with MS (using a MS model "activity progress" from a library)
Phase 1: Detect the need for change				
4	Head of the Packaging Dept (HPD)	Logon to open the agenda and performs the integration test.	Term APEL	We suppose that "TestIntegration" is the unique activity of the sub-activity "CADIntegration".The HPD receives the activity "TestIntegration" with "hoodCAD" as input.
5	Auto	Reports the clash problem.	APEL AMS	After the integration failed, the HPD reports the clash problem through a reporting message.
6	Auto	MS captures the event related to the clash problem detected at the packaging phase.	MS	MS captures the message on the clash problem and handles it..
7	Auto	The potential impact of the issue on the overall project is evaluated.	MS	MS analyses the clash event captured before and concludes that most likely there will be a delay for the hood redesign that might go beyond the fixed deadline (the situation is assessed in terms of effort, progress and state).
8	Auto	Send a notification to the Project Leader.	MS, ES	The MS notifies the project leader about the risk for the project to not meet the deadline.

Phase 2: Design the recovery Process				
9	PL	Search a corrective action by using ES. The PL decides to use DS/D2P support.	ES	The ES response to this feedback is to invoke Decision Support operating on the process model instance.
10	PL	A corrective action is searched.	DS	Values and alternatives are provided to DS by D2P. DS Experience DataBase suggests dealing with the problem by proposing several solutions: 1) carrying out an additional procurement process 2) redesigning 3) manage both tasks in parallel
11	PL	Decision is taken		PL decides to choose the running of the Design Process and the Procurement Process in parallel
12	PL	Ask for a recovery process.	ES DS	PL asks ES whether anything exists in the Experience DB. Return: Nothing!
13	PL	Browse the process database, visualise the nominal process to assess the situation. Create the model for the recovery process	ES APEL	Depending on the level of process description, the PL may use ProcessWeb or APEL for browsing the process DB starting from the car variant design , down to the hood design process. PL uses the Apel model editor to define the Hood Design Process and the Procurement Process running in parallel.
14	PL	Modifies the current flow of the nominal process by adding dynamically a new instance of the recovery process .	ES ->CS	The Change support attach the recovery process as a new activity to the nominal CAD integration process
15	PL	Requests ES to launch the recovery process.	ES APEL	All people that are part of the deviation process are notified. They receive the new process description (not automated).
16	Auto	Start in parallel the two design alternatives.	ES APEL	As soon as the deviation process is launched, the sub-processes "HoodCADProduction" for the revised hood design and "HeadlightDesignStudy" start. The second one is now monitored.

Phase 3: Enact the Recovery Process under MS control				
17		Setup Interaction Monitoring in the recovery process. The interaction to monitor is between PL and Hood design, and between PL and Headlight procurement.	MS	set up PieSlice MS(Interaction Monitoring) - Recovery Process, with interaction pattern to be matched
		To make the demo shorter, we suppose that the headlight study consists of three activities (rather than three sub-processes in the real scenario) "ProduceHeadlightSpec" carried out at the Engineering Dept, "FindAndSelectSupplier" at the Procurement Dept, and "SupplierProposal" performed by a supplier. Consequently, We will assume the first step has been completed, a Headlight Spec has been produced, and that the first activity of interest is "FindAndSelectSupplier".			
18	Head of Proc Dept (HPD)	The supplier selection activity "FindAndSelect Supplier" is started.	APEL	Following the assumption taken in the previous step, this step should be performed through the activity "FindAndSelectSupplier".
19	HPD	The multiple activity "Supplier Proposal" is started.	APEL	
20	HPD	The RFQ is sent to supplier candidates through process instances created at once along with the "headlightSpec".	ES APEL	The output RFQ from "FindAndSelectSupplier" activity is sent out to candidate suplliers in the same time.
21	HPD	The Procurement Department decides to evolve their process by incorporating an InternetAuction process.	ES APEL	For each supplier, the activity "SupplierProposal" is tracked continuously through progress reports. The final output of the activity is "headlightCAD". Once the RFQ has been sent out, and proposals received, this sub-process is evolved by: (a) using an external process "InternetAuction", (b) Diverting messages destined for FindAndSelectSupplier to InternetAuction (the Proposals), (c) sending messages from Internet Auction to Supplier proposal (OK / not OK). The final result (headlightCAD) is sent from the selected SupplierProposal to FindandSelectSupplier.

22	HPD	Installation of the process Internet Auction and of the redirection of the messages to IA process	ES Middleware	as defined above
23	Auto	Proposals are submitted and redirected to IA	Middleware	
24	Auto	MS is informed about the message pattern has been matched in the IA process in the procurement department	MS	likelihood Of Success is verified when at least one proposal of a Supplier is found "acceptable"
25	Auto	MS notifies the ES of the likelihood Of Success of the procurement.	MS	
Phase 4: Decision on Conciliation				
26	Auto	ES informs the PL that a decision is requested.	ES	
27	PL	Seek DS recommendatio n	ES DS	ES invokes DS. DS answers: Least risk with minimum cost and delay is to Buy-in headlights. PL interacts via DS UI
28	PL	PL accepts DS recommendatio ns: he requests ES to manage the new hood design discarding.	ES	
29	ES	ES cancels "HoodCADProd uction" and its monitoring.	ES MS	
30	HPD	Internet Auction selects a Supplier		In parallel with 26 to 29
Phase 5: Resumption of Integration Test				
31	Supplier	Finish the recovery process.	APEL	The selected supplier produces the "headlightCAD"
32	HPD	"CADIntegration Process" is resumed at the Packaging Dept. After	APEL	Using data "hoodCAD" (as the new hood design is dropped) and the "headlightCAD" supplier's design. Test OK: the process "SportCarDesignProcess" can continue.

		completion of the recovery process.		
33	PL	Records successful outcome to Experience DB	ES DS	

ES: Evolution Support	AMS: APEL Message Server
CS: Change Support	PS: Process Server
MS: Montoring Support	

Reflection and Reification in Process System Evolution: Experience and Opportunity

R. Mark Greenwood[1], Dharini Balasubramaniam[2], Graham Kirby[2], Ken Mayes[1],
Ron Morrison[2], Wykeen Seet[1], Brian Warboys[1], and Evangelos Zirintsis[2]

[1] Department of Computer Science, The University of Manchester,
Manchester, M13 9PL, UK.}
{markg,ken,seetw,brian}@cs.man.ac.uk
[2]: School of Computer Science, The University of St Andrews,
St Andrews, Fife, KY16 9SS, UK.
{dharini,graham,ron,vangelis}@dcs.st-and.ac.uk

Abstract. Process systems aim to support many people involved in many processes over a long period of time. They provide facilities for storing and manipulating processes in both the representation and enactment domains. This paper argues that process systems should support ongoing transformations between these domains, at any level of granularity. The notion of creating an enactment model *instance* from a representation is merely one special case transformation. The case for thinking in terms of model instances is weak, especially when process evolution is considered. This argument is supported by our experience of the Process*Web* process system facilities for developing and evolving process models. We introduce the idea of hyper-code, which supports very general transformations between representation and enactment domains, to offer the prospect of further improvements in this area.

1   Introduction

In the process modelling research community we often adopt a simplistic view that business, or software, process modellers aim to [3, 4, 5]:

1. Model a process using a textual or diagrammatic representation. (This model is often called a process model definition. It is at a class or type level and static.)
2. Translate (or compile) the model into some library form within a process support system (PSS).
3. Instantiate the library model to give a process model enactment. (This is often called a process model instance. It is dynamic and consists of some set of entity or object values within the PSS.)
4. The PSS runs the model enactment to support the process performance of a specific process instance.

There are of course design decisions about the important features of the process that we want to capture in our model, and support by process technology.

V. Ambriola (Ed.): EWSPT 2001, LNCS 2077, pp. 27–38, 2001.

The underlying assumption is that the textual or diagrammatic model represents current best practice, and one of the main benefits of modelling is to disseminate this to all process performance instances.

In this paper we argue that this view is a special case of a more general process support architecture. First, it is based on a single process class; we need to consider how a process support system will support many processes within an organization. Second, we should be thinking more generally about the relationship between the textual or diagrammatic representation, which we manipulate as process modellers, and the set of values within a process support system, which represent a specific model instance. In particular, we will argue that giving too much emphasis to the one-way translation from representation to values/entities places artificial limits on the potential of process support systems. We describe the hyper-code technology [2, 21] and illustrate how this promotes thinking about a more general two-way "round trip" translation, which can be performed many times throughout the lifetime of the process.

Two-way translation is important when we consider the wider context of observing enactment state, perhaps to debug it, and reusing code and data within a PSS. We will illustrate our argument using details from the ProcessWeb [14, 18] system with which we are most familiar. We believe that ProcessWeb is a reasonable representative of the state of the art, and our argument does not depend on the specific details of how various facilities are provided in ProcessWeb.

2   Process System Viewpoint

At any point in time a process support system (PSS) will include a set of process descriptions within its library. For each of these descriptions there may be zero or many process instances, each with their own specific state information. The PSS supplies some general environment facilities to all models. For example, most process instances may involve multiple users and each user may be involved in multiple process instances, not all from the same description. As a user logging on and off the PSS is orthogonal to the progress of the process instances, the logging on and off facilities apply across all models. Indeed users may log onto the PSS when they are not involved in any process instances. The PSS must also provide facilities that allow users to navigate around the current descriptions and instances, and to bind users to specific roles or activities in a process instance.

We can think of a PSS as a virtual machine, or operating system, that runs process services. Each process enactment instance is a process service and has a corresponding description.

The ProcessWeb system is based on the object-based language PML [13]. This has four base classes: roles, actions, entities and interactions. A role instance is an independent thread with local data and behaviour. An action instance is the PML equivalent of a procedure or method invocation. An entity instance is a data structure, and an interaction instance is a buffer for transferring data between roles. In ProcessWeb:

A Process description takes the form of a *set of PML classes*, and the name of a designated main class. There is a library structure of these descriptions, indexed by their main class name.

A Process instance consists of a network of PML role instances, linked by interaction instances. They are created by the built-in action *StartRole*. A unique name, provided at instantiation, is used to index each current process instance. (In Process*Web* the details of process instances are deleted when they complete, but they could be moved to a separate library of completed process instances.)

The environment facilities are provided in two ways. There is a set of Process*Web* specific PML classes that can be referenced by name in the process descriptions. These can be used for stateless information: for example, generic PML classes for the user interface, or accessing an external Oracle database. There are also environment facilities that provide information specific to the current state of the PSS as a whole. In Process*Web* these are provided by 'management roles'. Whenever a process instance is created it is given a link (interaction) with one of these. This *Manager* role gives the process instance access to environment information through a set of request types to which it will reply.

The key point for our argument is that while process enactment instances are independent of each other, they exist in a common environment. We do not expect a separate PSS, with its own users, state etc., for each instance. Conceptually the PSS is a virtual machine that runs forever. Even without considering process instance evolution, which we will return to in section 6, the PSS as a whole evolves: for example, through the introduction of new process descriptions, of new users, and the creation of new instances.

3   Reflection

The issue that we skipped in section 2 is how we get from a textual or diagrammatic process representation to a description as a set of classes within Process*Web*. In Process*Web* the technique used is linguistic reflection, which is defined as:

"the ability of a running program to generate new program fragments and to integrate these into its own execution" [10].

The PML language includes a built-in action *Compile*. PML is a textual language and the PML source for a model is input to the PSS as a *String*. *Compile* takes as input this source string and an environment, which is a *set of PML classes*. It produces either an error message, of type *String*, or a new environment, which consists of the input environment plus the newly compiled classes.

In terms of linguistic reflection, the program is the Process*Web* system itself. The Process*Web* models are the new program fragments through which it extends itself. Process*Web* includes in its description library a *Developer* model. This gives access to the *Compile* action, where the initial environment contains the PML and Process*Web* standard classes.

For this paper, the key point is not the choice of linguistic reflection (or the detail of its implementation in Process*Web*), but that there must be some mechanism so users can incrementally add new process descriptions into a running PSS. This will involve translating a model from the textual or diagrammatic representation used by a process modeller into the corresponding set of object/entity values within the PSS. In addition, there must be ways of establishing links with the generic environment provided by the PSS.

Linguistic reflection also offers benefits in terms of the ability of Process*Web* to evolve itself as well as its process models while still running and providing a service to its users.

4   Reification

It is no surprise to learn that not all Process*Web* models are perfect. Sometimes there are run-time programming errors. Sometimes the models just don't provide the expected process support for their users. When things go wrong a very important question is "What is the current state of this model instance?" The modeller needs information about the current state of the model, and possibly the PSS more generally. This can be provided by reification: the ability of a system to provide a concrete representation of aspects of its internal state. The full benefits of reification are available when these concrete representations can be manipulated as first-class language values.

If the current state is not deducible from the model's input, output and source text description then the modeller will usually resort to the diagnostic facilities. (The main advantage of the diagnostics is that they are interactive. There are programmable facilities for examining the current state, see section 6, but these are not as easy to use.) The Process*Web* diagnostic facilities provide text results in the general form:

```
<variable name> : <type name> = <string representation
                 of the value>
```

Where the value is a PML object, e.g. an interaction instance or a role instance, then the value string will contain a unique identifier that can be given as a parameter to the relevant diagnostic command to provide additional information.

By issuing a series of diagnostic commands and noting the answers a modeller can build up a picture of the model instance's current state. However, the representation provided for the results from diagnostics is quite different from the PML source text representation. In essence, we are doing the inverse of instantiation. We start with a set of values within the PSS, which are the process instance, and transform them into a representation of the current state for the modeller. When looking at the current state a modeller is often interested in a specific part of the model instance rather than the complete picture. It is often clear from the run-time error, or the observed problem, that it is a specific part of the problem that needs to be examined.

It is worth noting that errors do not have to be in the model instances. A specific model instance may expose errors in the general environment facilities. As more models are written new useful environment facilities that can be shared between models are discovered. In Process*Web* the diagnostic facilities can be used to give a representation of the state of the environment as well as the model instances since they are all written in the same language.

5   Hyper-Code

Hyper-code is a refinement of the concept of hyper-programming [8, 9, 20], in persistent programming language research. In hyper-programming a program is no longer a linear sequence of text, but contains both text and links to objects in the environment that exist when the program is being constructed. This takes advantage of the fact that, in persistent systems, programs can be constructed, stored and executed in the same environment. In traditional programs, where a program accesses another object during its execution, it contains a textual description of how to locate the object [11]. This is resolved to establish a link to the object itself. Typically this is during linking for code objects, and during execution for data objects. The benefits of hyper-programming include:

- being able to perform program checking early: access path checking and type checking for linked components may be performed during program construction
- increased program succinctness: access path information, specifying how a component is located in the environment, may be omitted
- being able to enforce associations from executable programs to source programs
- support for source representations of all procedure closures: free variables in closures may be represented by links

Hyper-code takes these final two benefits a step further. In hyper-code [21, 22] the programmer sees only a single, uniform, program representation throughout the software lifecycle. The Hyper-Code Representation (HCR) is presented at all stages of the software process: during process construction, enaction, debugging and the inspection of existing data and code values. The representation for creating new values and browsing existing values is the same. This maximizes simplicity for the programmer. It also means that there is no longer any distinction between an editor for creating new values, and an object browser for examining existing values. All programmer interaction with the system takes place through a single unified hyper-code editor. This blurs the distinction between compile time, bind time and run time.

In the hyper-code view of the programming lifecycle, any programming system can be described in terms of two domains and four primitive operations, which operate over the domains. The two domains are **E** (entities) and **R** (representations). **E** is the domain of language entities: all the first class values defined by the programming language, together with various non-first class entities, such as types, classes and executable code. **R** is the domain of concrete representations of entities in domain **E**. A simple example is the integer value *seven* in **E** and its representation 7 in **R**. The domain **E** can be divided into executable and non-executable subsets.

The four domain operations (illustrated in Fig. 1) are:

- *reflect*: maps a representation to a corresponding entity ($\mathbf{R} \Rightarrow \mathbf{E}$)
- *reify*: maps an entity to a corresponding representation ($\mathbf{E} \Rightarrow \mathbf{R}$)
- *execute*: executes an executable entity, potentially with side effects on the state of the entity domain ($\mathbf{E} \Rightarrow \mathbf{E}$)
- *transform*: manipulates a representation to produce another representation ($\mathbf{R} \Rightarrow \mathbf{R}$)

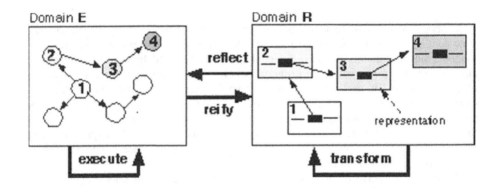

Fig. 1. Domains and domain operations

These abstract definitions may be interpreted in various ways for different concrete hyper-code systems. For example execute could involve strict, lazy or partial evaluation of an executable entity. The style of representation produced by reify could vary. The transform operation could be unconstrained, allowing any representation to be produced, or limit the possible representations as with a syntax-directed editor.

It is not intended that a user accesses these domain operations directly. A user only interacts with the system through an editor that manipulates HCRs. [21] proposes a set of hyper-code editor operations, based on the experience of building a hyper-code system for Java.

- Edit is essentially transform.
- Evaluate takes $r \in \mathbf{R}$, reflects r to the corresponding $e \in \mathbf{E}$, and executes e. If this produces a result $e_{res} \in \mathbf{E}$ then this is reified to $r_{res} \in \mathbf{R}$, and r_{res} is displayed in the editor.
- Explode and Implode respectively expand and contract a selected HCR to show more or less detail, while retaining the identities of any values referred to. They both use reflect and reify.

Note that in a hyper-code system, during design, execution, and debugging, users only see HCRs. Entities such as object code, executable code, compilers, linkers, which are artefacts of how the program is stored and executed, are hidden from the programmer, since these are maintained and used by the underlying system.

We return to the simplistic view from section 1, and review it from a hyper-code viewpoint.

1. Model a process using a Hyper-Code Representation (HCR) - (*transform*)
2. Translate this into a Process Support System (PSS) - (*reflect*)
3. Instantiate ? - (no corresponding primitive domain operation)
4. Run the model using the PSS - (*execute*)

There is a mismatch as there are no clear equivalents for instantiate and reify.

The purpose of instantiate is to get multiple process instances that follow the same definition. There are two ways this could be done without having instantiate built into the system. We could use transform to make a copy of a chosen representation and apply reflect to the copy, giving a distinct entity for execution. Alternatively, the representation could be not of a process instance, but of a process instance generator (constructor function). This could be executed many times; each execution having the side-effect of producing a new process instance within domain **E**.

As we have argued in section 4, reify is a familiar operation to those who develop and debug process models running on process support systems (although often only a limited form of reification is available). The fact that there is no corresponding transformation in the view, with which we started, is because of its simplified nature. There is an inter-relationship between instantiate and reify. Instantiation is often used as a way of keeping a reference between a model's source representation and its current enactment instances. However, in a system that supports reification the source representation can always be recovered. If required some source representation comparison tool could be used to identify whether or not two enactment instances belong to the same class.

The concept of developing a process model, represented in some source format, and then creating multiple model enactment instances to support the process embodies connotations of timing and granularity. The assumption is that there is some specific creation time at which this occurs, and that it occurs for the whole model at this time. The hyper-code viewpoint is more general in that reflection and reification can occur throughout the life-time of entities, and because they can be applied at whatever level of granularity not just at the model instance level.

One conclusion is that instantiation is not a fundamental concept that needs to be primitive within a process environment. It may be very useful in many modelling contexts, a common process design pattern perhaps? This is reinforced by the fact that there are some processes, e.g. a business's budget allocation process, for which there should only be one instance within a PSS. In addition, it is very much a business modelling decision whether an insurance company wants to think about one instance per policy, or one instance per customer, or indeed one instance for the whole company.

6   Evolution

Within process modelling, thinking about ongoing transformations between source representations and their corresponding PSS entity values is common in the context of process evolution. The arguments for evolution in process systems are based on three main themes. First, organizations evolve their processes and the models of these must be kept up to date, otherwise process support systems hinder rather than enhance process performance. Second, organizations frequently have management processes for monitoring and evolving their operational processes, and these meta-processes can be modelled and supported. Third, many processes are themselves long-lasting and incrementally developed, with later parts being dependent on results from earlier ones.

The simplest evolution for process systems to support is at the representation level. A modeller makes changes to the textual or graphical representation. This may then replace the changed process within the PSS library, or be made available through a new name or version identifier.

By allowing a lazy transformation from representations, a process system can support some evolution of a running model. Rather than have a single instantiation of the complete process at creation time, the translation from representation is done incrementally. The initial parts of the process may proceed at the same time as the representations for later parts are being created and changed. Indeed, if the environment provides a process with facilities to access and update representations that it will use in future, then earlier parts can create or modify the representations that will be used later. (This is analogous to many common situations, e.g. where part of a software development project is to define the testing procedures to be used by the project at a later date.) This approach blurs the distinction between process design and process execution. If we think of instantiation it is of process model fragments, which need to be combined with existing process enactment fragments, rather than instantiation of complete process models.

Both of the evolutions described above are in a sense anticipated. In Process*Web* terms they do not involve any new facilities that have not been described previously. They do not cater for the case where a running model needs to be changed to take unexpected requirements (including working around run-time model errors).

The facilities in Process*Web* for unexpected run-time (instance) evolution are based around being able to change the code for a PML role instance. More extensive changes consist of a number of related role instance evolutions. The evolution is programmed in PML. In essence, one PML process is the meta-process that is evolving another. The basic sequence is based on several pre-defined PML actions described in the following table.

(There is a simpler sequence *FreezeRole*, *ExtractRoleData*, manipulate table of data values, *InsertRoleData* and *UnfreezeRole* that can be used if only the unexpected change of local data values is required.)

Collectively these PML actions provide a powerful set of evolution mechanisms that have been exploited in research into process model evolution and its support [6, 7, 15, 18, 19]. They are however quite complex to use, and thus frequently the source of errors. When an error means that you need to evolve the meta-process, which you created to evolve another process because of its error, mistakes are easy to make.

PML is a textual language. This means that when writing the meta-process there is no way that the developer can refer directly, at development time, to the role-instances of the process being evolved. The binding between the meta-process and the process it changes is at meta-process run-time. The new PML source for a role instance cannot refer directly to any of its current values. This is why the code and data parts have to be treated rather differently in Process*Web* evolution.

Using the hyper-code terminology, the meta-process, when it runs, must reify the evolving process into a representation that it can manipulate, and then reflect to complete the evolution. The representation for code is a PML String and for data a PML table mapping resource names to values. For code, the reification is done by *GetRoleClasses* and *GetClassDefinition*, and part of the reflection is done by *Compile*. For data, the reification is done by *ExtractRoleData*. The final part of the reflection is done by *BehaveAs*. This must check the consistency of the new code and the data to which it refers. For example if the code includes the definition of an

Table 1. Basic sequence for evolving a PML role instance

Step	PML action	Effect
1	*FreezeRole*	This is used to suspend the role instance
2	*ExtractRoleData*	This returns the current local data values (resources) of the role instance as a PML *table (resouce_table)* indexed by the resource name.
3	*Compile*	The new code for the role instance is created and compiled (*Compile*) into a *set of PML Classes*
	(optional) *GetRoleClasses GetClassDefiniti on*	If required the current source for the role instance can be extracted. *GetRoleClasses* is used to get the *set of PML Classes* and the role class name given when the role was started (see *StartRole* in section 2). These can be passed to *GetClassDefinition* to get the role's current source as a PML String.
	(assignment command)	The *table* of local data values *(resouce_table)* extracted from the role is updated so that it contains those required when the role re-starts according to its new definition.
4	*BehaveAs*	This is used to change the code of the role instance. Its parameters include the new set of PML Classes and the new role class name, and the table of initial data values. *BehaveAs* also restarts the role instance so that its execution will continue

Integer resource named "x" and in the data table "x" has a String value then there is an error. (In PML, *BehaveAs* offers two options: fail if the code and data do not match, or just discard the data binding and continue.)

The experience of Process*Web* illustrates that reflection and reification are at the heart of effective process evolution support. The restrictions imposed by the linear textual nature of the PML language are a major factor behind the complexity of the facilities required to evolve Process*Web* models. One final note about evolution in Process*Web* is that it is supported at the granularity of the role instance. While one role instance is being evolved, others conceptually in the same model can still be running.

Process evolution at the enactment or instance level is normally thought of in terms of modifying code. There is some process code written that needs to be changed. Any required data modifications are a secondary effect. We can look at this from an alternative perspective. Process evolution involves the current process code being suspended (and never restarted) yielding a set of entities within the PSS that represent the current state. It is replaced by new process code that refers to as much of that current state data as required. The key problem is how to refer to the current state data when writing the source of the new process code. Clearly, a facility to include hyper-links to existing data in the source makes this much easier. With a hyper-code approach it would be possible to be constructing the new process code at the same time as the old process code is executing, and thus minimize the changeover time between old and new process code. Another advantage of hyper-code is the ability to reify and reflect at whatever level of granularity is appropriate for the required evolution. This contrasts with Process*Web* where the pre-defined PML actions for evolution (see Table 1) only operate at the granularity of roles.

7   Conclusion

At EWSPT'94 Dowson and Fernstrom's paper [3] discussed the idea of three domains: process definitions, process (definition) enactments, and process performance. Their diagram (page 92) includes one arrow from definitions to enactments. This is typical of the emphasis given to a single transformation from a representation domain (definitions) to an entity domain (enactments). We believe that a process support system needs to support the ongoing transformations between these domains. There is substantial benefit in thinking more generally about reflection, the transformation from representations to entities, and reification, the transformation from entities to representations. These are fundamental in a PSS. The one arrow in Dowson and Fernstrom's diagram is probably because their paper concentrates on the idea of separating the enactment and performance domains, and the relationship between these domains. They do later refer to the need for reification. "At the very least, a process manager making a change to an enactment needs to be able to inspect its current state, and tools supporting the presentation of views of enactment state are needed."

A hyper-code approach that would offer process modellers, using a PSS, a single source representation throughout the life of their model appears very promising. It means that developing, monitoring, debugging and changing can be interwoven as the modeller sees fit. The ability to link to existing entities within the PSS when constructing new hyper-code models would make re-use of model fragments easier. It would also greatly simplify the complexity the modeller currently faces when dealing with process evolution.

One issue to be resolved in how the primitive hyper-code domain operations should best be packaged and made available as concrete operations in a hyper-code process modeller. The concrete operations from the Java hyper-code system may not be the most appropriate. If we compare with Process*Web* there was a separation between suspending the thread associated with a role instance, and the reification to data structures that can be manipulated. Is this a separation that should be kept, should there be an option on the concrete operations that use reify? [21] reports some work on using a hyper-code representation (HCR) to trace the execution path of an entity during its evaluation.

This paper does not offer any measured benefits of the hyper-code approach. The importance of the underlying thinking certainly resonates with our experiences with the Process*Web* PSS. For example, the ability to reflect and reify at whatever granularity is appropriate, rather than just in terms of model instances. Our experience with Process*Web*'s facilities for evolution is that the problems of referring to existing data in new code are a major source of complexity.

The emphasis given to model instances seems to be closely tied to the single representation to entity transformation. In the context of ongoing transformations between the domains the case for instances is much weaker. Process evolution also weakens the concept of a instance, where it refers to identifying the generic process description that an enactment conforms to. We argue that model instances are not fundamental to a PSS. It is just as valid to think of describing and enactment as enacting a description. Less emphasis on instances also encourages us to think more generally about process fragments, in both the representation and entity domains, and how they can be developed, composed, separated and re-composed. This is one of the motivations for our interest in incorporating the benefits of architecture description languages (ADLs) in process modelling languages and support systems [1]

The final observation from this paper is that there are system as well as modelling language issues in the design of a PSS. In [17] we mentioned instances as an issue in our design of a second generation process language. Discussions at EWSPT'98 and the separation of process and language requirements discussed in [16] made us review this. Our preference is for a PSS that is a virtual machine [12], and therefore closely related to the language it executes. However the issues discussed in this paper are important to any PSS system, irrespective of its chosen implementation technology. On reflection, many of the issues around instances concern providing a process system supporting many models over time, rather than the expressive power of a process modelling language.

Acknowledgements. This work is supported by the UK Engineering and Physical Sciences Research Council under grants GR/M88938 and GR/M88945 (Compliant Systems Architecture).

References

1. Chaudet, C., Greenwood, R.M., Oquendo, F. and Warboys, B.C.: Architecture-driven software engineering: specifying, generating, and evolving component-based software systems. IEE Proc.–Software 147, 6 (2000) 203–214
2. Connor, R.C.H., Cutts, Q.I., Kirby, G.N.C., Moore, V.S. and Morrison, R.: Unifying Interaction with Persistent Data and Program. In: Sawyer, P. (ed): Interfaces to Database Systems. Springer-Verlag, In Series: Workshops in Computing, van Rijsbergen, C.J. (series ed) (1994) 197–212
3. Dowson, M., and Fernström B.C.: Towards Requirements for Enactment Mechanisms. In: Proceedings of the Third European Workshop on Software Process Technology, LNCS 775, Springer-Verlag, (1994) 90–106
4. Feiler, P.H., and Humphrey, W.S.: Software Process Development and Enactment: Concepts and Definitions. In: Proceedings of the 2nd International Conference on Software Process, Berlin, (1993) 28–40
5. Finkelstein, A., Kramer, J., and Nuseibeh, B. (eds): Software Process Modelling and Technology. Research Studies Press, (1944)
6. Greenwood, R.M., Warboys, B.C., and Sa, J.: Co-operating Evolving Components – a Formal Approach to Evolve Large Software Systems. In: Proceedings of the 18th International Conference on Software Engineering, Berlin, (1996) 428–437
7. Greenwood, M., Robertson, I. and Warboys, B.: A Support Framework for Dynamic Organisations. In the Proceedings of the 7th European Workshop on Software Process Technologies, LNCS 1780, Springer-Verlag, (2000) 6–21

8. Kirby, G.N.C., Connor, R.C.H., Cutts, Q.I., Dearle, A., Farkas, A.M. and Morrison, R.: Persistent Hyper-Programs. In Albano, A. and Morrison, R. (eds): Persistent Object Systems. Springer-Verlag, In Series: Workshops in Computing, van Rijsbergen, C.J. (series ed) (1992) 86–106.
9. Kirby, G.N.C., Cutts, Q.I., Connor, R.C.H. and Morrison, R.: The Implementation of a Hyper-Programming System. University of St. Andrews (1993)
10. Kirby, G.N.C.: Persistent Programming with Strongly Typed Linguistic Reflection. In: Proceedings 25th International Conference on Systems Sciences, Hawaii (1992) 820–831.
11. Morrison, R., Connor, R.C.H., Cutts, Q.I., Dustan, V.S., Kirby, G.N.C.: Exploiting Persistent Linkage in Software Engineering Environments. Computer Journal, 38, 1 (1995) 1–16
12. Morrison, R., Balasubramaniam, D., Greenwood, R.M., Kirby, G.N.C., Mayes, K., Munro, D.S. and Warboys, B.C.: A Compliant Persistent Architecture. Software Practice and Experience, Special Issue on Persistent Object Systems, 30, 4, (2000) 363–386
13. ProcessWise Integrator: PML Reference Manual, ICL/PW/635/0, April 1996. PML predefined class definitions available at http://processweb.cs.man.ac.uk/doc/pml-ref/Index.htm (accessed on 18 Jan 2001)
14. Process*Web*: service and documentation http://processweb.cs.man.ac.uk/ (accessed on 18 Jan 2001)
15. Sa, J., and Warboys B.C.: A Reflexive Formal Software Process Model. In: Proceedings of the Fourth European Workshop on Software Process Technology, LNCS 913, Springer-Verlag, (1995) 241–254
16. Sutton, Jr., S.M., Tarr, P.L., and Osterweil, L.: An Analysis of Process Languages. CMPSCI Technical Report 95-78, University of Massachusetts, (1995)
17. Warboys, B.C., Balasubramaniam, D., Greenwood, R.M., Kirby, G.N.C., Mayes, K., Morrison, R., and Munro, D.S.: Instances and Connectors: Issues for a Second Generation Process Language. In: Proceedings of the Sixth European Workshop on Software Process Technology, LNCS 1487, Springer-Verlag (1998) 135–142
18. Warboys B.C., Kawalek P., Robertson T., and Greenwood R.M.: Business Information Systems: a Process Approach. McGraw-Hill, Information Systems Series, (1999)
19. Warboys, B. (ed.): Meta-Process. In Derniame, J.-C., Kaba, B.A., and Wastell, D. (eds.): Software Process: Principles, Methodology, and Technology, LNCS 1500, Springer-Verlag (1999) 53–93
20. Zirintsis, E., Dunstan, V.S., Kirby, G.N.C. and Morrison, R.: Hyper-Programming in Java. In Morrison, R., Jordan, M. & Atkinson, M.P. (eds): Advances in Persistent Object Systems. Morgan Kaufmann (1999) 370–382
21. Zirintsis, E., Kirby, G.N.C., and Morrison, R.: Hyper-Code Revisited: Unifying Program Source, Executable and Data. In Proc. 9th International Workshop on Persistent Object Systems, Lillehammer, Norway, (2000)
22. Zirintsis, E.: Towards Simplification of the Software Development Process: The Hyper-Code Abstraction. Ph.D. Thesis, University of St Andrews, (2000)

Monitoring Software Process Interactions:
A Logic-Based Approach

Ilham Alloui, Sorana Cîmpan, and Flavio Oquendo

University of Savoie at Annecy - ESIA - LLP/CESALP Lab
B.P. 806 - 74016 Annecy Cedex - France
{alloui, cimpan, oquendo}@esia.univ-savoie.fr

Abstract. Due to distribution, complexity, heterogeneity and time consumption of nowadays processes, interaction of process elements has become a key issue to monitor. Process support environments are required that allow the process manager (typically a project manager) to continuously receive information from the enacting process (the subject process) in order to detect both problematic situations such as deviations with regard to interactions that are considered as valid and "improvable" situations where better use can be done of project resources. This position paper claims that to this problem, logic-based approaches represent a suitable solution. A formalism for defining interaction monitoring models and the interaction management system that enact them are briefly presented. The industrial relevance of this work is currently being demonstrated in the framework of the PIE ESPRIT IV 34840 LTR Project.

1. Introduction

Distribution, complexity, heterogeneity and time consumption of nowadays processes have led to the need for process support environments that enable the follow-up and monitoring of such processes. Process monitoring aims to prevent from/detect deviations that may cause the failure of the whole project, especially for real industrial processes which are complex and subject to permanent change [1]. Among aspects to be monitored, interaction of process elements appears as a key issue. By interaction we mean both direct message exchange and the consequence of an action on a process element (i.e. not necessarily through message sending).

An important requirement is therefore:

Process support environments should provide means both to define monitoring models for process elements' interactions and to follow up ongoing interactions during process enactment.

Indeed process support environments are required that allow the process manager (typically a project manager) to continuously receive information from the enacting process (the subject process) in order to detect: (a) problematic situations such as deviations with regard to interactions that are considered as valid; (b) "improvable" situations, i.e. situations that can optimise utilisation of project resources (e.g. human, time, etc.).

V. Ambriola (Ed.): EWSPT 2001, LNCS 2077, pp. 39–46, 2001.

Validity of interactions can be either at a syntactic level, i.e. related to ordering constraints on message exchange or on a semantic level, i.e. related to the state of achievement of the intention that motivated a message sending. Examples are when a process element requests information or a service from another process element, the process manager needs to know if the intention behind the request has been achieved or not, if it has been withdrawn, if it is impossible to achieve, etc. As other intentions may rely on these results, support is needed by the process manager to be informed of all consequences on the remaining ongoing interactions. Examples of situations that could lead to optimising resource consumption are when an interaction becomes useless, i.e. the intention to be achieved is no longer necessary or when it has already been achieved by another process element (e.g. an experienced performer may be allowed to issue a document for very common requests using predefined standard documents, therefore bypassing the work of the person usually assigned to this task).

In both kinds of situations (problematic and improvable) monitoring provided to the process manager may range from very simple tracing to more sophisticated system able to automatically elaborate new information on process elements' interactions. For instance, the monitoring can compute consequences of a deviation on other interactions to prevent from future deviations.

In the existing process support environments one generally can never know at every moment if requests being performed by the others have been successful or not. This usually relies on human way of working. A computerised support would not be needed if users systematically communicate with each other the interaction state of process elements they are responsible for. Therefore to meet the requirement cited-above, our approach is to provide users (i.e. process managers) with an active guidance[1] [2] during process enactment. This position paper introduces IML (Interaction Modelling Language) formalism for defining interaction monitoring models and IMS (Interaction Management System) that enact them. Both are logic-based. Section 2 describes the background as well as the key features and concepts of IML for meeting the requirement cited above. Section 3 summarises the main contribution of our approach to the stated problem and presents ongoing work.

2.   A Logic-Based Approach for Process Interaction Monitoring

Process interaction monitoring is itself process-oriented as depicted by Fig. 1. Indeed the chosen lifecycle consists of: (a) a modelling phase, where the interaction models are defined by a process engineer using IML; (b) an enactment phase where defined models are instantiated for a given subject process, and afterwards enacted by IMS in order that a process manager monitors the process elements' interactions. The definition, instantiation and enactment of interaction models are orthogonal to the enactment of the subject process. That means that we can define monitoring on processes that are already being enacted.

---

[1] Active guidance is defined as the ability of process enactment mechanisms to provide the users with advises or information relevant to the current performance state.

The proposed approach for interaction monitoring is based on intentions (i.e. it is goal-driven) [3, 4]. Among the key concepts of IML is the concept of message that contains the intention that motivates the sending of the message by a process element.

The reference model for monitoring considers a software process as a set of process elements that interact by means of message passing in order to achieve some process goals.

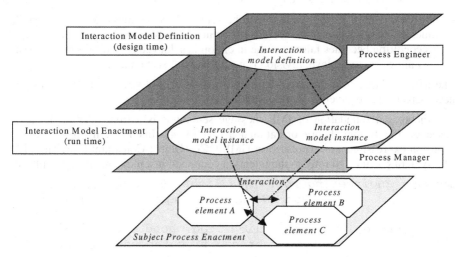

Fig. 1. Interaction monitoring life-cycle

The process engineer can use IML: (a) to attach to each request, order, notification, agreement, etc. an intention to be honoured; (b) to define valid sequences of messages. The goal of IMS is to maintain the network of intentions depending on the current state of the whole process. It collects information on the state of the process elements' interactions, computes consequences on the process of the success, failure, etc. of an interaction and publishes both acquired and elaborated information. As a monitoring tool for the process manager, IMS does not enforce any model. Interaction patterns can be defined or modified at any moment during enactment.

2.1 Defining Interaction Monitoring Models

IML allows process engineers to describe different interaction monitoring models based on the concepts of *Interaction Interface*, *Message*, *Port*, *Interaction*, *Attachment* and *Container*. Only the concepts relevant to the scope of this paper will be presented. A detailed description of IML can be found in [5]. Examples presented in this section are extracted from an automotive industry scenario provided by an industrial partner [6].

Using IML, the process engineer can define: (a) the types of messages to monitor; (b) to each process element an interaction interface with a given number of ports (i.e. interaction points) and a set of protocols (valid sequences of messages). Message types define the semantics of messages that are exchanged. Protocols define ordering constraints on messages when they are exchanged between process elements.

Message Types

A message type is defined by its name, a set of typed input parameter declarations, its intention (*intends*), a maintenance condition for the intention (*while*) and the facts that are asserted by the message type (*asserts*).

A message intention expresses a goal to be achieved by the message destination. At runtime, an intention persists as long as its maintenance condition is evaluated to true. If this condition becomes false or if the intention is achieved or if it fails or it appears that is impossible to achieve, revision is performed (cf. section 2.2.).

The asserts clause in a message definition is used to add new information (asserts new facts) to the receiver of messages of that type.

The theoretical foundation of IML message semantics is a first-order modal logic based on the formal theory of rational action [3, 4]. Intention, maintenance and assertion expressions are expressed in UML/OCL (Object Constraint Language) [7]. The symbol § is used to refer to the intention contained in a message. An example is:

```
message EngineeringOrder (headlight: Headlight,
                hood: Hood, clashReport: ClashReport)
{
        intends exists(headlight.cad, hood.cad |
                headlight.cad.fits includes hood.cad)
}
```

EngineeringOrder message type has as input parameters three typed artefacts: *headlight* of type *Headlight*, *hood* of type *Hood*, *clashReport* of type *ClashReport*. The intention of an *EngineeringOrder* message is that it exists a headlight CAD that fits a hood CAD. Notice that as expressed, the intention is honoured the first time such artefacts exist.

RequestForStudyNewHeadlightDesign contains the intention that a new headlight CAD is created and that it fits the hood CAD *hoodCAD* given as parameter.

```
message RequestForStudyNewHeadlightDesign
            (headlight:      Headlight,      hood:      Hood,
            clashReport: ClashReport, hoodCAD: HoodCAD)
{
        intends (headlight.cad.isNew) and
                (headlight.cad.fits includes hoodCAD),
        while not §EngineeringOrder
}
```

This intention is honoured once such headlight CAD is produced. If not honoured yet, it persists while not *§EngineeringOrder* (i.e. the intention of *EngineeringOrder*) is true. This way dependency between intentions of different messages can be expressed by the process engineer.

Another example is *HeadlightCAD* message that asserts the fact that a new headlight CAD is created and that it fits the hood CAD given as parameter:

```
message HeadlightCAD (headlight: Headlight, hood: Hood,
   hoodCAD: HoodCAD, clashReport: ClashReport,
   hoodSketch: HoodSketch,
            headlightCAD: HeadlightCAD)
{
      asserts (headlightCAD.isNew) and
                 (headlightCAD.fits includes hoodCAD)
}
```

Port Types

A port type is defined by its name, the set of messages types that it can send ('!' symbol is used) or receive ('?' symbol is used) possibly under certain conditions expressed as a precondition that is necessary but not sufficient. Preconditions define conditions that must be fulfilled by message parameters.

The example:

```
port type Recov-prt
   {
         (message ?EngineeringOrder
          precondition clashReport.isNew),
         message !RequestForStudyNewHeadlightDesign,
         message !RequestForStudyNewHoodVersion,
         message ?RevisedHoodCAD,
         message ?HeadlightCAD
}
```

defines a port type called *Recov-prt* that can receive instances of *EngineeringOrder*, *RevisedHoodCAD*, *HeadlightCAD* message types and can send instances of *RequestForStudyNewHeadlightDesign*, *RequestForStudyNewHoodVersion* message types. Receiving messages of type *EngineeringOrder* is subject to the condition that its parameter *clashReport* is newly created.

Protocol Types

A protocol type expresses a set of constraints on the ordering of message types that can be sent/received among the interaction interface ports. Among binary operators to express the ordering constraint are: sequential (->), alternative (|) or concurrent (||).

In the following protocol type named *rec*:

```
protocol rec = (p-recov-prt?EngineeringOrder ->
      (p-recov-prt!RequestForStudyNewHeadlightDesign ||
           p-recov-prt!RequestForStudyNewHoodVersion)
              ) ->
      ((p-recov-prt?HeadlightCAD ->
                              p-recov-prt!HeadlightCAD) |
       (p-recov-prt?RevisedHoodCAD ->
                              p-recov-prt!RevisedHoodCAD)
       ) -> rec
```

an example of constraint is that sending a *RequestForStudyNewHeadlightDesign* message and *RequestForStudyNewHoodVersion* can be done concurrently in any order from the same port *p-recov-prt* but after receiving an *EngineeringOrder* message at that port. Notice that *rec* may recursively apply.

Once defined models for interactions are instantiated and enacted, the monitoring becomes effective. The next section gives an overview of how at runtime IML intentional semantics is carried out by IMS.

2.2 Enacting Interaction Monitoring Models

At runtime, To each interaction interface instance (associated to an enacting process element) is associated an intention base containing the intentions to be achieved, the maintenance condition that are associated to them and the facts to be asserted.

To monitor interactions, IMS uses a graph of intention dependencies, a truth maintenance system (TMS) like [8] where dependencies are represented by oriented graphs where edges represent intentions and arcs represent consequence relationships between intentions. The graph is constructed starting from the underlying logic theory and from user-defined rules that are supplied at system customisation time. An example of such rules is:

```
(achieved(A) and achieved (B)) -: nolongerequired(C)
```

where the user expresses that *C* is no longer required if achievement of *A* and achievement of *B* are true.

Predicates to express goal states are defined as facts depending on the state of their achievements: *achieved(I), failed(I), nolongerequired(I)* and *impossible(I)*. A, B, C and *I* are logical expressions. Each time a fact is added or a conclusion is inferred, truth values are calculated for all affected conclusions. Results of such revision are provided to the process manager.

The message exchange sequence shown in table 1 is a possible conversation that starts with sending a message of type *EngineeringOrder* from *p-mngt-prt port* and ends when receiving a message of type *HeadlightCAD* by *p-recov-prt* port. The intentions, associated maintenance conditions and information that are added to interaction interfaces' intention bases are updated all along the conversation.

According to what has been defined in the interaction monitoring model, tests are performed by IMS at each port on the message to see whether it conforms to the defined port type or not (valid message type, valid precondition), and, if ordering constraints defined by the protocols are respected or not.

Tests on the message semantic level are performed each time a new information is asserted to an intention base through a message (*asserts* clause). IMS revises then all intention bases that are involved within the current conversation. For instance when receiving the message *RequestForStudyNewHeadlightDesign* (4), its associated intention (*§4*) together with its maintenance condition (*not §2*) are added to the corresponding intention base.

When receiving the message (7), a new information is asserted expressing that *§4* has become true. Therefore IMS sends a message *IML-achieved(§4)* to *p-recov-prt* and revises all the intention bases involved in the conversation: as *§4* implies *§2* and *§4* has been achieved, this implies that *§2* has also been achieved. Then as *not §2* is

Table 1. Intention management during a conversation

Message	Interaction interface intention base		
	Intends	While	Asserts
1: p-mngt-prt ! EngineeringOrder (headl, hood, cl)			
2: p-recov-prt ? EngineeringOrder (headl, hood, cl)	exists(nheadlightCAD: HeadlightCAD, nhoodCAD: HoodCAD | nheadlightCAD.fits includes nhoodCAD)		
3: p-recov-prt ! RequestForStudyNewHoodVersion (headl, hood, cl, hoodcad, headlcad)			
3: p-recov-prt ! RequestForStudyNewHeadlightDesign (headl, hood, cl, hoodcad)			
4: p-heades-prt ? RequestForStudyNewHeadlightDesign (headl, hood, cl, hoodcad)	(headlightCAD.isNew) and (headlightCAD.fits includes hoodCAD)	not §2	
5: p-hoodes-prt ? RequestForStudyNewHoodVersion (headl, hood, cl, hoodcad, headlcad)	(nhoodCAD.isNew) and (hoodCAD.status = revised) and (nhoodCAD.fits_too includes headlightCAD)	not §2	
6: p-heades-prt ! HeadlightCAD (headl, hood, hoodCAD, cl, hoodsketch)			
7: p-recov-prt ? HeadlightCAD (headl, hood, hoodCAD, cl, hoodsketch)			§4

false, the maintenance condition associated to *§5* no longer holds, consequently *§5* is no longer required. IMS sends the following messages to the process manager: *IML-achieved(§2)* then *IML-nolongerequired(§5)* with reference of concerned interaction interfaces. At the end of this conversation, all intentions underlying process elements' interactions are labelled by the IMS either as achieved or failed or no longer required or impossible to achieve.

3. Concluding Remarks

This position paper briefly presents a logic-based approach for monitoring interactions that are performed among distributed software processes. The proposed process support environment allows, on the one hand, process engineers to define interaction patterns using IML language and on the other hand process managers to continuously receive information on the enacting process through IMS. Provided information can be used to detect both problematic and "improvable" situations. The main contribution of this approach is that monitoring of interactions focus is not only on syntactic aspects of messages but also on their semantic. In some sense, this approach complements existing Interface Definition Languages that classically focus on the container aspects, with, a contents language based on an intentional semantic. Another feature is that monitoring can be done on-line unlike systems such as Balboa [9] where information exploitation is posterior to the process enactment.

With regard to interaction-based approaches, other systems have been proposed founded on process algebras like Wright [10], Darwin [11] and π-SPACE [12].

Wright for instance, is based on CSP for modelling interactions while Darwin and π-SPACE use the π-calculus to cope with requirements on software architecture evolution and dynamism. The main difference with IML is that in such approaches, no assumption is made on interactions' duration, in particular time consuming interactions are not managed. IML is therefore more suitable for long-time consuming software processes.

This work is currently being implemented and evaluated as part of the process monitoring support within the framework of the ESPRIT IV PIE (Process Instance Evolution) project [13,14, 15]. Implementation is based on the refinement of IML models to process-centred environments in ProcessWeb/PML [16]. The communication with other software components (including the subject process elements) is done via a communication layer founded on JMS (Java Message Service).

References

1. Lehman, M.M.: Software's Future: Managing Evolution. IEEE Software, vol. 15 no. 1, IEEE Computer Society, January/February 1998.
2. Dowson, M., Fernström, C.: Towards Requirements for Enactment Mechanisms. Proceedings of the 3rd European Workshop on Software Process Technology (EWSPT'94), Villard de Lans, February 1994.
3. Cohen, P. R., Levesque, H.J.: Rational interaction as the basis for communication. Intentions in Communication. P.R. Cohen, J. Morgan, and M.E. Pollack (Eds.), M.I.T. Press, Cambridge, 1990.
4. Cohen, P. R., Levesque, H. J.: Intention Is Choice with Commitment. Artificial Intelligence, 42(3), Elsevier Science Publishers (North-Holland), 1990.
5. Alloui, I., Oquendo, F.: Definition of the process interaction language. D3.04 Deliverable, PIE LTR ESPRIT IV Project No. 34840, 1999.
6. User requirements - consolidated version Deliverable, PIE LTR ESPRIT IV Project No. 34840, 1999.
7. UML Object Constraint Language Specification version 1.1, 1 September 1997.
8. Doyle, J.: A Truth Maintenance System. Artificial Intelligence, No. 12, 1979.
9. Cook, J. E., Wolf, A. L.: Toward Metrics for Process Validation. Third International Conference on the Software Process, Virginia, USA, October 1994.
10. Allen, R., Garlan, G.: Formalizing Architectural Connection. Proceedings of the Sixteenth International Conference on Software Engineering, Sorrento, Italy, May 1994.
11. Magee, J., Kramer, J.: Dynamic Structure in Software Architectures. Proceedings of ACM SIGSOFT'96, Fourth Symposium on the Foundations of Software Engineering (FSE4), San Francisco, October 1996.
12. Chaudet, C., Oquendo, F.: π-SPACE: A Formal Architecture Description Language based on Process Algebra for Evolving Software Systems. Proceedings of ASE'2000 International Conference on Automated Software Engineering, Grenoble, France, September 2000.
13. Alloui, I., Beydeda, S., Cîmpan, S., Gruhn, V., Oquendo, F., Schneider, C.: Advanced Services for Process Evolution: Monitoring and Decision Support. Proceedings 7th European Workshop on Software Process Technology. Lecture Notes in Computer Science, Vol. 1780, pp 21 - 37, Springer Verlag, February 2000.
14. Cîmpan, S., Oquendo, F.: OMEGA: a language and system for on-line monitoring of software-intensive processes. ACM SIGSOFT Software Engineering Notes, July 2000.
15. Alloui, I., Oquendo, F.: Supporting Decentralised Software-intensive Processes using Zeta Component-based Architecture Description Language. Proceedings of the 3rd International Conference on Enterprise Information Systems (ICEIS'01), 7-10 July 2001, Setúbal/Portugal. (to appear)
16. Warboys, B. C., Kawalek, P., Robertson, I., Greenwood, R. M.: Business Information Systems: a Process Approach. McGraw-Hill, 1999.

Experiences with Behavioural Process Modelling in FEAST, and Some of Its Practical Implications

Meir M. Lehman, Juan F. Ramil, and Goel Kahen

Department of Computing
Imperial College of Science, Technology and Medicine
180 Queen's Gate
London SW7 2BZ, United Kingdom
{mml, ramil, gk}@doc.ic.ac.uk

Abstract. The FEAST/1 (1996-1998) and FEAST/2 (1999-2001) projects have been investigating the role and impact of feedback and feedback-based system dynamics as reflected by attributes of the long term evolution of industrial software and the behaviour of the processes that evolve them. The investigation was triggered by the hypothesis that, with the possible exception of the least mature processes, software processes are multi-agent, multi-level, multi-loop feedback systems that must be managed as such to achieve sustained process improvement. This paper summarises some of the findings of the FEAST projects to date with emphasis on the process modelling methodology that were adopted and that have evolved over the duration of the two projects. Such procedures encompass both metric based black-box and white-box (*system dynamics*) behavioural modelling. It will also draw attention to the practical industrial application of the results obtained in the form of over thirty-five rules and guidelines for software evolution planning and management.

1 Introduction

It has been universal experience since the start of the digital computer age that computer systems addressing real world applications, termed *E*-type systems [22], must be continually adapted and enhanced, that is *evolved*, if they are to remain effective. The reasons for this have been well understood for many years and the phenomenon is recognised as *intrinsic* to such systems. Such systems are judged by the results they deliver in relation to attributes such as performance, functionality delivered, behaviour in execution, ease of use, reliability and so on. The criterion of acceptability of such systems is that users and, in general, stakeholders are *satisfied* with present system behaviour, are able to live with the results of system execution and successfully use the results delivered, even while recognising system shortcomings and hoping for better things to come. In this, *E*-type systems differ from *S*-type systems [22] where, by definition, the criterion of acceptability is that of *mathematical correctness* relative to a *program specification*. The majority of systems upon which businesses and organisations rely are of type *E*, even though system constituents might be, indeed, at the

V. Ambriola (Ed.): EWSPT 2001, LNCS 2077, pp. 47–62, 2001.
© Springer-Verlag Berlin Heidelberg 2001

lowest component level, should be of type S [22,31]. Hence the importance of the former type and the study of the processes by which they are evolved.

Complex software can, in general and at least in the long run, be no better than the process by which it was developed and is evolved [40]. To ensure effective process enactment and management, however, requires *inter alia* appropriate process models [9,20]. Different approaches to process modelling have been discussed in the literature [e.g. 9] and in workshop series such as the present European Workshop on Software Process Technology and the series of International Workshops on Software Process, for example. In this paper we limit ourselves to the discussion of one important role of process modelling, that of identifying process changes that are likely to lead to the improvement of process and product attributes. In this connection, the paper summarises lessons learnt during the modelling of evolutionary behaviour inspired by observation of systems addressing disparate applications and evolved by different types of organisations, and the phenomenology derived therefrom. The observations and conclusions were acquired over many years of investigation; most recently in the FEAST (*Feedback, Evolution And Software Technology*) projects [12]. They, in turn, have yielded candidates for practical industrial application through the adoption of over 35 rules and guidelines for software evolution planning and management.

2 Feedback in the Software Process

In 1993 one of the authors (mml) asked himself the question, why, in spite of the emergence of new software engineering approaches and techniques (e.g. object orientation, CASE tools, design methodologies, software patterns and so on), it is still generally so difficult to achieve major *sustained* software process improvement? In response he proposed the following FEAST hypothesis: *As complex feedback systems, global E-type software processes evolve strong system dynamics and with it the global stability characteristics of other such systems. The resultant stabilisation effects are likely to constrain efforts at process improvement* [27,29]. This hypothesis is consistent with observations first made in 1972 [3] when discussing the implications of a *ripple* observed in the growth trend of IBM OS/360-70 when plotted over release sequence numbers. The term *global process* is used here in the system-theoretic sense to refer to the *system*, that encompasses the activities and influences of all those involved in the evolution of a system. These include analysts, designers, implementers, testers, sales personnel, users, user support and their line and executive managers.

The FEAST hypothesis and its implications have been discussed in four international workshops to date [11,26]. The hypothesis has been investigated by two successive UK EPSRC funded projects, FEAST/1, from 1996 to 1998 [29], and FEAST/2, from 1999 to 2001 [30]. The projects focussed on the study of software systems developed, marketed, supported and evolved by ICL, Logica, Matra-BAe and more recently (FEAST/2) BT. Lucent Technologies have also provided data on two of their real time systems[1]. The data and observations emanating from these projects have provided evidence that overall can be interpreted in terms of the feedback nature of the evolution process. Thus, the results achieved are, in general, consistent with observations made during the seventies and eighties [23]. They include, for example, support for at least six of eight behavioural patterns encapsulated in *laws of software evolution*[2]. Findings of the projects to date are summarised in numerous publications [12].

Behaviours that complex feedback systems are likely to display, include:
- constraints on and/or stabilisation of process performance as a consequence of the dominance of *negative* feedback loops[3]
- the dominant role of outer loops of the system that may , determine (possibly constraining) observable *global process* behaviour

From the above one can derive the following consequences:
- localised, attenuated impact of forward path changes on the process; thus *local* changes may have little impact on *global* behaviour
- achievement of significant change in process performance is likely to require adjustment of feedback loops; the consequences and impact of feedback paths should not be neglected in either process planning or process improvement. Note however that the role and impact of individual loops in a multi-loop system is in general difficult to determine without appropriate process modelling techniques, for example, process behavioural models
- outer, i.e. global, process loops, require particular attention. These include, but are not limited to, those involving the final users and marketeers, that reflect the business, contractual, financial and marketing framework within which the merely technical evolution process operates

Evidence consistent with the feedback nature of the software process has, in FEAST, come from several sources, including:
- reasoning about process activity, in the abstract and during the construction of *system dynamics* (SD) models [8,13], *invariably* reveals process loops that involve humans. For example, deployment of a system in its operational domain changes the domain and contributes, therefore, to a further cycle of the evolution process [23,27]. Whether feedback control loops in the strict classical sense can be identified in existing processes or deployed in newly designed processes is still an open question [28]
- results of building and executing simulation models based on SD and other techniques[4], that include feedback loops
- observations of decaying growth rate and the successful modelling of growth trends over releases using inverse square models over segments (one, two) of system lifetime suggest the role of system size (and size inherited complexity) as a constraining factor in long-term evolution

---

[1] Thanks to the good offices of one of two FEAST Senior Visiting Fellows.

[2] The laws are stated and discussed in [23] and in numerous papers [12,31].

[3] The composite effect of positive and negative feedback involves also characteristics such as gains and delays of forward and feedback paths. See [8] for details.

[4] See [20] for a survey of process simulation modelling.

- observed patterns of behaviour such as ripples or other oscillatory behaviour on plots reflecting metric data of evolving software process behavioural trends [3,23,32,33]. Such behaviour about otherwise smooth trends suggests feedback-controlled self-stabilisation though other interpretations are possible, such as the role of a random component in the release interval, the time between individual software releases [44]

In summary, on the basis of such evidence the results of the FEAST projects have greatly strengthened the view of the present authors that, *apart from the most primitive[5], software processes are complex multi-level, multi-loop, multi-agent feedback systems[6]*. FEAST provides a theoretical framework within which process improvement, and in particular the role of feedback in such improvement, can be explained.

From a more practical perspective, the feedback-system nature of the software processes explains *part of* the difficulties encountered in the search for industrially effective process modelling formalisms. Whilst there has been work on process models aimed at fine grained *process description*, the work on models of process and product attribute *behaviour* [36] has been much less. It must be much more widely recognised, in industrial process modelling and otherwise, that both aspects can be important contributors to achieving disciplined planning, management, execution and control of the process. Behavioural modelling is seen to be an important tool that can materially assist the achievement of sustained, significant process improvement. Possible roles of behavioural quantitative models include:

- encapsulation of past process performance to provide a means for forecasting as, for example, when addressing cost, interval and quality issues
- establishment of baselines for process performance monitoring and evaluation
- process initial design or subsequent re-design by pursuit of 'what-if' questions related to changes in process elements and policies

The world at large, has developed well known procedures such as CMM [10,40,49], SPICE, Bootstrap and ISO9001 to assist organisations in process improvement through achievement of increasingly high levels of process maturity [40]. Some of these paradigms have explicitly recognised the role of feedback, in particular at the higher maturity levels (e.g. CMM). The development of these paradigms has been influenced by concepts of quantitative statistical control [e.g 4] and guidelines for *measurement* have been provided [e.g. 49]. It appears, however, that guidelines for quantitative *behavioural modelling* to support process improvement needs wider investigation and discussion [41].

The survey that follows is intended to introduce some of the practical experiences with and implications of modelling and analysis effort such as undertaken in the FEAST projects and in over two decades of individual, small scale, effort prior to their initiation. We do not, therefore, include here any of the modelling results or of the data and other evidence obtained. These have been covered in past publications, some referenced here and more generally those listed and, in part obtainable, from the FEAST and source web sites [12].

---

[5] In the sense of low degree of process maturity [40].

[6] This statement has been included as an eighth law of software evolution.

3   Behavioural Process Modelling

Two classes of models appear to be relevant to the present discussion. *Black-box* models encapsulate relationships between attributes, as, for example, when one seeks to build regression and other statistical models directly from a data set. Primarily, they reflect structure, trends and correlation *in* the data. *White-box* models, on the other hand, seek to reflect elements and mechanisms within the real process. They convey, therefore, insight into the internals of the process being modelled[7]. Within the software engineering community, black-box and white-box modelling of the software process have largely been treated independently. The former is exemplified by the work reported in a series of International Symposia on Software Metrics, the latter by the series of International Wokshops and Conferences on the Software Process and by the ProSim Workshops on Software Process Simulation and Modelling. There are, however, potential and significant links between black-box and white-box approaches as discussed, for example, in [7,16]. White-box models have been proposed as a means for the identification and definition of indicators and metrics, [16], with the metrics derived therefrom having a *systemic* character.

As will be further explained in section 6, the present authors submit that the iterative and/or combined use of both classes of models can effectively address some of the modelling challenges imposed by the feedback nature of the software process, and in so doing, help towards the achievement of sustained process improvement.

4   Black-Box Modelling

In the FEAST approach black-box models are used to characterise global process behaviour, to establish baselines and determine whether a change in behaviour has happened or not. One starts with a set of key process attributes expressed as series of (generally numeric) values and then derives mathematical models that encapsulate patterns and trends.

To maintain discipline it is advisable to start data collection in *top-down* fashion. That is, begin with a small set, of probably not more than five or ten, different attributes and acquire metrics to reflect externally observable, global, data that appears to reflect process behaviour, in terms for example, of effort applied, product size, quality and schedule. This is particularly important when resources for data extraction and processing are severely limited. The starting set of behavioural metrics can be progressively refined as the cycle proceeds through the acquisition of additional data. Model building and the development of further insight drive each other. Note, however, that in situations in which one must rely on data collected and stored in the past, particularly important when studying evolution, one will be constrained, both in initial model construction and in model refinement, by what is available in the source data bases. In FEAST, a suite of evolution metrics [12,32,42], including system *size* measured in

---

[7] For a discussion of related topics the interested reader is referred to [19].

module counts as inspired by previous experience, has been used with success to characterise and model software evolutionary behaviour. For reasons discussed in the literature [e.g. 31], *module* counts were preferred to lines of code or function points [37] in the context of the FEAST analyses. In fact, selection of the FEAST suite was strongly influenced by that used in the 70s studies that yielded the laws of software evolution. An alternative approach to metrics selection is provided by GQM [47].

When initiating a new study that is to extend over the years, one will wish to select the most useful metric, in the context of the objectives of the planned study, the data already available and that which can be identified and captured. In general evolution studies, however, one will normally wish to initiate study of the behaviour immediately and must, as already indicated, rely on existing data sources for historical data. In that event one can only use what has previously been obtained or deduced from stored data. Thus, for example, metrics can also be extracted from sources such as configuration management databases or change-log records, which tend to be long lived. In one particular case-study [42] *Perl* scripts [45] were developed to extract and parse tens of thousands of change log entries automatically and derive system size in modules and other indicators. Other scripts permitted determination of approximate indicator of effort applied from analysis of developer identifiers. Together these scripts have enabled the reconstruction of process performance over many years of system evolution, when it was believed that no records were available. Such scripts however, rely on records that satisfy a degree of regularity in format and must be customised to individual systems. Generic procedures for historical data collection and metrics formalisation are an interesting topic for further research.

In either case, that is whether directly accessible or whether by deduction, and for any given evolution (or other) process attributes, one may be left with a choice of alternative measures that are appropriate. It is, in general, well worth exploring the benefits of the alternatives.

Data acquisition, particularly when retrieved from historic data not initially designed for any specific study or, for that matter, established without informed thought as to the purpose for which it was to be used, must often be followed by data cleansing, filtering and/or smoothing. It may be difficult for the unassisted eye to detect trends or changes in them. Thus, procedures for use in the treatment of noisy software engineering data have been proposed [43]. These are particularly relevant when the real, but random, effects or process noise contributions to process behaviour are large, for example, with respect to a deliberate change in policy or resources that has or is being applied. This problem is especially acute when noise is relatively large or changes are small. In the latter case, change detection approaches such as those described in [2,4] can also be useful [12].

Once data as retrieved from, say, a historical database is cleansed, one can proceed to search for behavioural patterns, regularities or other trends in the evolutionary behaviour of a system. If several systems are being studied in parallel one may also begin to identify any common patterns of behaviour, with the ultimate aim of identifying behavioural invariants. The discovery of any such patterns, regularities or invariants can then initiate a search for models that reflect the observations and/or the rates of change of associated attributes. Techniques such as the ones used in FEAST [12] or their equivalent can be applied. Statistical or other methods, those based on *fuzzy dynamics* [15], for example, may be useful for development of models for use in the planning and management of system evolution.

The above has provided brief guidelines for the application of black-box models to the study of software system evolution. It may be thought that such relatively simple techniques do not have much value. The FEAST experience to date indicates otherwise [12,33,42]. Procedures, analysis and interpretation as outlined above, has permitted the modelling of growth trends and trends in other process performance indicators over long periods of system evolution with reasonable accuracy. Further analysis has suggested that the observed behaviour is related to the effects of self-stabilising feedback, and in particular, of *global* process dynamics and must, therefore, be considered in software evolution planning and management [34].

It is to be noted that from the black-box models one can also recognise change points in process dynamics as time progresses, and hence to identify, for example, changes in process performance. The analysis of *why* such changes have happened usually requires the study of the relationships between several attributes within the *global* process. The investigation of such influences is, however, more appropriately pursued by means of white-box modelling, as briefly discussed in the next section.

5   White-Box Modelling

White-box modelling can help answer questions about the implications of introducing, modifying or eliminating process constituents, including steps, or the policies by which the process is directed, managed and controlled. It is, of course the impact of such changes on process behaviour, as when seeking process improvement, that is the matter of real interest, of concern. Such models can be constructed using, for example, system dynamics (SD) [8,13], discrete-event simulations or other techniques [20]. In FEAST, four important issues in white-box modelling have been identified.

The first, which is reflected in the other three, is whether construction is to proceed *bottom-up* or *top-down*. Does one attempt to construct the model in all its gory detail or should one first attempt to achieve a gross model that reflects gross system behaviour and then gradually add detail by refinement to achieve gradual convergence of model behaviour to that of the real world process. This issue was first considered by Zurcher and Randell [50] and is closely related to the approach described by Wirth [48]. At first sight and ignoring global issues, the bottom-up approach, as in general taken by the process programming community [e.g. 38], would seem to be preferable since it permits one to model the mechanisms, procedures and the elements of which they are composed, in exquisite detail. If, however, one accepts that the software process is a complex feedback system one must also accept that the bottom-up approach cannot easily reflect all the many facets and effects of the feedback forces, mechanisms and loops and their, largely unknown, impact. Nor will mastery of the individual open loop mechanisms facilitate understanding of total system properties or even higher level sub-systems. Moreover, it is widely recognised that people, individually and collectively, play a crucial, probably decisive, role locally in the process. At the lower levels that are encountered when one models process behaviour bottom-up, and which will often reflect or be dependent on individual behaviour and performance, one is forced to use statistical approximations to model the likely or average behaviour or performance of the human participants. This clearly constitutes a major challenge [e.g. 17]. It is our contention that while people behaviour, whether as *doers* or as managers, has a direct and visible impact locally in and on the process, meaningful aggregate human impact at the global level is possible because of the moderating and stabilising influence of feedback. Scaffolding around the model can only reflect a best guess as to the magnitude and relationships between the various feedback induced forces. Convincing *validation* and *calibration*, of the model in operation, in part and as a whole, as it mimics process behaviour, is well nigh impossible. Even when exploring, specific low level issues, the models should, as far as possible, reflect the aggregated activity of individuals. In summary, given the nature of the software process we opt unequivocally for the top-down approach.

The second issue relates to the complexity of the model itself and is closely bound up with issue one. The value of a model is as a tool to support achievement of understanding of the process or other system being modelled. Models produced from the bottom-up inevitably become more and more complex as one develops process descriptions that reflect current understanding of system behaviour. And this is, in practice, what one will do because that is where the focus of the modeller is. In the top-down approach, on the other hand, detail is progressively added only as one seeks to bring model behaviour to more closely reflect reality. Thus any increases in model complexity is not spurious. It directly reflects the increasing understanding of the complexity of the real world process being modelled. The direct benefits of model simplicity are clear.

Moreover to be of practical value, the model must be validated and calibrated against its subject. The simpler the model, the more straight forward and convincing the calibration, the less the ambiguity, alternative interpretations of what is being observed. FEAST project experience in constructing and interpreting SD models and their behaviour under execution has by-and-large confirmed the benefit of starting with the simplest possible model. In the first instance such models address the issue or mechanism of immediate interest. Detail may then be added to the model and to its behaviour bit by bit to achieve greater precision or more precision in reflecting real world behaviour. Analysis of this issue confirms our earlier recommendation to approach process simulation top-down.

The third issue refers to model validation. In the foregoing, we have referred repeatedly to the need for validation and calibration. The basic problem arises from the fact that, in general, a model is assessed by the closeness of its behaviour to that of the system being modelled. One can, in general, achieve behaviour as close as desired simply by introducing enough detail and complexity in the model through the addition of ever more parameters or variables. But that merely indicates success in mimicking behaviour. It does not (necessarily) imply greater correspondence between the model, its parts and their respective behaviour on the one hand and the process, its sub processes and mechanisms and their behaviour on the other. Once again, and as already indicated, the solution of this issue, lies in restricting the detail and complexity of the model to that required for solution of the problem or for the feature being addressed. General techniques for validating the results from simulation models and for establishing the credibility of the results may be found, for example, in [14], and this must be followed when possible.

The final issue is how the potential role of simulation models varies as process maturity increases [7]. On the one hand a more mature [40] process will tend to control the use of feedback information in a more disciplined and predictable manner and is thus more amenable to being modelled. The individual manager is, however, more likely to apply individual judgement based on information fed to him or her from various sources. That is he/she acts as a feedback mechanism in a way that may be difficult to predict but that can have significant impact at the global level. For less mature processes feedback is likely to be less disciplined and hence represent a greater challenge to meaningful modelling. This and related issues require further investigation.

The preceding has briefly discussed some basic issues that arise when constructing simulation models that seek, for whatever reasons, to reproduce system behaviour. In the case of the FEAST studies of the software process the object of study was the *phenomenon* of software evolution. The principle goals included identification of the drivers of evolution and of the mechanisms that control and direct it, to learn to control those mechanisms and to improve direction, planning and management of product evolution to serve the best interests of the determining stakeholders. In pursuing those goals SD models have played an important role [e.g. 5,18,36,46]. The models that have been developed and themselves, evolved, are remarkably simple when one compares them with other SD models reported in the literature, e.g., [1]. In particular, as recommended above, the models have all been developed top-down, were seeded by very simple aggregated structures with model detail restricted to the minimum necessary to identify a meaningful process. In the spirit of the top-down approach the initial model elements included elements from the global process, external that is, to the immediate technical software process. Only when the initial models displayed behaviour that was meaningful in our understanding of the process did we plan, as recommended, the gradual refinement of the models to reproduce behaviour that could be validated by, *inter alia*, discussion with the collaborators. Examples of white-box modelling in FEAST are provided in [5,18,36,46].

6   Iterating Black-Box and White-Box Modelling

Process iteration, the repeated execution of process elements appears to be a property of the engineering of software, at least, as we currently know it. At the coding level, for example, iteration occurs when a software module is modified and recompiled again and again in a search for desired behaviour. It can of course occur at all levels and even across levels. Another example of iteration is provided by the planned evolution of a new version of some software system. This is achieved by means of a series of releases, that is, an initial release and a series of upgrades.

It has been argued that system evolution tends to become more difficult as a system ages [21,39] and often calls for process *improvement*, even change, to cope with, for example, growing complexity. Indeed, it has been widely recognised that every time the evolution process is enacted, as for example, in the preparation of a new release, there is an opportunity to introduce process changes and to assess their effects by means of comparison with performance over past releases or process iterations.

Within this context, black-box and white-box techniques display complementary features that can be used in an iterative fashion [41]. Fig. 1 displays a suggested software process modelling cycle with alternating phases of black-box and white-box modelling. Each release cycle offers an opportunity to complete one modelling cycle and to achieve further refinement and validation of the models.

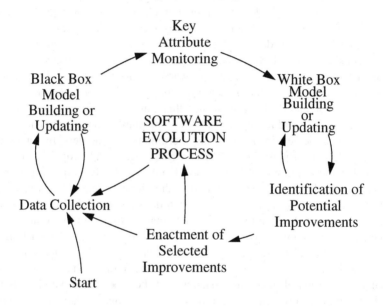

Fig. 1. Iterating Black-Box and White-Box Modelling

In Fig. 1 black-box models are used to generate baselines and, in further cycles, also to assess the continuing effectiveness of the process. White-box models serve primarily as a basis for identification of potential improvements and of evaluation of the benefit derived. What-if experiments and sensitivity analysis can be performed to assess, for example, various changes to forward and feedback paths. Once the selected changes to the process have been implemented and when new data is available, black-box models are updated as a result of the new observations. This provides an independent assessment of the effects of the process changes being undertaken. White-box models can now be updated as required and the cycle repeated.

7   Guidelines for Software Release Planning and Management

A recent paper [34] collects together over 35 guidelines and rules (see Table in the Appendix) for software evolution planning and management as derived from the FEAST observations and earlier work [12,21,23]. In association with literature references extending over a 30 year period, the paper [34] provides an outline of the observations and phenomenological reasoning that has led to the recommendations in the table. Some of the items on the lists that follow will appear intuitively self-evident. Others may, at first sight, seem without technical foundation or justification but this is not so. The above paper infers them from the empirical generalisations derived from the FEAST and earlier studies. We now suggest that they can be formally derived from and be based on a unified and coherent conceptual framework, a *theory of software evolution*, still to be fully developed and formalised [35].

8   Implications for Software Process Technology

Amongst their results the FEAST studies have identified a meaningful number of behavioural invariants as implied, for example, by the laws of software evolution [21,23,33] and the principle of uncertainty [24,25]. These invariants are largely related to various properties of the real world and human-organisational activity in that domain. This is what provides the basis of the theory of software evolution mentioned in the previous section. It is expected that the theory will be, at least in its basic premises, technology independent. Current approaches to the study of software evolution tend to adopt either the *what* and *why* approach on the one hand or the *how* on the other [35]. By providing a formal conceptual framework for the former, the proposed theory will also clarify and support mastery of the latter and contribute to the advance of software technology. One of the benefits of such a theoretical framework, if successfully accomplished, would be to provide a *rationale* for good practice. But one of its practical applications could be in the rationalisation and justification of development and adoption of specific software technology and tools (e.g. technology for the capture and update of assumptions embedded in programs and specifications [35]).

9   Final Remarks

Some fundamental limitations of models, in general, have been discussed in, for example, [23, chapter 11]. Even considering these limitations, behavioural process models are a means towards improving and disseminating understanding of the process, building a common language and sharing concepts and views amongst those involved. Many organisations have established infrastructures to capture, preserve and evolve relevant process-related experiences derived from past projects or releases [6]. Quantitative models may also play a useful role if considered as part of such schemes. One of the barriers to achieve success in this regard comes from the knowledge burden imposed by the modelling process and modelling tools. It is, however, possible to envisage that quantitative process modelling support systems of the future will offer the practitioner a suite of ready-to-be-used black-box and white-box models and tools for their use. An essential requisite for such tools is to be intuitive and user friendly. It must also be sophisticated enough not to impose an excessive knowledge-burden on the model builder and process improvement analyst. It seems that there is still a long way to go before achieving these in the field of software engineering.

It is hoped that following completion of the FEAST/2 project, the experience and guidelines summarised in this paper will be refined and other relevant aspects documented in future activity. Though the main focus in FEAST has been on the study of evolving systems, many of the experiences derived and conclusions reached to date have implications in the context of *ab initio* software development. The value of these is expected to remain significant with the current move to Component and COTS based development [31].

Acknowledgements. Many thanks are due to the other member of the FEAST team, Professors D. Perry and W. Turski for having shared with us their insights in regular meetings over several years and for many useful discussions and to Ms Siew F. Lim for her support in all our activities. We are grateful to our industrial collaborators for providing data and for discussions that have been essential for the progress made. Financial support from the UK EPSRC through grants GR/K86008 (FEAST/1), GR/M44101 (FEAST/2), and GR/L07437 and GR/L96561 (SVFs) is gratefully acknowledged.

References[8]

1. Abdel-Hamid, T.K. and Madnick, S.E.: Software Project Dynamics - An Integrated Approach, Prentice-Hall, Englewood Cliffs, NJ (1991)
2. Basseville, M. and Nikiforov, I.V.: Detection of Abrupt Changes: Theory and Application. PTR Prentice Hall, Englewood Cliffs, NJ (1993)
3. *Belady, L.A. and Lehman M.M.: An Introduction to Program Growth Dynamics. In Freiburger, W. (ed.): Statistical Computer Performance Evaluation, Academic Press, NY, (1972) 503–511
4. Box, G. and Luceño, A.: Statistical Control by Monitoring and Feedback Adjustment. Wiley, New York (1997)
5. Chatters, B.W., Lehman, M.M., Ramil, J.F. and Wernick, P.: Modelling a Software Evolution Process. ProSim'99 Workshop, Silver Falls, Oregon, 28-30 June 99. Also as Modelling a Long Term Software Evolution Process. J. of Software Process - Improvement and Practice, vol. 5, iss. 2/3, July (2000) 95 - 102
6. Chatters, B.W.: Implementing an Experience Factory: Maintenance and Evolution of the Software and Systems Development Process. ICSM 99, 30 Aug. to 3 Sept. Oxford, UK, (1999) 146–151
7. Christie, A.: Simulation in support of CMM-based Process Improvement. Journal of Systems and Software, Vol. 46, No. 2/3 (1999) 107–112

---

[8] References indicated with '*' are reprinted in [23]. Those indicated with '**' are available from [12].

8. Coyle, R.G.: System Dynamics Modelling - A Practical Approach. Chapman & Hall, London (1996)
9. Curtis, B., Kellner, M.I., and Over, J.: Process Modeling. Commun. ACM, Vol. 35, No. 9, Sept. (1992) 75–90
10. El Eman, K. and Madhavji, N.H. (eds.): Elements of Software Process Assessment and Improvement. IEEE CS Press, Los Alamitos CA (1999)
11. FEAST 2000 Workshop on Feedback in Software and Business Processes, July 10-12 2000, Imperial College, London, UK, call and selected contributions, <http://www.doc.ic.ac.uk/~mml/f2000>
12. FEAST, Feedback, Evolution And Software Technology, project web page including publications listings at <http://www.doc.ic.ac.uk/~mml/feast>
13. Forrester, J.W., Industrial Dynamics. MIT Press, Cambridge MA (1961)
14. Forrester JW and Senge P, Tests for Building Confidence in System Dynamics Models. In System Dynamics, Legasto AA Jr., Forrester JW, Lyneis JM (eds.) TIMS Studies in the Management Sciences, Vol. 14. North Holland, New York, (1980) 209–228
15. Friedman, Y. and Sandler, U.: Evolution of Systems under Fuzzy Dynamics Laws, Fuzzy Sets and Systems vol. 84, (1996) 60–74
16. Huff, K.E.: Process Measurement though Process Modelling and Simulation. ISPW 10, Proc. of the 10th International Software Process Workshop "Process Support of Software Product Lines", Ventron, France, June 17 - 19 (1996) 97–99
17. Humphrey, W.S. and Singpurwalla, N.D.: Predicting (Individual) Software Productivity, IEEE Trans. on Softw. Eng., vol. 17, No. 2, (1991) 196–207
18. Kahen, G., Lehman, M.M., Ramil, J.F. and Wernick, P.: Dynamic Modelling in the Investigation of Policies for E-type Software Evolution. ProSim Workshop, July 12 -14, 2000, Imp. Col., London UK (2000), a revised version to appear in J. of Syst. and Softw. (2001)
19. Kaposi, A.A. and Myers, M.: Systems, Models and Measures. Springer-Verlag London (1994)
20. Kellner, M.I., Madachy, R.J. and Raffo, D.M., Software Process Simulation Modelling: Why? What? How? J. of Syst. and Softw., Vol. 46, No. 2/3, April (1999) 91–106
21. *Lehman, M.M.: Programs, Cities, Students, Limits to Growth?. Inaugural Lecture. In Imperial College Inaugural Lecture Series, Vol. 9, 1970 1974, 211–229. Also in Gries D. (ed.): Programming Methodology. Springer Verlag, (1978) 42–62
22. *Lehman, M.M.: Programs, Life Cycles and Laws of Software Evolution, in Proceedings of IEEE Special Issue on Software Engineering, September, 1060-1076. With more detail as "Programs, Programming and the Software Life-Cycle,". Also in System Design, Infotech State of the Art, Rep, Se 6, No 9, Pergamon Infotech Ltd, Maidenhead, 1981, 263–291
23. Lehman, M.M. and Belady, L.A.: Software Evolution - Processes of Software Change. Academic Press London (1985)
24. Lehman, M.M.: Uncertainty in Computer Application and its Control through the Engineering of Software, J. of Software Maintenance, Research and Practice, vol. 1, 1 September (1989), 3–27
25. Lehman, M.M.: Uncertainty in Computer Application, Technical Letter, Comm. ACM, vol. 33, no. 5, pp. 584, May (1990)
26. **Lehman, M.M. (ed.): Preprints of the three FEAST Workshops. Dept. of Computing, Imperial College (1994/5)
27. Lehman, M.M.: Feedback in the Software Evolution Process. Keynote Address, CSR 11th Annual Workshop on Software Evolution: Models and Metrics. Dublin, 7-9th Sept. 1994. Also in Information and Softw. Technology, sp. is. on Software Maintenance, Vol. 38, No. 11 (1996) 681–686

28. **Lehman M.M., Perry D.E. and Turski W.M.: Why is it so hard to find Feedback Control in Software Processes?, invited talk, Proc. of the 19th Australasian Comp. Sc. Conf., Melbourne, Australia, 31 Jan. - 2 Feb. (1996) 107–115
29. **Lehman, M.M. and Stenning, V.: FEAST/1 Case for Support. Dept. of Comp., Imperial College, London, March (1996)
30. **Lehman, M.M.: FEAST/2 Case for Support. Dept. of Comp., Imperial College, London, July (1998)
31. **Lehman, M.M. and Ramil, J.F.: Implications of Laws of Software Evolution on Continuing Successful Use of COTS Software. Dept. of Computing, Res. Rep. 98/8, Imperial College, London, June (1998). A revised version as Software Evolution in the Age of Component Based Software Engineering, IEE Proceedings - Software , Vol. 147, No. 6, 249 - 255, December (2000)
32. Lehman, M.M., Perry, D.E. and Ramil, J.F.: Implications of Evolution Metrics on Software Maintenance. ICSM 98, Bethesda MD, 16 - 18 Nov. (1998) 208–217
33. *id.* On Evidence Supporting the FEAST Hypothesis and the Laws of Software Evolution, Metrics 98, Bethesda MD, 20-21Nov. (1998) 84–88
34. Lehman, M.M.: Rules and Tools for Software Evolution and Management. FEAST 2000 Workshop. Pre-prints. July 10 - 12, Imperial College, London (2000).
<http://www.doc.ic.ac.uk/~mml/f2000> A revised and extended version (with Ramil, J.F.) to appear in Annals of Software Engineering, special volume on Software Management (2001)
35. **Lehman, M.M. and Ramil, J.F.: Towards a Theory of Software Evolution - And Its Practical Impact, invited talk, Pre-prints of the International Symposium on the Principles of Software Evolution, ISPSE 2000, Kanazawa, Japan, Nov 1-2, (2000)
36. **Lehman, M.M., Ramil, J.F., and Kahen G.: Thoughts on the Role of Formalisms in Studying Software Evolution, International Special Session on Formal Foundations of Software Evolution, Lisbon, Portugal, 13 Mar., 8 pps. (2001)
37. Low, G.C. and Jeffery, R.D.: Function Points in the Estimation and Evaluation of the Software Process. IEEE Trans. on Softw. Eng. Vol. 16, Jan. (1990) 64–71
38. Osterweil, L: Software Processes Are Software Too, Proceedings of the 9th International Conference on Software Engineering, (1987), 2–12
39. Parnas, D.L., Software Aging. ICSE 16, Sorrento, Italy, May 16-21, (1994) 279–287
40. Paulk, M.C. et al: Capability Maturity Model for Software, Version 1.1. Software Engineering Institute Report, CMU/SEI-93-TR-24 (1993)
41. Ramil, J.F., Lehman, M.M. and Kahen, G.: The FEAST Approach to Quantitative Process Modelling of Software Evolution Processes, Proc. PROFES'2000 2nd Intl Conference on Product Focused Software Process Improvement, Oulu, Finland, 20 - 22 Jun. 2000, in Frank Bomarius and Markku Oivo (eds.) LNCS 1840, Springer Verlag, Berlin (2000) 311–325
42. Ramil, J.F. and Lehman M.M.: Metrics of Software Evolution as Effort Predictors - A Case Study, Proc. ICSM 2000, Int. Conf. on Software Maint., 11-14 Oct., San Jose, CA (2000)
43. Tesoreiro, R. and Zelkowitz, M.A.: Model of Noisy Software Engineering Data. ICSE 98, Kyoto, Japan, April 19-25 (1998) 461–476
44. Turski, WM: The Reference Model for Smooth Growth of Software Systems Revisited, submitted for publication, March (2001)
45. Wall, L., et al: Programming Perl. O'Reilly & Associates, Sebastopol CA (1996)

46. Wernick, P. and Lehman, M.M.: Software Process White Box Modelling for FEAST/1. ProSim 98 Workshop, Silver Falls, OR, 23 June (1998). Also in J. of Sys. and Softw., Vol. 46, No. 2/3, April (1999)
47. Wernick, P.: Identifying and Justifying Metrics for Software Evolution Investigations Using the Goal-Question Metric Method. FEAST 2000 Workshop. July 10 - 12, Imperial College, London (2000). http://www.doc.ic.ac.uk/~mml/f2000
48. Wirth, N: Program Development by Step-wise Refinement, Comm. ACM, Vol. 14, No. 4, April (1971) 221–227
49. Zahran, S.: Software Process Improvement - Practical Guidelines for Business Success. SEI Series in Software Engineering, Addison-Wesley, Harlow, England (1997)
50. Zurcher, F.W. and Randell, B.: Iterative Multi-Level Modeling - A Methodology for Computer System Design. IBM Res. Div. Rep. RC-1938, Nov. (1967). Also in Proc. IFIP Congr. 1968, Edinburgh, Aug. (1968), D138–D142

Appendix

Table. A Summary of Guidelines for Software Release Planning and Management[9]

Item	Description
1	Prepare comprehensive specifications and maintain them updated
2	Formalise program specification (long term goal)
3	Capture, document, structure and retain assumptions in specification
4	Verify assumptions as part of verifying specification
5	Continuing capture, updating and full documentation of assumptions during design, implementation, integration and validation work
6	Develop and use tool support for specification work and recording of assumption throughout process in structured form (as database), classified by categories
7	Create and update comprehensive documentation to minimise impact of growing complexity
8	Apply conscious effort to control and reduce complexity and its growth
9	Document assumptions and design and implementation rationale underlying a change
10	Periodically review assumption set
11a	Plan for clean-up releases after major increments in functionality
11b	Observe safe change rate limits in planning and implementing change and evolution
12	Constrain scope and size of a release increment based on past system successful incremental growth
13	Alternate major (functional enhancement, extension) and minor (clean-up, restructuring) releases
14a	Change validation must address change interaction with & impact on that part of system that is not changed
14b	Change validation must include continued validity of assumptions
15	Assess domain and system volatility and take this into account in implementation

---

[9] For further details on these guidelines see [34].

Table (cont). A Summary of Guidelines for Software Release Planning and Management

Item	Description
16	Manage and control complexity in its many aspects
17	Pursue active complexity control (anti-regressive work)
18	Determine and apply an appropriate level of anti-regressive work
19	Collect, plot and model historical data to determine patterns, trends and rates of change and growth
20	Establish baselines of key measures over time and releases
21	Use new data to assess, recalibrate and improve metric-based (black-box) planning models
22	Use 'm+2s' criterion or similar to determine safe, risky or unsafe growth increments
23	When required increment is large split into several releases as in evolutionary development
24	Develop automatic tools to support data collection, modelling
25	Follow established software engineering principles when implementing and evolving functionality (e.g., information hiding) to minimise interaction between system elements
26	Consider, model, manage global process embedding technical process
27	Consider, model, manage informal organisational links as part of global process
28	Model dynamics of global process
29	Use dynamic models to plan further work
30	Use dynamic models to identify interactions, improve planning and control strategies
31	Use dynamic models when seeking process improvement
32	Estimate likelihood of change in areas of application domain and their impact on assumptions
33	Periodic and event-triggered review and assessment of likelihood of change in assumption sets
34	Improve questioning of assumptions by, for example, using independent implementation & validation teams
35	Provide ready access by evolution teams to all appropriate domain specialists

Software Process Technology Transfer: Using a Formal Process Notation to Capture a Software Process in Industry

Ulrike Becker-Kornstaedt[1], Holger Neu[1], and Gunter Hirche[2]

[1] Fraunhofer Institute for Experimental Software Engineering (Fraunhofer IESE),
Sauerwiesen 6, D-67661 Kaiserslautern, Germany
{becker, neu}@iese.fhg.de

[2] Thales (former Thomson-CSF Elektronik)
Elisabethstraße 6, D-24143 Kiel, Germany
gunter.hirche@thomelektronik.thomson-csf.com

Abstract: Industry seems to be reluctant to use software process modeling technology. This paper reports on a case study in the context of the software process technology transfer project. For the target organization, the aim of the project was to develop a detailed description of their processes. For the research organization involved, the goal of the case study was to determine whether a process modeling method and tool, based on a graphical, yet formal notation could be used by industrial organizations to capture their processes.

1 Motivation

Software process models play an important role in process improvement programs. An explicit representation of the development process as it is performed or as it should be performed is a key to software process improvement. The models are the basis for understanding and analyzing processes, improving existing processes, designing new ones, as a basis for process changes, or for disseminating process knowledge. Software development has become increasingly complex, requiring larger teams. Often, these teams are distributed across different locations. In order to coordinate such large development teams, a common understanding of the development process is necessary.

Industry best practices have shown that a defined process to be followed is key to successful software development. Process assessment schemes, such as SPICE [Col95] or BOOTSTRAP [Boo93], that assess the maturity of development processes based on industrial best practices recommend explicit descriptions of the processes to be followed.

A key concept for process improvement is to incrementally incorporate experience gained and lessons learned from carrying out the process. Capturing the process 'as is' in an explicit description, in a descriptive software process model, is therefore a first step. Changes to this as-is process can then be incorporated into the model, and the updated and improved process can be disseminated to Process Participants [Huf96]. A new model, describing the process as it should be performed, allows to

V. Ambriola (Ed.): EWSPT 2001, LNCS 2077, pp. 63–76, 2001.

guide Process Participants through a common process and facilitates coordination among project members.

Real-world software processes are complex. Complex software processes lead to complex software process models. To deal with the complexity of these models, model creation and presentation often requires tool support. Many of these tools require the models to be described in a formal notation. Benefits from formal notations are that inconsistencies or ambiguities in the model can be identified and reduced or removed, and weaknesses in the process can be assessed more easily [VM97].

Based on our own experience, very few companies use formal notations and process modeling tools to document their processes – despite the advantages of formal notations and the risk of an ambiguous process description. Most enterprises prefer to use drawing tools or text editors to describe their processes for their everyday work – typically the processes are described in process handbooks. These tools lack process domain knowledge and do not provide mechanisms to detect ambiguities or weaknesses in the process model. As a result, the handbooks are often of poor quality, having inconsistencies or ambiguities.

There are only few examples reported in literature, where software process technology (i.e., software process methods and tools) has been successfully transferred from research into industrial practice. [JCD00] describes several cases on software process technology usage in industry. [BDT96] used a formal notation (MVP-L) in an industrial project, but reports that for communication with Process Performers, a graphical notation was more useful.

This paper presents a case study on process technology transfer into industrial practice. From the technology providers' point of view the goal was to determine whether a formal process modeling notation and supporting tool that had been developed in research could be used by people who had a general background in software process improvement, but were not process modeling experts. This technology transfer included additional support, such as training, by the process technology providers.

For this project, a formal (graphical) notation was used to create the process model. The model was then used to support process guidance during enactment in the form of a web-based process guide [KBKR+98] to guide Process Participants through the process. The notation and tool, as well as the web-based process guide were still used after the end of the project. For us, this is an indication that a formal process technology can be introduced into industrial practice.

The paper is structured as follows: The next section gives the background information, such as the organizational context in which the case study was conducted. Section 3 introduces Spearmint, the notation and tool used. Section 4 describes the procedure followed for process modeling and process technology transfer at the target organization. Finally, Section 5 gives a summary of the paper and the major lessons learned from the project.

2 Context of the Case Study

To better understand the procedure followed in the case study, this section briefly introduces the project and the participating organizations.

The case study involved two partners, Fraunhofer IESE, an organization involved in applied research, and Thales (former Thomson-CSF Elektronik), whose processes were to be captured.

Thales is involved in the development of defense systems, it is a German subsidiary of a worldwide operating company in professional electronics. Thales has some 150 employees.

At Thales, a Software Engineering Process Group (SEPG) was set up to trigger process improvement activities.

The SEPG decided to use the assessment recommendations to trigger concrete process improvement activities. One of the suggested actions from the assessment at Thales was that an explicitly documented process was a key factor to reach a higher SPICE level. However, an explicit process description was needed not only to reach a higher SPICE level in a re-assessment, but SEPG decided that the process model should serve as a starting point for further improvement activities. Thus, the process description had to be developed in a way that it could support Process Participants in their everyday work. SEPG decided to make the process description available as an on-line handbook.

A key issue for Thales was that the process model was not maintained by outside experts, but that the SEPG within Thales became owner of the model. Thus, the process model was to be created, maintained and extended by members of the SEPG of the software development organization. To achieve this ownership, the members of SEPG at Thales had to be able to use the tool and had to understand how to do process modeling in order to perform it on their own. Therefore, a major goal of the project – besides providing the process model – was the transfer of software process technology into the target organization. In this context, it was not only important to show whether the concepts provided by the tool were sufficient and helpful to capture real-world processes. In addition, the case study was to explore whether the use of the tool could be adopted by non - process - modeling experts.

For Fraunhofer IESE the major goal of the tech transfer case study was to assess the applicability of the tool and methodology to capture real-world software processes and develop an explicit process description.

This led to the following major requirements for tool support and the for modeling procedure. The first set of requirements is related to the software process modeling domain:

- Take into account **specifics of software processes**: Software processes are complex, human-based, creative, and cooperative processes. This involves concepts that are beyond the 'typical' process entities such as activities and artifacts. To support creativity, control flow had to be described using entry and exit criteria. As models may have to be changed frequently, for instance to match project specifics or to reflect changes in technology, the tool had to support consistent process change as well as consistency checks on the model.
- Ability to deal with **complex process models**: The process to be described consisted of several subprocesses that were interconnected through common artifacts. Many roles participated in the process. Thus, the tool had to provide

mechanisms to manage this complexity, such as a view concept, where a *view* denotes any subset of the overall process model.

The following set of requirements results from the project context - the usage at the customer site:

- Provide **detailed descriptions** of the process entities (i.e., activities, artifacts, and tools): Guiding Process Participants through their everyday work required detailed descriptions regarding certain activities or artifacts. This included information such as task lists or entry criteria for activities, as well as references to artifact templates and examples.
- Ability to **present the process model on-line** as a process handbook: The process model was to be used to support Process Participants in their everyday work. Therefore, the model had to be available to everyone within the organization in an easy way. Within the organization, it had been opted that ideally, the process model would be available on the company Intranet.
- **Ownership** of the model **within** the **target organization**: Thales wanted to remain independent of anybody from outside their organization to maintain or elaborate the process models. Thus, the process model was to be maintained within the organization by members of the SEPG. This required a tool and notation that was easy to learn and to use by people who had a good general background in software engineering and process improvement, but who were not experienced Process Engineers.

3 The Spearmint Notation and Tool

Based on the requirements for tool support, the tool suite Spearmint/ EPG [BHK+99] was selected to document the current software process at Thales. Spearmint[1] is a tool to support a Process Engineer in the creation of software process models. Spearmint was especially designed to help a Process Engineer capture complex software process models. The tool provides mechanisms such as different views on the process model, where a view can be designed in a way that it shows exactly the subset of the process information that is relevant to the person, therefore avoiding information overflow.

Spearmint uses a graphical notation based on a formal syntax to describe the structural properties of process models. Spearmint reduces the complexity of the process models via the build in refinement and containment hierarchy. Spearmint provides a flexible attribute concept that allows to include additional information to the different entities of the process model. For guiding Process Participants through the process, Spearmint provides the EPG Generator. The different components of the tool are briefly described in the following sections. A more detailed description of the tool can be found in [BHK+99].

---

[1]Spearmint = Software Process Elicitation, Analysis, Review, and Measurement in an Integrated Environment. Spearmint is a registered trademark of Fraunhofer IESE.

3.1 Notation

This section describes the Spearmint syntax. Spearmint uses a graphical notation to document the processes. For the notation, icons were selected that are intuitively understandable. Nevertheless, there are strict syntax rules on how process models can be constructed from these symbols. The major advantage of this graphical notation is that it is formal while still understandable for novice users. Based on the formal notation consistency rules have been defined, allowing consistency checks to performed. To show the basic relationships, Spearmint has four entity types (*Artifact, Activity, Role* and *Tool*) and six relationship types (*consumes, produces, modifies, involves, uses,* and *contains*) between those entities. Activities and Artifacts can be connected using the product flow relationships *consumes, modifies* and *produces.*

Spearmint uses the following four notational symbols for the entities:

Spearmint uses the following four notational symbols for the entities:

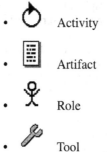

- Activity

- Artifact

- Role

- Tool

The notation for the relationships are

- Consumes: only possible from an Artifact to an Activity
- Produces: only possible from an Activity to an Artifact
- Modifies: only possible between Activity and Artifact
- Involves: only possible between Activity and Role
- Uses: only possible between Activity and Tool
- Contains is only visible in a tree, there is no explicit graphical symbol for it.

This set of symbols and relations makes it easy to understand and model a process. Figure   shows a simple example of the notation. Activity 1 consumes Artifact 1 and Role 1 is involved in this Activity. Activity 1 also creates Artifact 2, which is modified by Activity 2 by using Tool 1.

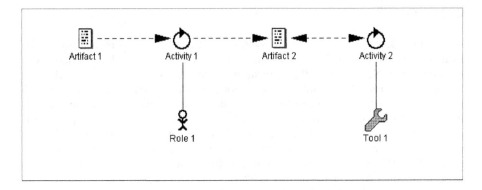

Fig. 1. Example Notation with all entities and relations

With this concept and the graphical representation of the model, it is possible to present to the user an understandable user interface with the possibility to perform checks according to formal rules.

The Entities Artifact and Activity can be refined into sub - Artifacts and sub - Activities and can, therefore, contain multiple entities of their own type. Figure shows a simplified version of the Spearmint schema that defines the formal syntax of Spearmint process models.

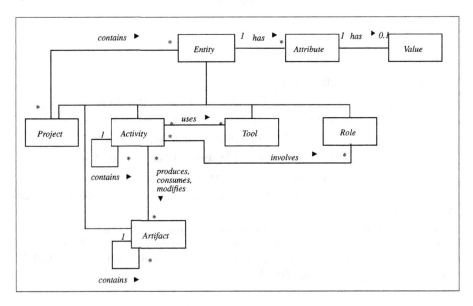

Fig. 2. The conceptual model of Spearmint

Each entity can have different Attributes. The user can enter a value for each of these attributes to further describe the entity . Each entity type has a set of predefined attributes, such as name or description. In addition, a user can define his/her own attributes, or delete existing ones. The attribute concept makes it easy to create detailed descriptions of the entities in the process model.

3.2 Reducing the Complexity of Models through a View Concept

The Spearmint tool knows two ways to reduce the complexity in models: decomposition, and a view concept. A *view* shows a subset of the overall process. The major views supported by Spearmint are *ProductFlowViews*, *ProcessViews*, *ArtifactView*, and *ActivityView*. Artifact- and *ActivityViews* show the decomposition hierarchies of activities and artifacts. The *Artifact-* and *ActivityView* are structured like a file tree to show the decomposition hierarchy. The *Roles-* and *ToolsView* are simple lists, because tools and roles can not be decomposed according to the Spearmint syntax. Besides these views Spearmint has two other views, the *PropertiesView* for editing various Attributes and the *HypertextView* for discussing the process model over the Internet.

- A *ProductFlowView* shows Activities, Artifacts, as well as the relations consumes, produces and modifies between these Entities. The tool supports refinement of activities. The refinement of the Activity is shown in a new *ProductFlowView*. This *ProductFlowView* shows the product flow of that activity at the next lower level of abstraction, i.e., the product flow of all sub - activities and the artifacts involved. Consistency between these views is maintained by the tool. If, for example, a new *ProductFlowView* is being constructed for an activity A, all activities that are modeled in this new *ProductFlowView* are automatically inserted as sub - activities of A into the corresponding activity hierarchy. The mechanism of the *ProductFlowView* and the interplay with the hierarchy views reduce the complexity of the model by consistently maintaining different abstraction levels of the process model. Spearmint enforces the rule that an Activity is contained in only one *ProductFlowView* to keep the model consistent.

- Besides the *ProductFlowView* Spearmint knows *ProcessViews* showing product flow, Role, and Tool assignment. Whereas the contents of *ProductFlowViews* is enforced by the tool, the user may decide which Entities and Relations are displayed in the *ProcessView*.

- For editing the Attributes and their values, the *PropertiesView* is used. This view shows all Attributes that are connected with the currently selected entity. The Process Engineer can edit the values of a predefined Attribute set, create new Attributes, or delete existing Attributes and their Values. The main advantage of this view is that the View is only visible if the user wants to edit an Attribute and shows only the Attributes of one Entity.

Using the view concept, the Process Engineer is able to model subsets of the process model. The Process Engineer sees only an understandable amount of information, he/she can either see a rough overview of the whole process or drill down through the refinement hierarchy to see details of a specific part of the process model.

3.3 Consistency Rules

Spearmint checks during the creation of the process model whether or not the modification of the model intended by the user is allowed or not. There are different degrees of enforcement of these rules: enforced rules, recommended rules, and optional rules. Most of the enforced rules related to product flow and refinement are enforced by the tool, so that the process model is always correct regarding these concepts. If a user tries to violate an enforced rule, the input is simply ignored. For example, Spearmint prevents a product flow between two activities or two artifacts. A violation of a recommended rule produces warnings by the system. For example, Spearmint warns that an artifact is already produced by an activity, and the user adds a second 'produces' relationship between that artifact and another activity. Optional rules can only be invoked by the user. Well-formedness rules regarding the process model are optional rules. For instance, entities must have unique names.

3.4 EPG

The EPG (Electronic Process Guide) is a web-based assistant for process navigation, allowing its users to browse through process information. The EPG is implemented as a set of HTML pages. When an EPG is generated from a Spearmint process model, relationships such as product flow, role assignment, or refinement appear as hyperlinks. The information described in the attributes appears as text in the EPG. To further allow to customize EPGs, it can be determined during generation which attributes are to be generated into the EPG. A more detailed description of Spearmint and the EPG can be found in [BHK+99].

4 Case Study

This section describes the case study. The goal of the case study was to determine the applicability of the Spearmint method and tool in an industrial context. In particular, we wanted to examine the suitability of the approach for people who have a general background on software process improvement but are not especially familiar with process modeling concepts. The case study involved the following roles: two Process Engineers from FhG IESE, who acted as providers of process technology, three SEPG members at Thales who were to become process modeling experts, and several Process Participants at Thales. Note that the SEPG members are a subset of the Process Participants.

For the case study, five major stages could be identified: preparation, training, initial process modeling, process model elaboration, and model review. In the early stages, the process modeling activities were done by the technology transfer organization, who coached the SEPG. Gradually, the SEPG members became process modeling experts and took over modeling activities, while the technology transfer organization withdrew. The stages and the involvement of the different parties in these stages had been agreed upon by the two organizations.

1. **Preparation**: To make process elicitation more efficient for Process Experts, the Process Engineers should have some background information about the process

before doing interviews [BB00]. The assessment report and sample documents such as a problem change request provided valuable background information on the process for the outside Process Engineers before the start of the process modeling activities. Analyzing these documents took approximately two days, one of them on site.

The resulting model had to describe the major activities, artifacts, and roles, as well as product flow (consumes, produces, modifies) between activities and artifacts, and assignment of roles to activities. The attributes to be modeled included long descriptions for activities, artifacts, and roles, and entry and exit criteria for activities.

2. **Training**: In order to transfer process technology into an organization, training is necessary. Thus, a one-day workshop was held by the Process Engineers from Fraunhofer IESE on site to enable SEPG members and Process Participants to attend. The workshop consisted of teaching process modeling concepts to the Process Participants, doing excecises with the tool, and exemplary modeling of one process by the Process Engineers. The general process modeling concepts familiarized the attendees with information such as why to model software processes, what to model, recommended steps, and typical information sources for software process information. The purpose of the training was twofold: The SEPG members were shown by the training how to obtain the information needed to create a process model from the information gained in an interview, while the Process Participants learned what was expected from them in the course of the process modeling activities: which information they had to provide in the interviews, how the information was elicited, and how the process information was to be used afterwards.

3. **Initial process modeling**: As part of this process technology transfer project, one process was to be modeled by the Process Engineers from Fraunhofer IESE as an example process. For the other processes, FhG IESE had to provide assistance to SEPG in modeling. Thus, the modeling of one process was integrated into the training to show in a concrete example how information was extracted from an interview and subsequently expressed as a Spearmint process model. For this purpose, one of the Process Participants volunteered as an interview partner for a Process Engineer. In a group exercise, led by the Process Engineers from IESE, the information from the interview was afterwards formalized into the first version of a process model using the Spearmint tool.

At first the major activities, artifacts, roles were elicited and the structure of the model (i.e., product flow and role assignment between them) was documented with Spearmint. To visualize the development of the process model, a beamer was used to show all attendees the model. This promoted discussion about the model because every attendee could see the model and suggest changes and extensions. Simultaneously, the most important attributes, such as detailed descriptions for activities and artifacts, and entry/exit criteria for activities were filled in to capture the information that was discussed during the development of the model. Control flow between different activities was described using a natural language description (*entry criteria* and *exit criteria*). Note that product flow only defines an implicit order of activities, i.e., if an activity produces an artifact that is consumed by a second activity, there is an implicit order that the first activity has to be completed before the second can start. However, sometimes start conditions for activities have to be defined more explicitly, for instance, an activity may not start before a contract has been signed. Such a condition could not be expressed via product flow relations, because the contract would not be an input document to that activity.

As the model started to get too complex, the experts of Fraunhofer IESE recommended refining some of the activities into a refining *ProductFlowView* to reduce the complexity of the top level process.

The first version of the model showed the rough structure of the process, especially the product flow relationships.

4. **Model Elaboration**: The further elaboration of the model as well as the complete creation of other sub - models was done completely by SPEG at Thales. For problems with Spearmint and help for the elaboration of the process, Fraunhofer IESE provided help via phone. Typical questions addressed to IESE included strategies on when to use refinements, or which attributes to fill in. The tool was viewed as very helpful by SEPG. The final model consisted of two sub - processes, 30 artifacts (all at top level), 24 activities (9 at top level), and four roles. It was not necessary to use sub - artifacts because SEPG decided not to differentiate between parts of documents and the complete document. During this stage, the focus was not so much on the structural properties of the process model, but on detailed descriptions of the process, which would facilitate process guidance during enactment.

5. **Review**: Review of the model was done by the Process Engineers off-line, using the graphical representation of the model together with a hypertext version of the process model, generated from the Spearmint model. This hypertext version showed the attribute values. The built-in consistency checks provided by Spearmint had already been performed by SEPG, leading to a process model that was structurally correct. Thus, we checked for inconsistencies in the textual descriptions. Typical 'errors' in the model were inconsistencies between the graphical product flow and the textual description. For instance, although the artifact description stated that the artifact was to be used in Activity A, there was no product flow relationship between the artifact and A, or an artifact that was modified – according to the textual description – was consumed according to the graphical view. Feedback on the model was provided to SEPG via phone.

When we, i.e., the Process Engineers, got the final version of the process model, we were surprised at the level of detail that was incorporated into the model. Apart from those attributes that had been attached in the early version during the workshop, a lot of new attributes had been defined and used, yielding a very detailed picture of the process regarding the description.

Figure 3 shows two of the process models in Spearmint.

Nearly one year after the beginning of the project, Thales keeps using Spearmint/EPG to maintain, elaborate, communicate their process within the organization, and provide process guidance.

By the way: A SPICE re-assessment, conducted one year after the first one, showed significant improvement in the level reached. This may not only be due to the introduction of a documented process, however, developing a detailed description of a software usually increases 'process awareness' in organizations.

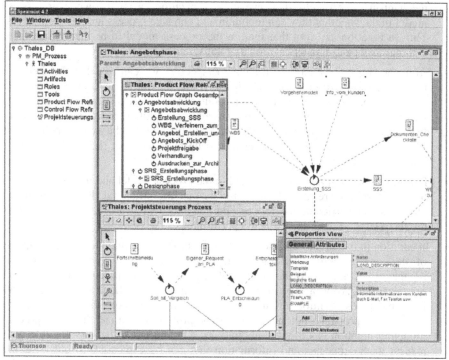

Fig. 3. Spearmint model for the processes at Thales

The major advantage of the Spearmint notation for Thales is that the description with the easy understandable notation helps the process participants to identify the expected in- and output and the roles and tasks involved of the Process. The model explains: Who is involved. What are the Tasks. What is the necessary input and the expected output of the process.

5 Lessons Learned

This section presents the lessons learned from the case study. The lessons include experience solely related to the usage of Spearmint as well as more general experience regarding process technology transfer.

The first set of lessons learned are related to the modeling task, the model, and tool support for process modeling.

- From our case study we can conclude that Spearmint is feasible to model real-world processes, and its concepts proved helpful to capture those aspects that were felt to be important by SEPG.

- It is possible to introduce a formal process modeling notation and tool from research into industrial practice, to be used by non-researchers. Such a notation has to be easily understandable or learnable for users of the model, who are often no experts in the area of process modeling. For instance, a simple visualization mechanism is very helpful. However, organizations want to own their process model in the way that they can maintain and enhance process models themselves. Thus, a notation and tool that require the process model to be maintained from external Process Engineers is probably not suitable.

- From the process technology transfer perspective we can say that the concepts that were most difficult for participants were the refinement concept and the difference between product flow and control flow. The difficulty for the users was the fact that a product flow defines only an implicit order (i.e., an activity that depends on the output of another activity may not be started before that activity) and that an explicit order has to be modeled with the Attributes entry criteria and exit criteria.

- The high amount of attributes attached to the process model and the extended textual descriptions are an indication for us that the structural description of the model is not sufficient for Process Participants who want to use the process model to support their daily process performance.

- In addition to the structural description of the model, a detailed textual description of the various entities is important. Processes differ a lot across different organizations, and so do the needs and requirements for process models within organizations. A lot of the process information is very difficult to formalize, and for some types of information (such as guidelines on how to perform certain tasks) it is probably not necessary or helpful to formalize them. A process modeling notation has to take this into account and has to be very flexible with respect to the concepts and information that can be expressed. In our case, the formal approach to describe the structural properties of the model, enhanced by informal textual descriptions, has shown to be a very good combination. Other usages, however, may require a different degree of formality.

- Keeping the right balance between formality and informality is one key for obtaining a model that is useful and is being used. The formality in the model facilitates structuring the model and ensures a certain quality of the model, and a higher degree of formality enforced by the tool might have eliminated the errors detected in the review phase. On the other hand, a process model that is intended to support Process Performers in their daily work needs a lot of information that is rather 'vague', such as guidelines or hints. This information in itself is very difficult to structure and formalize, as it is usually presented in natural language. Using the Spearmint attribute concept, these 'information chunks' can be integrated into the process model, and the formal approach helps to locate this information.

- The case study showed that tool support is very helpful in modeling complex processes. Once processes – and their models – get more complex, tool support becomes extremely helpful if not necessary to reach a certain quality of the model. Using a formal approach allowed for formal consistency checks that proved to be very helpful in our case.

- In the beginning, Spearmint was, for Thales, more a tool for visualizing the model than for finding inconsistencies. Spearmint made it easier to create and display the model because the inherent restrictions of Spearmint helped to achieve a complete but short description of the process. The modeling of new parts or extensions of the process is now easier because Spearmint keeps the model consistent.

The following experience is related to process technology transfer into industrial practice.

- One key issue we have learned from this project is that process technology transfer requires systematic introduction of both the tool and the underlying concepts. To reach long-term results and ensure that an organization really adopts process technology in their daily practice, the target organization needs intensive support. This support includes general training with process modeling concepts as well as training with the tool and the notation to be used. Once the organization starts to use the tool itself, support such as a helpline or review of the model by the organization providing the technology is necessary to reach long-term achievements.

- For us, the detailed elaboration of the model is an indication that the notation, although it has a certain degree of formality, can be adopted easily. With brief training, the usage of the tool can be learned rather fast by people who have a background in process improvement.

6 Summary

The experience reported in this paper described a successful example of the transfer of software process technology into industrial practice.

The Spearmint concepts have shown to be useful in modeling real-world software processes. Using a formal approach has shown to be applicable in industrial practice, because it allowed for formal consistency checks that proved to be very helpful in our case. However, a formal notation has to be supported by a tool to be accepted in industry. Furthermore, the case study showed that with a small amount of training, the usage of the Spearmint tool could be learned.

Unfortunately, we do not have any data on the effort spent on the development of the model. For us, it would be interesting to find out how much effort could be saved due to the formal approach, allowing, for instance, consistency checks. It remains to be investigated in which situation a formal approach is more helpful, and which information can be better captured and represented using an informal approach.

We want to stress one aspect we regard as crucial for the success of process technology transfer. When transferring process technology results from research into industry, the transfer should be planned thoroughly in order to achieve long-term results. It is not enough to simply provide a tool for an organization. Introducing process modeling concepts should include training with the new concepts. The transfer is further facilitated by providing additional support, such as examples, or a 'hotline'. Such additional support is necessary to make the technology transfer a long-term success, that is, the tool is still used after the transfer phase when the supporting organization withdraws.

Acknowledgments. The authors would like to thank the people involved in this study at Thales for their cooperation. We would like to thank Dirk Hamann who provided us with background information on assessments and Jürgen Münch for his valuable comments on an earlier version of the paper.

References

[BB00]   Ulrike Becker-Kornstaedt and Wolfgang Belau. Descriptive Process Modeling in an Industrial Environment: Experience and Guidelines. In Reidar Conradi, editor, *EWSPT 7*, pages 176–189. Lecture Notes on Computer Sciences, Springer–Verlag, 2000.

[BDT96]   Alfred Bröckers, Christiane Differding, and Günter Threin. The role of software process modeling in planning industrial measurement programs. In *Proceedings of the Third International Software Metrics Symposium*, Berlin, March 1996. IEEE Computer Society Press.

[BHK+99] Ulrike Becker-Kornstaedt, Dirk Hamann, Ralf Kempkens, Peter Rösch, Martin Verlage, Richard Webby, and Jörg Zettel. Support for the Process Engineer: The Spearmint Approach to Software Process Definition and Process Guidance. In *Proceedings of the Eleventh Conference on Advanced Information Systems Engineering (CAISE '99)*, pages 119–133, Heidelberg, Germany, June 1999. Lecture Notes on Computer Sciences, Springer–Verlag.

[Boo93]   Bootstrap Project Team. Bootstrap: Europe's Assessment Method. *IEEE Software*, 10(3):93–95, May 1993.

[Col95]   Antonio Coletta. The SPICE Project: An International Standard for Software Process Assessment, Improvement and Capability Determination. In P. Nesi, editor, *Proceedings of the Conference on Objective Quality Techniques and Acquisition Criteria*, pages 49–63, Florence, Italy, May 1995. Springer Verlag.

[Huf96]   Karen E. Huff. Software process modelling. In Alfonso Fuggetta and Alexander Wolf, editors, *Software Process*, Trends in Software, chapter 1, pages 1–24. John Wiley & Sons, 1996.

[JCD00]   M. Letizia Jaccheri, Reidar Conradi, and Bard H. Dyrnes. Software Process Technology and Software Organizations. In Reidar Conradi, editor, *EWSPT 7*, pages 96– 108. Lecture Notes on Computer Sciences, Springer–Verlag, 2000.

[KBKR+98] Marc I. Kellner, Ulrike Becker-Kornstaedt, William E. Riddle, Jennifer Tomal, and Martin Verlage. Process Guides: Effective Guidance for Process Participants. In *Proceedings of the Fifth International Conference on the Software Process*, pages 11–25, Chicago, IL, USA, June 1998. ISPA Press.

[VM97]   Martin Verlage and Jürgen Münch. Formalizing software engineering standards. In *Proceedings of the Third International Symposium and Forum on Software Engineering Standards (ISESS '97)*, pages 196–206, Walnut Creek, California, USA, March 1997. IEEE Computer Society Press.

An Evaluation of the Spearmint Approach to Software Process Modelling

Louise Scott, Lucila Carvalho, Ross Jeffery, and John D'Ambra

Centre for Advanced Software Engineering Research
University of New South Wales, 2052, Sydney, Australia
{L.Scott, R.Jeffery, L.Carvalho, J.Dambra}@unsw.edu.au

Abstract. Over the years the process modelling community has proposed many languages, methods and tools for capturing, analysing and managing software processes. It is important that as new approaches are proposed they are evaluated in real software process modelling projects so that users can tell which approaches they should consider using and researchers can decide which approaches warrant more investigation and development. This paper presents an evaluation of the Spearmint approach to software process modelling in two software process modelling projects. The evaluation identifies strengths and weaknesses of the approach and possible areas for improvement.

1   Introduction

Descriptive software process modelling is an important part of any software process improvement programme. Descriptive modelling allows process engineers to understand existing processes, communicate process and analyse existing practices for improvement. Much work has been done on proposing languages, techniques and tools for descriptive software process modelling (see, for example, [2,5,6,7,11]) and many claims have been made about the advantages of particular approaches. Among these approaches is Spearmint [1] [3], motivated by a desire to provide integrated support for process definition and process guidance.

Spearmint comprises a modelling language and a graphical tool to support the use of the language and incorporates many features that claim to support the descriptive modelling of large, complex, real-world software processes. These features include a comprehensive language for software process modelling based on product flow, a visual language to assist process communication and the use of decomposition, multiple representations and partial views of processes to help manage complexity. Spearmint also has the ability to generate an Electronic Process Guide (EPG) (a web-based, hyperlinked process handbook) automatically from Spearmint models. The purpose of this evaluation is to use Spearmint in real process modelling projects in order to shed light on the relevance and usefulness of the Spearmint features to process modelling in general.

---

[1] Spearmint is a registered trademark of Fraunhofer IESE, Kaiserslautern, Germany.

V. Ambriola (Ed.): EWSPT 2001, LNCS 2077, pp. 77–89, 2001.

The evaluation is based on two case studies where Spearmint was used for software process modelling. The first case study involved the recovery, modelling, documentation and communication of a process for a web application development project. The goal of this project was to capture the process model used and communicate it to the customer as the first step in process improvement. This project tested Spearmint's support for creating, editing, documenting and communicating web application development processes. In the second case study, Spearmint was used to capture and document the ISO 12207 Software Life Cycle Processes Standard [9]. The goal of this project was to communicate the ISO Standard to a customer, identify possible ways of improving their process, and then produce a process guide of the new, improved process. This case study tested the expressive power of the Spearmint language to see if it could capture all of the information in the standard, its ability to communicate a process to a customer, the performance of the EPG generator and the usefulness of the generated EPG as a process guide. It also tested Spearmint's ability to manage large process models. The two studies represent a broad spectrum of the possible uses of Spearmint. In general we found the language supported these projects well, the visual representation was invaluable for communicating with customers, the tool features of decomposition, multiple and partial views provided good support for the management of the large models, the EPG generator performed well saving a lot of work in producing a process guide and the resultant EPG was well accepted by the process participants.

The next section describes the Spearmint approach with special emphasis on the features that are evaluated in this report. Then, in sections 3 and 4, the two projects that form the basis of the evaluation are described. In Section 5 the evaluation method is presented and the results are reported in Section 6. A summary of our results is given in Section 7 and Section 8 concludes the paper.

2   The Spearmint Approach

The Spearmint approach supports process definition and process guidance as vehicles for improving understanding and communicating software processes. Spearmint is designed to support process engineers in the elicitation, editing, review and analysis of large, complex process models. It also supports the generation of web-based Electronic Process Guides for process guidance.

To support such a broad base of activities, Spearmint incorporates many features, some of which are unique to Spearmint and all of which are specifically designed to improve support for the descriptive process modelling of large, complex process. The following list summarises these features and the claims made about each feature.

C1 - Comprehensive language for descriptive process modelling [14]: The language underpinning Spearmint is a descriptive process modelling language based on a product flow modelling (as opposed to workflow modelling) approach. Processes are modeled as activities that can be decomposed into component activities. Activities produce, consume or modify artifacts that can be decomposed into component artifacts. Roles take responsibility for activities and tools are used during activities. Any model built from these components is called a product flow model. An activity can be refined by a product flow model that shows in more detail the component activities and their product flow relationships to artifacts. It is claimed that this schema provides a comprehensive language for describing software processes (note: it is not claimed that this language would be good for prescriptive process modelling or supporting process execution).

C2 - Visual language [12]: Spearmint uses a visual language based on the comprehensive schema for process modelling. The visual modelling language shows activities, artifacts, roles and tools and the relationships between them as graphs. An example of such a graph is shown in Fig. 1. It is claimed that this visual presentation assists in the communication of process models to non-expert process participants (e.g. customers).

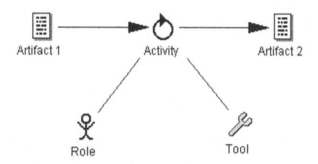

Fig. 1. An example of the visual language used in Spearmint.

C3 - Decomposition [3]: The language supports decomposition of activities into sub-activities, artifacts into sub-artifacts and activities into more detailed product flow models. It is claimed that these decomposition features help manage large, complex process models.

C4 - The Spearmint tool [15]: Spearmint is embodied in an integrated graphical modelling tool that supports the visual language and allows users to create, edit, analyse and document process models. Users can create and edit their models in the visual modelling language using a graphical editor as shown in Fig. 2. Analysis is both dynamic (users are prohibited from making relationships not defined in the language) and user invoked in the form of a checker that checks models against pre-defined well-formedness rules. Documentation can be generated by the document generator in a variety of formats including RTF and HTML.

C5 - Different representation types [3]: The modelling tool provides many different view types for creating and editing process models. View types include graph views, lists of entities and tree views for hierarchical structures. This feature is designed to make complex models more manageable by giving users a range of different ways of visualising different aspects of the model.

C6 - Partial views [3]: The modelling tool allows users to create partial views on a process model. This is designed to help manage complexity by allowing users to view and edit only small parts of large complex models at any one time.

C7 - EPG Generator [4]: The tool automatically generates Electronic Process Guides from Spearmint models. These guides are generated according to a pre-defined format with project specific data included from the model. The purpose of this functionality is to make the generation of process guides from the Spearmint model quick and error free (as opposed to coding the web pages by hand).

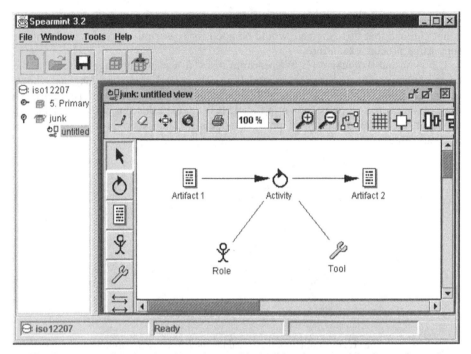

Fig. 2. A screen shot showing the major graphical editing features of the Spearmint tool.

Our evaluation explores the effectiveness of the features of Spearmint so that more understanding of process modelling tools can be gained. It concentrates on the process modelling language, the tool and the ability to generate EPGs. The EPG framework itself and its effectiveness as a process guide is not evaluated in this paper (see [13] for an evaluation of the effectiveness of the EPG). The next two sections describe the projects that were used as the basis for this evaluation.

3   LTS Project

A small Australian electronic publishing company was the source of the data for the first case study. The project of interest was the development of a web application for on-line processing of applications for credit products such as home and personal loans. The project was considered typical by the company of its web development projects for the following reasons: the project
- had a short and very strict deadline
- concerned only a small team
- proceeded "fairly chaotically" (where chaotic implies little formal process)
- involved a customer naive about web development but very involved in the project.

During the case study data was collected from the project in the form of e-mail passing through the project manager and documents that were produced for the project. The e-mails were analysed to recover the process model and in some cases supplemented with interviews of process performers. The e-mails contain many instances of processes that were identified and then abstracted into a process model. The Spearmint language was used to express the process model and the tool was used to capture and edit the process model. The goal of the LTS project was to capture the existing process model and present it to the customer so that they could learn about and understand their existing processes as a first step towards process improvement.

The process model that resulted was not large (about 30 activities) and contained only three levels of decomposition. However, this model was reworked many times during its construction, testing the editing and restructuring features of the tool extensively.

4   ISO 12207 Software Life Cycle Processes Standard

The ISO 12207 Software Life Cycle Processes Standard is a comprehensive standard specifying the processes that should/can be applied during the acquisition, supply, development, operation and maintenance of a software system. It defines processes at a high level, prescribing only what should be done, not necessarily how these tasks should be done.

The ISO 12207 Standard was captured in the Spearmint modelling language using the Spearmint tool. Since the process was already defined, the modelling process was largely one of capture, requiring little rework and restructuring. The resulting process model contained many activities, artifacts and roles and many layers of product flow refinement. This tested Spearmint's ability to deal with large process models. When the ISO model had been captured, the EPG generation feature was used to produce an EPG that was then installed on the company's intranet to guide a software development project.

5   Evaluation Method

The evaluation of Spearmint is based on our experiences with using Spearmint in the above two projects. The main tasks in these projects were process recovery, process model creation, restructuring and communication. For each task, the approach was evaluated by the process engineers against its published claims. Some of the results are objective, such as the ability of the language to capture process concepts and the reliability of the tool, but most are subjective (e.g. Did this feature help you to deal with the complexity of the model? Did this feature help you discuss process models with customers?). In these cases we have tried to articulate the reasons for our conclusions about the approach.

Two process engineers were involved in the project and sometimes their subjective evaluations differ significantly. We attribute this largely to different levels of experience with process modelling and Spearmint. One engineer had no previous experience with process modelling or Spearmint while the other was heavily involved in the construction of the Spearmint tool. In our discussion we call these the novice and expert users respectively.

6   Evaluation

The evaluation is structured into observations on the language and observations on the tool. As well as evaluating with respect to the claims made, we also include sections for "other comments". These comments identify features that are not present in Spearmint that we would have found useful. A summary of the results of our evaluation is given in Table 1.

Table 1. A summary of the Spearmint claims vs evaluation results.

Spearmint Feature	Claim	Expert user	Novice User
C1.Comprehensive language	Comprehensive for descriptive process modelling	Four important concepts missing	Two important concepts missing
C2. Visual language	Helps communication	Confirmed	Confirmed
C3. Decomposition	Manages complexity	Confirmed	Confirmed
C4. Integrated Spearmint tool	Create, edit, analyse, document models	Creation and editing good, analysis ok, documentation poor	Creation and editing good but difficult to learn, analysis not used, documentation poor
C5. Different representation types	Manages complexity	Partially confirmed	Confirmed
C6. Partial views	Manages complexity	Confirmed	Not used
C7. EPG generation	Easy EPG generation	Confirmed	Not used

6.1   Evaluation of the Language

C1 Comprehensive language: The literature claims that the Spearmint schema provides a comprehensive language for process modelling [14]. We found that for reasonably unstructured processes such as those observed in the web development project product flow modelling was a good paradigm for modelling. In these kinds of processes an emphasis on process order would be misleading and at times impossible to specify. The product flow approach, with the emphasis on input and output artifacts, suits the descriptive nature of the model developed for the LTS project. The product flow approach also proved adequate for the ISO model since the standard does not emphasise order of tasks and at times explicitly states that tasks need not be performed in any particular order.

Although the language was adequate, some extra modelling concepts would have been useful especially when the model is used to guide a process. In particular, the ability to model optional activities and artifacts and conditional paths through the product flow models would have added significantly to the expressiveness of our models. For example, consider the requirements process shown in Fig. 3. The activities, artifacts and product flows that continue on from "Accept, reject or rework" are optional - if a requirement is rejected then no further action is taken. Also, the product flows from "Accept, reject or rework" are conditional - either a "Rejected requirement" OR an "accepted requirement" is produced, but not both. We also saw examples in our models where products may be consumed by different activities depending on their nature. It would be useful to be able to specify these conditional and optional product flows in the visual model.

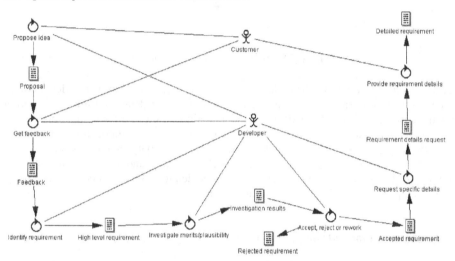

Fig. 3. The product flow capturing the requirements elicitation and refinement processes in the LTS project.

Another shortfall of the product flow modelling approach defined by Spearmint was that there was no simple way to capture the concepts of versions and iterative processes, which were central to the LTS Project. Consider the "Demo phase" product flow shown in Fig. 4. The product "version" in this model represents the many versions of the application produced during its construction. The whole process is highly iterative and a new version may contain only minor changes to a previous one. Therefore, many versions are produced during the course of the project. Neither the concept of iteration or versions is adequately captured in this visual model.

C2 Visual language: The Spearmint approach claims that its visual language helps to communicate processes, especially to people who are not very familiar with process modelling concepts. It was our experience that the graphical representation of the language and its inherent simplicity does make it easy to understand, especially when discussing processes with customers. We discussed our process models with our clients and, after a brief introduction to the language, we had no trouble communicating our ideas. On the other hand, the visual language alone is not

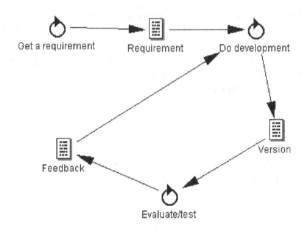

Fig. 4. The demo phase of the LTS project.

sufficient to capture all of the details of the model required for proper understanding. The description attributes were used extensively to input detail and referred to often by the customer to get a more detailed understanding of the entities in the models.

C3 Decomposition: The Spearmint language supports decomposition of activities, artifacts and process models to help contain the complexity of process models. We used these features extensively when modelling and found them invaluable. The ability to decompose allows different levels of detail to be captured in the models which helps understanding and communication.

6.2   Other Comments on the Language

Supporting abstraction: We found Spearmint provided no support for abstracting generic process models from instances of processes. This is an important and challenging task for the process engineer that could be well supported in a tool such as Spearmint. Take, for example, the model shown in Fig. 5 which represents an instance of a process observed in the given data. It is the task of the process engineer to abstract such instances into a more generic process model. An example of an abstract model that represents the instance is shown in Fig. 6. The model and instance relate according to several well-defined rules, the most basic being that each entity in the instance is represented by an entity in the abstraction, and that each entity in the abstraction has at least one corresponding entity in the instance. The same applies for the relationships between entities. Support for checking these rules would greatly assist the process engineer and help to eliminate some of the variance found in process models due to the interpretation of the engineer.

Well-formedness rules: Spearmint defines a series of well-formedness rules for models designed to increase the quality of model by detecting errors, omissions and inconsistencies in the models. We found some of the well-formedness rules defined by Spearmint very useful for analysing the models. Applying these rules helped to structure the LTS model and actually detected inconsistencies in the ISO Standard.

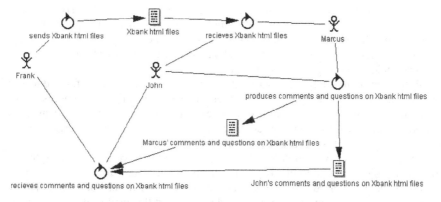

Fig. 5. An example of an instance model created from the e-mail data in the LTS project.

6.3   Evaluation of the Tool

C4 Integrated environment: The Spearmint tool is designed to provide an integrated environment for the creation, editing, analysis and documentation of process models. In our case studies we performed these activities extensively, and found the tool supports the creation and editing of models extremely well. During the LTS project we continually restructured the model as it evolved from the instances and the tool supported this well. We also found that different people working on the model preferred different ways of constructing the model (one preferred to work bottom up and the other top-down). We found that the flexible approach to refining models in Spearmint supported all of these activities very well.

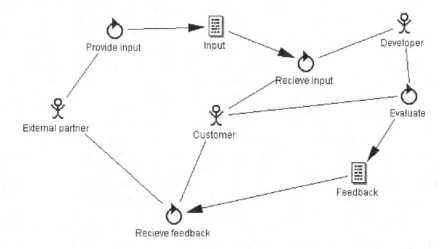

Fig. 6. An example of an abstract process model built from the instance data shown in Fig. 5.

As we restructured the LTS model we used copy and paste extensively to try out new structures. The extended copy and paste provided in Spearmint (where relationships between entities are copied as well as the entities themselves) supports this kind of reuse exceptionally well and saves time for the user to identify all of the relevant links and components for copying.

With regards to analysis, Spearmint enforces some of the well-formedness rules defined in the method, warns about others, checks for some and ignores some. In general, the behaviour of the tool in this respect was satisfactory. The way the tool enforces rules on refinement structures and uses it to automatically create and keep structures consistent is a great help to the process engineer.

Once the model was captured the reporting facilities were a disappointment. In both our projects it was crucial to be able to show the models to our industry partners to communicate our ideas to them. For this we needed sensibly formatted word documents for presentation. Spearmint did not support this well as it doesn't provide a well formatted way of combining textual descriptions with graphical representations in a useful output format (e.g. RTF). We constructed our reports by saving individual diagrams, using the report generator to extract attribute text and then handcrafting the reports (including headings). This was very time consuming.

C5 Multiple views: The claim that the multiple view/representation approach is a good tool for managing the complexity of models was only partially validated in our experience. It is true that having many different representations of the process model does help to visualise and understand complex models, but it adds significantly to the complexity of the tool. A large portion of the complexity is transferred from complex views of the model to the complexity of managing many different views. The tool helps with this by providing a view explorer and some useful navigation facilities, but the user must still maintain a consistent model of the views and the relationships between them in order to use the tool effectively. It is also our experience that this feature adds significantly to the effort required to learn the tool.

C6 Partial views: The claim that creating partial views on the model helps manage complexity was mostly supported in the experience of the expert user. Once again, though, there is a trade-off in that reducing the complexity of one view increases the number of views the process engineer needs to work with. The tool helps manage the complexity of many views by automatically keeping all views consistent with the underlying model. It also provides a view explorer to assist with navigation, however, much of the functionality to manipulate partial views is very subtle (such as include/exclude). The novice user did not reach a level of expertise with the tool even after extensive use to be able to exploit the partial view functionality.

C7 EPG Generation: The claim that Spearmint provides an efficient and accurate way to generate EPGs was confirmed. The advantages gained by such automatic generation over hand-coding of EPGs is enormous. Once the software process model had been captured in Spearmint it was a simple matter to generate a well-structured, functional, high-quality process guide. The generation of hundreds of hyperlinked web-pages with links to templates, examples and tools took a matter of seconds. Once installed, the EPG was well accepted by the process participants [13]. The advantages of the ability to generate a valuable software process improvement tool such as the EPG so quickly and easily cannot be overstated.

6.4   Other Comments on the Tool

Learning the tool: The tool and the language are non-trivial and need to be learnt before the tool can be used effectively. Understanding the underlying concepts and rules is central to being able to use the tool. The novice user (especially being new to process modelling) had trouble using the tool. The user documentation was not used much (even though many of their problems were specifically addressed in that document). The ScreenCam demo was used extensively by the novice to understand how to use Spearmint and the different functionality. Apart from understanding the conceptual use of the tool, there is also a lot of functionality and many different views to be learnt. Even after quite extensive use, some of the more subtle (but important) features of Spearmint (like the include/exclude features, XML export and report function) were not being utilised by the novice user. Some basic usage scenarios, described step-by-step, may have helped with the learning difficulties.

In our experience there are four different things to learn in order to be able to use the tool:
- the process modelling concepts including the language,
- the different views supported by the tool,
- the many different features for drawing, analysing, reporting and saving models,
- the subtle behaviour of the tool (e.g. include/exclude, copy/paste, the rule checking and enforcement).

All these areas need to be well understood before the tool can be fully utilised and suitable learning material should be available.

7   Lessons Learned

Through our use of Spearmint in these two projects we have formed a picture of what we believe are the most useful features of the approach and where we think improvement could be made. We have summarised these opinions below. Although a complete evaluation/comparison of Spearmint with other process modelling tools is beyond the scope of this paper, we recognise that many tools are available with similar features that may be considered for purchase ([1,8,10]). We would strongly recommend that people looking to purchase a software process modelling tool consider our experience when selecting a tool.

"Must have" features
- Visual modelling – this is invaluable for communicating with the customer.
- An expressive language – while the product flow approach was mostly suitable for our needs we would have liked some dynamic concepts to support the process execution through the process guide.
- Decomposition/modularity – if the language/tool does not support decomposition large models will quickly become unmanageable.
- Checking – checking models against an accepted set of well-formedness rules can help identify errors and hence increase the quality of the models.
- Good reporting facilities – if you can't produce a nice report for your customer there is little point in using a tool to capture your models.

- Support for learning the language and the tool – standard documentation like on-line help as well as tutorials and wizards should be provided.
- EPG generation – if your goal is to use the process model as a guide then put this feature at the top of your list – it is invaluable.

Useful features
- Multiple views – although they add to the complexity of learning and using the tool the multiple views really help to manage the complexity of the model. It is important that they are automatically kept consistent by the tool.
- Partial views – once again, partial views add to the complexity of learning and using the tool but are useful in managing complexity.
- Support for abstraction (of a process model from a process instance) – would have greatly assisted the creation of the process models from the e-mail data.

8   Conclusion

The Spearmint approach to software process modelling has, in general, proved very successful in these two studies for supporting the creation and representation of descriptive process models. We have found the language supported these projects well with some minor exceptions that we have suggested for improvement. We found the visual representation truly invaluable for communicating with customers which was an important part of both our projects. We found the tool features of decomposition, multiple views and partial views provided good support for the management of the large process models, even though the multiple and partial views add to the complexity of learning and using the tool. We also found that the EPG generator performed well saving a lot of work in producing a process guide and that the resultant EPG was of a high quality and well accepted by the process participants. Having said that, we found the reporting facilities disappointing and would have benefits from more learning material, but these are a side effect of the immaturity of the approach rather than serious defects.

For the future we believe that the language should be fine-tuned to include more support for concepts required for a process guide such as allowable paths through the models and the specification of optional activities. Support for abstraction from instance models would have been a useful feature for us in the tool and would have reduced the workload of the process engineers significantly.

Acknowledgements. We would like to thank Allette Systems (Australia) for providing the e-mail data for the LTS Project case study, and the Fraunhofer Institute for Experimental Software Engineering, Kaiserslautern, Germany for supplying the Spearmint/EPG tool for evaluation. Funding for this project was provided through a collaborative SPIRT grant by the Australian Government (DETYA), University of Technology Sydney, University of New South Wales, AccessOnline Pty Ltd Sydney and Allette Systems (Australia).

References

1. ARIS. www.ids-scheer.de (29/11/00)
2. Sergio Bandinelli, Alfonso Fuggetta, Carlo Ghezzi and Luigi Lavazza, " SPADE: An Environment for Software Process Analysis, Design and Enactment", GOODSTEP Technical Report No 020, March 1994.
3. Ulrike Becker-Kornstaedt, Dirk Hamann, Ralf Kempkens, Peter Rösch, Martin Verlage, Richard Webby, Jörg Zettel. "Support for the Process Engineer: The Spearmint Approach to Software Process Definition and Process Guidance". Matthias Jarke, Andreas Oberweis (Eds.): Advanced Information Systems Engineering, Proceedings of the 11th International Conference CAiSE'99, Lecture Notes in Computer Science, Vol. 1626, pp. 119-133. Springer, 1999.
4. Ulrike Becker-Kornstaedt, Louise Scott and Jörg Zettel, "Process engineering with Spearmint(/EPG", Proceedings of the 22nd International Conference on Software Engineering, pp. 791-792, 2000.
5. B. Curtis, M. I. Kellner and J. Over. Process Modelling. Communications of the ACM, 35(9):75-90, September 1992.
6. Xavier Franch and Josep M. Ribo, " PROMENADE: A Modular Approach to Software Process Modelling and Enaction" Department de Llenguatges: Sistemes Informatics, Universitat Politecnica de Catalunya Technical Report No LSI-99-13-R, 1999.
7. D. Höltje, N. H. Madhavji, T. Bruckhaus, W. Hong, "Eliciting Formal Models of Software Engineering Processes", Proceedings of the 1994 CAS Conference, 1994.
8. INCOME V4. www.promatis.com (29/11/00)
9. ISO/IEC 12207:1995 Information Technology - Software Life Cycle Processes, International Standards Organization, 1995.
10. IThink. www.ithink.com (29/11/00)
11. M.L. Jaccheri, P. Lago, G.P. Picco, Eliciting Software Process Models with the E3 Language, ACM Transactions on Software Engineering and Methodology, 7:4, October 1998, pages 368-410.
12. Peter Rösch, Martin Verlage and Richard Webby, "SPEARMINT - A Prototype Tool for Visualising Complex Software Processes", Fraunhofer IESE Report 058.97/E, 1997.
13. L. Scott, R. Jeffery and U. Becker-Kornstaedt, "Preliminary Results of an Industrial EPG Evaluation", Technical Report Number 01/1, Centre for Advanced Software Engineering Research, University of New South Wales, Sydney, 2052, Australia.
14. Richard Webby and Ulrike Becker: "Towards a Logical Schema Integrating Software Process Modeling and Software Measurement." Presented at PMESSE '97 at ICSE 19, Boston, USA, May 1997.
15. Richard Webby, Peter Rösch and Martin Verlage, "Spearmint: an Integrated Approach to Software Process Visualisation", accepted for publication in the Transactions of the Society for Design and Process Science Journal of Design & Process Science.

A Software Process for an Integrated Electronic Commerce Portal System

Volker Gruhn[1] and Lothar Schöpe[2]

[1] Universität Dortmund, Fachbereich Informatik, Lehrstuhl Software-Technologie
Baroper Str. 301,
D-44227 Dortmund, Germany
volker.gruhn@uni-dortmund.de
[2] Informatik Centrum Dortmund e.V., Abt. Software-Technik
Joseph-v.-Fraunhofer-Str. 20,
D-44227 Dortmund, Germany
schoepe@icd.de

Abstract. In this paper we discuss that software processes for the development of electronic commerce systems are different from software processes for other kinds of information systems. We underpin this assumption by discussing an example software process and software architecture. This example is driven by real-world requirements. It is the development of a portal solution which is to be used by sales staff of an insurance company.

1 Introduction

Conventional business transactions – i.e. transactions not supported by information technology (IT) – are conducted nowadays by media like paper, telephone or fax [27],[28]. IT-supported business transactions use media like electronic mail, EDI, WWW and other Internet services [6],[7]. On an abstract level, partners in business transactions – either electronic or conventional – are supplier and customer. In special businesses, however, they can be called supplier and consumer, addressee and provider, or producer and supplier but also management and employee.

These roles – supplier and customer – can be taken by companies, administrations or private persons. If the role of the supplier as well as the role of the customer is taken by a company, the business transaction is called business-to-business (B2B). If the role of the customer is taken by a private person, the business transaction is called business-to-consumer (B2C). Analogously, the roles can be taken by an administration. In that case, the business transactions are called administration-to-consumer (A2C), administration-to-administration (A2A) or business-to-administration (B2A). Business transactions within a company – between management and employees, without external partners – are called business-to-employee (B2E). From a supplier's point of view, electronic commerce includes marketing, sales, distribution and after-sales support of products or services [21]. Electronic commerce primarily supports busi

V. Ambriola (Ed.): EWSPT 2001, LNCS 2077, pp. 90–101, 2001.

ness-to-consumer (B2C) or administration-to-consumer (A2C) business transactions. Electronic business, on the contrary, does not involve private customers but supports electronic business transactions between companies, administrations or between management and employees.

In electronic commerce as well as electronic business, suppliers and customers communicate electronically by means of a data communications network [1]. The Internet with its protocols (TCP/IP, FTP, NNTP, SMTP, HTTP, etc.) and services (Usenet, e-mail, WWW, etc.) represents such a data communications network.

The business transactions conducted between two partners in electronic commerce or electronic business are supported entirely or in part by different software systems. Each partner of the electronic business transaction uses individual and specific, simple or complex software systems to support his own business transactions. These systems do not only support the external business transactions with other partners, but often also the internal business transactions (B2E). Electronic commerce systems and electronic business systems may integrate the different software systems of the different partners of electronic commerce or electronic business transactions in a rather tight or more loose way. In this sense, an electronic commerce portal is an integration platform for different software systems like legacy, web, Internet or office systems. This structure of a typical electronic commerce system illustrates that software processes for this kind of systems differ from software processes for more traditional information systems. Key differences are:

- System integration is even more important than for traditional information systems. Systems to be integrated do not necessarily have a long lifetime. It should be planned that they are replaced after a while. This is true in the area of electronic commerce systems, because many predefined building blocks, like shop systems, content management systems, etc., are developed by small software companies. Users generally do not want to be dependent on these small suppliers.
- Users of the system are not known personally, feedback is more difficult to get.
- Besides of traditional software development skills, skills about graphical design are needed in order to provide attractive user interfaces.

Software processes take place in a more distributed way. While software components are developed by software houses, graphical features for the interface are developed by multimedia companies or marketing departments.

2 Architecture of the IPSI System

During a software engineering project an electronic commerce portal for insurances has been designed and realized. This portal – called Internet Portal System for Insurances (IPSI) – will support insurance agents with their daily work. The main goal of the portal is to support business-to-employee (B2E) processes. Thus, the communication between management and employees (e.g. insurance agents of an insurance company), but also between different employees, is supported by providing information about the product portfolio, tariffs, customers and contacts by the electronic commerce portal and its subsystems.

During the information analysis of the software engineering project, it was recognized that the electronic commerce portal serves as an integration platform for different heterogeneous subsystems. Based on a 3-tier-architecture, the user interface and data repository are separated from the functional application logic [15]. On the level of the functional application logic, the following subsystems of an electronic commerce portal have been identified:

Office System:[1] The office system manages contact addresses and scheduled appointments. For addresses, remote data and local data are distinguished: While remote data is managed by the partner management system of the insurance company, local data is managed by an office system on the user's computer in order to satisfy his privacy requirements.

Content Management System: Information of any kind is supplied by the content management system. Each employee of a company (e.g. management, back office employees or agents of the insurance company) can provide information for all others. Governed by individual access rights, every employee can get information from or put information into the content management system for every other employee (e.g. new product portfolio, handbooks, marketing materials, comments to the law, decisions in the context of insurances, etc.). The content management system will organize this information using different views and access rights.

Procurement System: The procurement system offers consumer goods (e.g. laser printers, toner, pencils, etc.) and services (e.g. courses, trainings, seminars, etc.). Every insurance agent can order consumer goods for his daily work. The management can monitor the orders and control the costs caused by the insurance agents.

Communications system: The communications system represents the interface to telecommunications media like mobile phones, fax and e-mail. The communications system is able to send documents, notifications or reminders by e-mail, Short Message Service (SMS) or fax. Notifications and reminders are sent at a pre-defined time set by the office system.

Portal Administration System: The portal administration system serves as the single point of login, i.e. the user of the electronic commerce portal does not need to authorize himself at each subsystem of the portal. The second purpose of the portal administration system is the analyzation and presentation of the log files of the subsystems.

Search System: The search system allows the user to search for information in the entire electronic commerce portal, based either on full text scan retrieval or predefined keywords. The results of a search request can be appointments, addresses of customers, information from the content management system, ordered goods or a combination of these elements.

---

[1] The management of addresses is realized by a traditional host system like IBM MVS (for remote data) and additionally by a local office system like Lotus Organizer or Microsoft Outlook (for local data). Access to the remote data is provided by the electronic commerce portal via an XML interface. The synchronization of remote and local data is also guaranteed by the electronic commerce portal.

Legacy System[2]: A legacy system is an external system not included in, but connected to the electronic commerce portal. Legacy systems are realized as host applications [8].

The portal user interface consists of web pages written in Hypertext Markup Language (HTML). For data management, a relational database management system is used if the subsystems do not have their own repository. Now, let's take a closer look at the system architecture (Figure 1).

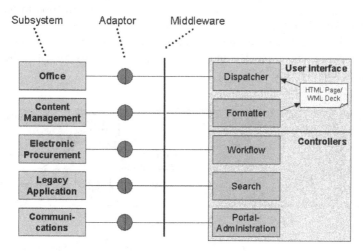

Fig. 1. System Architecture

Office, content management, procurement, legacy and communications are all external systems. To avoid building these from scratch, it was decided to integrate existing solutions into the electronic commerce portal.

Since the interfaces used to access the external systems are very different, each one is connected to the central middleware „backbone" via an individual adaptor. Each adaptor provides a set of methods to the middleware that encapsulates the native interface of the external system. This way, the (possibly complicated) native interface does not need to be publicly known in order to access its functionality. Instead, other subsystems can simply use the methods provided by the adaptor. For example, to send an e-mail via the communications system, it is sufficient to call the respective method of the communications adaptor which will then take care of constructing a RFC822-compliant message [9] from the supplied parameters, setting up a session with the SMTP server and sending the e-mail. Furthermore, the encapsulation allows for an

---

[2] In case of an integration in an existing infrastructure methods, concepts and software tools have to be provided an used. For this electronic commerce portal IPSI an integration by conventional domain specific highly individual application systems are necessary. These individual application systems are already used in insurance companies, authorities and financial organizations, etc.. These systems are also called legacy systems, e.g. partner management database in insurance companies or a billing system.

easy change of external systems: If a system's native interface changes, only its own adaptor must be rewritten while all other subsystems remain untouched.

The user interacts with the electronic commerce portal primarily via a web browser (other user agents such as mobile phones are also allowed by the system architecture). This has important implications for the control flow within the system: In traditional software systems, the dialog can be controlled by the system to a large extent: For example, the system can open a modal dialog box at any time, forcing the user to take some specific action before he can do anything else [17]. On the web, however, all actions are initiated by the user. The server cannot push information to the browser that the user did not request.[3]

Consequently, the external systems (office, content management etc.) of the electronic commerce portal remain passive and act only on user requests passed to them via the path depicted in Figure 2:

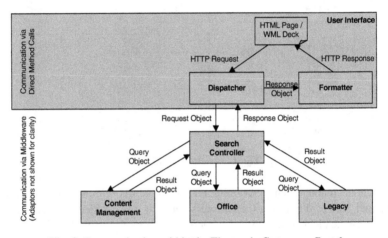

Fig. 2. Communication within the Electronic Commerce Portal

Every user action like clicking on a link or submitting a form generates an HTTP request [11] which is received by a central dispatcher. The dispatcher parses the HTTP request string, builds a request object from its contents and passes it to the controller that is responsible for handling the requested task. The search controller and admin controller implement the functionality of the search and portal administration systems mentioned earlier; all other transactions involving the external systems are handled by the workflow controller.

---

[3] This is true for a user interface built from plain HTML pages. Of course, one might conceive a client-side Java applet displaying information pushed to it by the server. However, this would require a Java-capable user agent, ruling out most of the currently available mobile agents like WAP phones, organizers etc. Plain HTML, on the other hand, makes the least assumptions about the target platform, and the subsystems producing it can easily be adapted to generate similar formats like Wireless Markup Language (WML).

The controllers might be considered the brains of the electronic commerce portal: They evaluate the request objects passed by the dispatcher. Depending on the type of request, they send commands to or query information from the external systems, consolidate the results and return them to the dispatcher. To achieve this, the specific workflow necessary to fulfill any given request is hard-coded into the respective controller. For example, upon receiving a request to search for a particular person in all the external systems, the search controller queries the office, content management and legacy systems and returns the combined results to the dispatcher.

The dispatcher then forwards the response object received from the controller to the formatter. This subsystem is responsible for converting the information contained in the response object into a format the user agent can render. In most situations, the preferred output format will be Hypertext Markup Language (HTML) [18] which is accessible with a wide range of user agents. For more exotic user agents such as WAP phones and organizers, other formatters can generate output formats like Wireless Markup Language (WML) [26]. This flexibility is one main advantage of the separation between formatters and controllers: Since the implementation of the user interface is concentrated in one dedicated system, the visual presentation of information can be changed or expanded without touching any of the systems actually providing the information.

Because of performance considerations and special system requirements, most external subsystems and the web server run on separate computers. This distributed architecture requires a middleware like CORBA to coordinate the calling of methods and passing of objects among the different subsystems. Of course, using the middleware is not necesssary within single subsystems such as the user interface: For example, the dispatcher calls a method of the formatter directly to pass a response object received from a controller.

The dispatcher and the controllers, however, might run on different machines. Thus, they exchange objects via the middleware. Two models of communication were considered during the design phase of the project:

1. **Publisher/Subscriber Model:** The dispatcher publishes a request object via the middleware and announces its availability with an event that describes the type of request. Controllers can subscribe to events that are relevant to them and get a copy of the respective request object from the middleware.
2. **Explicit Call Model:** Based on the type of request, the dispatcher decides which controller(s) it must call to pass the request object to via the middleware.

In the publisher/subscriber model, the dispatcher is effectively reduced to a mechanism for converting HTTP request strings to request objects since it does not know which controller is responsible for which type of request. While this may at first seem like an elegant decoupling, there are some pitfalls: Although the "sending" part of the dispatcher does not need to be changed when a new controller is added to the subscriber list, the "receiving" part must still be prepared to accept result objects from the additional controller. Regarding the effort for defining interfaces between the dispatcher and the controllers, the publisher/subscriber model holds no advantage over the explicit call model: Both dispatcher and controllers need to know which attributes are defined for request objects of any type, regardless of the means by which the objects are transported. More problems arise from the multi-user environment of the electronic commerce portal: The dispatcher needs to know which result object returned by the controller corresponds to which request object passed to it. In the explicit call model, this mapping is implicitly provided by the call stack of the middleware. In the publisher/subscriber model, each request object (and the objects passed between controllers and subsystems) would have to be tagged with a unique identifier in order to track the incoming result objects – an unnecessary overhead.

Controllers and subsystems communicate by exchanging "business objects" [2], i.e. entities that are central to the workflow in the electronic commerce portal. The following business objects are therefore known to all controllers and subsystems:

- User
- Contact
- Appointment
- Task
- Message
- Shop Item
- Order
- Order History
- Search Request
- Search Result

To schedule an appointment, for example, the workflow controller creates an appointment object from the data received by the dispatcher and passes it to a method of the office subsystem that adds the appointment to the user's calendar. If the user chooses to be reminded of the appointment by e-mail in time, the workflow controller additionally creates a message object, connects a copy of the appointment object to it and passes it to the communications system which will queue it for e-mail delivery at the time requested by the user.

3 Realization

The first phase in the process of realizing the electronic commerce portal was an analysis of the content and function requirements. To gain insight into the portal users' needs, the project team visited several insurance companies. Through demonstrations of systems currently used by insurance agents and discussions with developers, the team learned about the typical tasks an insurance agent performs in his daily work and how these can be supported by software solutions. The results of the analysis were organized by breaking the more comprehensive tasks down into singular activities which were then prioritized and documented in requirement forms.

Based on the requirement forms, the subsystems office, content management, procurement, communications, legacy, search and administration were identified. For each of these subsystems, a make-or-buy decision had to be made. After evaluating existing solutions and considering the effort for developing a subsystem from scratch vs. integrating the existing solution, the team chose the integrative approach for most systems, namely:

- **Office**   Outlook 98 by Mircosoft Corporation [5]
- **Content Management** Pirobase 4.0 by PiroNet AG [19]
- **Procurement**   SmartStore 2.0 by SmartStore AG [22]

- **Communications**

E-mail	JAVA-Mail by Sun Microsystems, Inc. [23]
Fax	Sendfax – Freeware Linux 6.3 (i386) by SuSE GmbH [24]
SMS	Sendfax – Freeware Linux 6.3 (i386) by SuSE GmbH [25]

- **Legacy** sample partner database of the Continentale Versicherung

The search and administration systems were not classified as external systems but as controllers since they actively request or modify information of the other systems.

To test the feasibility of these decisions, the team programmed cut-through prototypes, i.e. "quick-and-dirty" implementations of the adaptors described in the system architecture. The goal of these prototypes was to prove that it is possible to encapsulate the native interfaces of the external systems and make their key features accessible via the adaptors. This goal was met for all subsystems, clearing the way for the next phase of the software development process.

For the object oriented design phase, the team used the Unified Modeling Language (UML) [3]. The key features of all subsystems were modeled in use cases in order to identify business objects and possible dependencies between the subsystems. Based on the insights gained in this step, concrete classes were defined for each subsystem. To ensure an easy consolidation of the results and allow for later changes to the subsystems without touching any dependent classes, each subsystem is represented at the "outside" by one boundary class. This class provides all methods other classes need to access the subsystem. As an example, let's consider a search request handled by the legacy system (Figure 3):

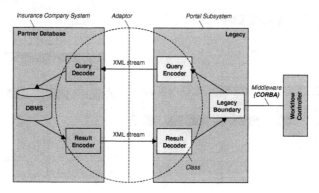

Fig. 3. Integration of Legacy System

The large box in the middle is a view inside the legacy subsystem that we know from previous figures. The smaller boxes inside represent classes. Because only the legacy boundary class is connected to the workflow controller via the middleware, in our example the controller does not pass the search request object directly to the query encoder. Instead, the search request is passed to the legacy boundary class which then passes it to the query encoder. This class is a part of the adaptor that, as discussed earlier, hides the native interface of the external system from the portal subsystem: In the case of the legacy system, queries and results of the insurance company's partner database are XML-encoded [4] for maximum platform and transport independence. The XML-encoded search query is run against the insurance company's database, and the encoded result is returned to the legacy subsystem where the result decoder (another part of the adaptor) creates a search result object and passes it to the legacy boundary class, which returns it to the workflow controller.

After consolidation of the designs for subsystems, controllers and user interface, the team entered the implementation phase. Most classes were implemented in the Java programming language [12], only the adaptor for the office system uses Microsoft Visual C++ [14] code to access the Microsoft Outlook 98 API.

Figure 4 shows the homepage of the electronic commerce portal. After logging into the system, the insurance agent is presented with all information that is relevant to him that time: Personal messages, articles of interest from the content management system, scheduled appointments and due tasks from the office system, events and items from the procurement system. Legacy applications like the partner database and a provisioning system are accessible via links on the homepage. A search interface allows for meta searches in selected areas of the portal.

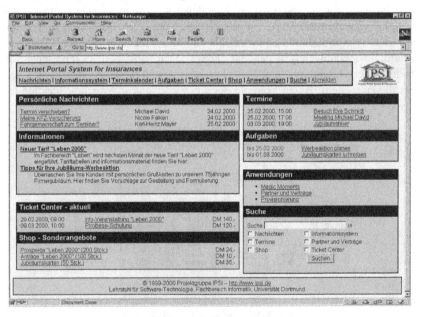

Fig. 4. Electronic Commerce Portal

The process model for the development of the electronic commerce portal IPSI will be shown in a rough scheme in figure 5. Funsoft-Nets are used for process modeling [10]. The process model consists of the subprocess models (requirement specification, subsystem evaluation, system design, prototype development, realization, integration- and system test, user interface development and realization).

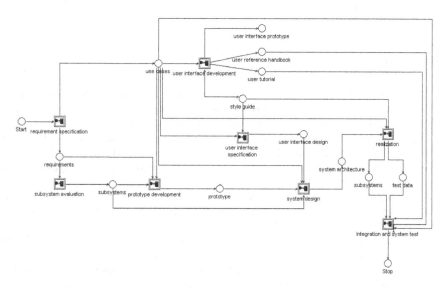

Fig. 5. Software Development Process for the Electronic Commerce Portal

4 Conclusion

In building the IPSI system we had to recognize that the implementation of a portal system is an integration engineering task. This had an important impact onto the software process deployed. Backend integration is based on middleware, frontend integration is based on a commonly used user interface which demanded for careful design.

Most requirements for IPSI were fulfilled by integrating standard tools. In order to effectively plan the software process for building IPSI, it was crucial to use prototypes (compare above). Only after implementing these prototypes we were able to assess the feasibilty of the architecture and only then we were able to calculate duration of the tasks identified and efforts needed for these tasks. The productive use of IPSI showed that the openness of the architecture is a crucial issue. Many further legacy systems had to be added after the initial release, standard tools were exchanged for individual customers. All these modifications depend on a clear and modular architecture. With hindsight, it would have been useful to develop IPSI as a component-based system on the basis of a standard component model like JavaBeans or COM [13].

Summing this up, the effort for implementing was lower than initially expected, simply because we were able to benefit from standard tools. The kind of tasks was different from what was initially planned, more tasks than initially planned were integration tasks. In the end only a few thousand lines of software were written, but this software was used as glue between existing systems and therefore required extremely detailed design and careful testing.

References

1. Adam, N., Yesha, Y. (ed.): Electronic Commerce: An Overview. In: Adam, N, Yesha, A.: Electronic Commerce. Lecture Notes on Computer Science, Vol 1028, Springer-Verlag, Berlin Heidelberg New York (1995) 4–12
2. Baker, S., Geraghty, R.: Java for Business Objects. In: Carmichel, A.: Developing Business Objects. SIGS Cambridge University Press USA (1998) 225-237
3. Booch, G., Jacobson, I., Rumbaugh, J.: The Unified Modeling Language User Guide. Addison Wesley, Reading, MA, USA (1999)
4. Bray, T., Paoli, J., Sperberg-McQueen, C.M.: Extensible Markup Language (XML) 1.0 W3C Recommendation 10, Feb. 1998, http://www.w3.org/TR/1998/REC-xml-19980210 (cited: March 2000)
5. Byne, R.: Building Applications With Microsoft Outlook 2000 Technical Reference, Microsoft Press (2000)
6. Chesher, M., Kaura, R.: Electronic Commerce and Business Communiations. Springer Verlag, Berlin Heidelberg New York (1998)
7. Connelly, D.W.: An Evaluation of the World Wide Web as a Platform for Electronic Commerce. In: Kalakota, R., Whinston, A.: Readings in Electronic Commerce. Addison Wesley Longman Inc. reading, MA, USA (1996) 55-70
8. Coyle, F.P.: Legacy Integration –Changing Perspectives. In: IEEE Software, Vol. 17, No. 2 (2000) 37-41
9. Crocker, D.H.: RFC822: Standard for the Format of ARPA Internet Text Messages. ftp://ftp.isi.edu/in-notes/rfc822.txt (cited: March 2000)
10. Deiters, W., Gruhn, V.: The Funsoft Net Approach to Software Process Management. In: Int. Journal of Software Engineering and Knowledge Engineering, Vol. 4, No. 2 (1994) 229-256
11. Fielding, R., Gettys, J., Mogul, H., Frystk, L., Masnier, P., Leach, T, Berners-Lee, H.: RFC2616: Hypertext Transfer Protocol – HTTP 1.1.
12. ftp://ftp.isi.edu/in-notes/rfc2616.txt (cited: March 2000)
13. Gosling, J., Joy, B., Steels, G.: The Java Language Specification. Addison Wesley Longman, Inc. Reading, MA, USA (1996)
14. Gruhn, V., Thiel, A.: Komponentenmodelle – DCOM, JavaBeans, Enterprise Java-Beans, CORBA. Addison-Wesley, München (2000)
15. Kruglinski, D.J.: Inside Visual C++ Version 5. Microsoft Press, 1999
16. Lewandowski, S.: Frameworks for Computer-Bases Client/Server Computing. In: ACM Computing Surveys, Vol 30, No. 1 (1998) 3-27
17. Lincke, D., Zimmermann, H.: Integrierte Standardanwendungen für Electronic Commerce – Anforderungen und Evaluationskriterien. In: Hermanns, A., Sauter, M. (Hrsg.) Management-Handbuch Electronic Commerce, Verlag Franz Vahlen München (1999) 197-210
18. Nielsen, J.: The Difference Between Web Design and GUI Design. Alertbox for May 1, 1997 http://www.useit.com/alertbox/9705a.html (cited: March 2000)

19. Pemberton, S. (et.al.): XHTML™ 1.0: The Extensible HyperText Markup Language. A Reformulation of HTML 4 in XML 1.0. W3C Recommendation 26 January 2000 http://www.w3.org/TR/2000/REC-xhtml1-20000126 (cited: March 2000)
20. PiroNet AG: Pirobase© System Architecture. http://www.pironet.com (cited: March 2000)
21. Rhee, H., Riggins, F.: Toward a unified view of electronic commerce. In: Communications of the ACM, Vol. 41, No. 19 (1998) 88-95
22. Schmidt, B., Lindemann, M.: Elements of a Reference Model for Electronic Markets. In: Proceedings of the 31st Annual International Conference on Systems Science HICSS'98, (1998) 193-201
23. SmartStore AG: SmartStore Standard Edition 2.0. http://www.smartstore.de
24. (cited: March 2000)
25. Sun Microsystems Inc.: JavaMail 1.1.3™ Release. http://java.sun.com/
26. (cited: March 2000)
27. SuSE GmbH: SuSE Linux 6.3 (i386) – November 1999 "sendfax"
28. http://www.suse.de/en/produkte/susesoft/linux/Pakete/paket_sendfax.html
29. (cited: March 2000)
30. SuSE GmbH: SuSE Linux 6.3 (i386) – November 1999 "yaps"
31. http://www.suse.de/en/produkte/susesoft/linux/Pakete/paket_sendfax.html
32. (cited: March 2000)
33. Wireless Application Forum: Wireless Application Protocol: Wireless Markup Language Specification. Version 1.1, 16 June 1999.
34. http://www1.wapforum.org/tech/documents/SPEC-WML-19991104.pdf (cited: March 2000
35. Zwass, V.: Electronic Commerce: Structure and Issues. In: International Journal of Electronic Commerce, Vol. 1, No.1 M.E. Sharpe, Armonk, NY, USA (1996) 3-23
36. Zwass, V.: Structure and Macro-Level Impacts of Electronic Commerce: From Technological Infrastrukture to Electronic Marketplaces. In: Kendall, K.E.: Emerging Information Technology Sage Publications (1999)

A Mobile Agent Approach to Process-Based Dynamic Adaptation of Complex Software Systems

Giuseppe Valetto[1,2], Gail Kaiser[1], and Gaurav S. Kc[1]

[1]Columbia University, Department of Computer Science, 1214 Amsterdam Avenue, Mail Code 0401, New York, NY, 10027, United States
{valetto, kaiser, gskc}@cs.columbia.edu
[2]Telecom Italia Lab, Via Guglielmo Reiss Romoli, 274, 10148, Torino, Italy
Giuseppe.Valetto@tilab.com

Abstract. We describe an approach based upon software process technology to on-the-fly monitoring, redeployment, reconfiguration, and in general dynamic adaptation of distributed software applications. We choose the term *dynamic adaptation* to refer to modifications in structure and behavior that can be made to individual components, as well as sets thereof, or the overall target system configuration, such as adding, removing or substituting components, *while the system is running and without bringing it down*. The goal of dynamic adaptation is manifold: supporting run-time software composition, enforcing adherence to requirements, ensuring uptime and quality of service of mission-critical systems, recovering from and preventing faults, seamless system upgrading, etc. Our approach involves dispatching and coordinating software agents - named Worklets – via a process engine, since successful dynamic adaptation of a complex distributed software system often requires the concerted action of multiple agents on multiple components. The dynamic adaptation process must incorporate and decide upon knowledge about the specifications and architecture of the target software, as well as Worklets capabilities. Dynamic adaptation is correlated to a variety of other software processes - such as configuration management, deployment, validation and evolution - and allows addressing at run time a number of related concerns that are normally dealt with only at development time.

1 Motivation

Distributed software systems are becoming increasingly large and difficult to understand, build and evolve. The trend towards integrating legacy/COTS heterogeneous components and facilities of varying granularity into "systems of systems" can often aggravate the problem, by introducing dependencies that are hard to analyze and track and can cause unexpected effects on the overall system functioning and performance.

A number of best software engineering practices attack this challenge, such as component-based frameworks, Architectural Description Languages (ADLs), Aspect-Oriented Programming (AOP), etc. They mainly operate on the specification of the software at some level, aiming at better describing, understanding and validating software artifacts and their interrelationships. Those practices must be incorporated

V. Ambriola (Ed.): EWSPT 2001, LNCS 2077, pp. 102-116, 2001.

into and enacted by the development process in order to enable the creation and maintenance of quality systems, and in general result in new iterations of the lifecycle spiral when any corrective, adaptive and perfective needs arise.

A complementary avenue for addressing the aforementioned complexity is represented by the introduction of run-time automated facilities that enable some form of monitoring, control and adaptation of the software behavior – including re-deployment and reconfiguration of components without bringing the system down. Such dynamic adaptation assumes that systems can gauge their own "health" (i.e. run-time quality parameters) and take action to preserve or recover it, by rapidly performing suitable integration and reconfiguration actions.

The scope of dynamic adaptation is necessarily limited with respect to full-fledged re-engineering, but it can still alleviate or resolve at lesser costs a wide range of maintenance, evolution and operation problems, such as supporting run-time software composition, enforcing adherence to requirements, ensuring uptime and quality of service of mission-critical systems, recovering from and preventing faults, seamless system upgrading, etc.

Numerous research initiatives are active on these themes. The DARPA DASADA program [14] – for instance - has recently promoted a large number of efforts aimed at achieving and maintaining high levels of assurance, dependability and adaptability of complex, component-based software at all phases of the system's life cycle: before, during and after system assembly time, including provisions for on-the-fly re-assembly and adaptation. The ESPRIT project C3DS [6] similarly tackles dynamic composition, (re)configuration and execution control of componentized services. Also other research efforts address various facets of the same challenge, such as automatic software configuration and deployment (SoftwareDock [18]), rapid composition of heterogeneous software with federations (PIE [13.]) or workflow-aware middleware (Opera [2]), dynamic layout (re)programming for distributed systems (FarGo[20]), and many others.

Successful dynamic adaptation requires a considerable knowledge of the specifications and architecture of the system, in order to detect inconsistent or undesired structure/behavior and decide what to do. Hence, it builds upon approaches that encourage the formalization of such knowledge during development, but aims at extending their usefulness to the realm of software operation. Moreover, automating the dynamic adaptation of a non-trivial system requires the presence of a sophisticated process engine to handle the intricacies and dependencies of adaptation procedures. Hence, we present an approach to dynamic adaptation that is based upon process and agent technologies. On the one hand, it proposes to exploit distributed process technology to efficiently build and operate reliable and robust software products. On the other hand, it is positioned at the intersection between software processes such as evolution, configuration management, deployment, and validation, and allows addressing several of their concerns not only at development time but also at run time.

2 Approach

We envision an approach that explicitly takes advantage of process technology to automate the dynamic adaptation process with a community of software agents, whose activities are orchestrated by a distributed process engine.

We employ Worklets [22] as our dynamic adaptation agents: Worklets carry self-contained mobile code that can act upon target components and follow directives indicating their route and operation parameters. Worklets were originally conceived as a means for flexible software (re)configuration, with effects local to the target component. Each Worklet would work with the component needing configuration, deciding what to do on the basis of the component state and its own capabilities. Moreover, a Worklet could "hop" from a component to another, carrying out at each location a portion of a predetermined multi-step configuration sequence. A very simple example of this kind of reconfiguration would be dispatching a Worklet to modify the ports used for inter-communication by two components of the target system: the Worklet would carry information about the various port numbers and code to activate new ports and deactivate old ones.

The careful reader may notice that even this simplistic scenario actually calls for some degree of coordination, since the Worklet must be instructed to avoid disrupting any outstanding communications (or enable their recovery), and the switch to new ports must happen at both sites in an "atomic" way, to preserve at all times the correctness of the inter-component interaction.

In Section 3.3, we propose a more comprehensive scenario that exemplifies the kind of problems that any dynamic adaptation mechanism must resolve and technically clarifies our approach. However it is clear that when the target system becomes substantially large and complex, with various interwoven aspects of adaptation that involve a multiplicity of components, individual Worklets cannot simply go off and do their job autonomously, neither the subtleties of that job can be practically hardcoded or scripted into them *a priori*. Successful dynamic adaptation demands that a number of interdependent actions be performed in a concerted and timely way: some kind of "guiding hand" is necessary, which in our belief can conveniently take the form of a process enactment engine.

Process- and agent-based dynamic adaptation derives from considerations advocating the separation of concerns between coordination and computation in distributed programming [7]. On the one hand, Worklets deliver the computational units that carry out the mechanics of modifying the system behavior. Such computational code can be written in principle in any conventional programming language that allows Worklets to interact with the target components: we currently employ Java because Java as a platform inherently offers considerable mileage with respect to the kind of mobile distributed computation that we envision. On the other hand, the dynamic adaptation process provides the coordination context: it does not deal with the local operation of a Worklet on a target component, but rather with enacting cooperative reactive and proactive dynamic adaptation procedures, scheduling and committing the overall work of cooperating Worklets, handling contingencies and exceptional courses of action, etc.

Dynamic adaptation processes are defined by codifying multi-faceted predefined and/or accumulated knowledge about the system (e.g. requirements, composability, architecture, configuration, distribution, operation) and their intended variation in an enactable process language, which becomes the coordination "programming" language for the Worklets community.

Notice that at this stage we are not overly concerned about evaluating or producing process modeling and enacting formalisms particularly suited for dynamic adaptation. Rather, we focus on how an "ideal" or "generic" process technology can be employed to implement systems with the specific kind of *process awareness* [33] required for dynamic adaptation.

The target system must be process-aware in the sense that its components and connectors must be able to accommodate dynamic adaptation agents and expose to them appropriate internal reconfiguration functionality. However, they do not need to incorporate any process enactment capabilities, nor know anything about the dynamic adaptation process: process-awareness is provided for them by a completely external and separate process enactment engine.

Such process engine must be decentralized in many senses, since scalability, responsiveness and fault tolerance are crucial for effective dynamic adaptation. Therefore, we envision a set of distributed task processors - typically co-located with major target system components - that coordinately take up "local" fragments of the overall dynamic adaptation process and orchestrate worklets accordingly; moreover, they contribute to maintaining a distributed process state and handle a variety of widely dispersed resources and artifacts.

Additionally, it is critical that the process engine distribution architecture can change in correspondence to changes in the target system, such as dynamism and mobility of components as well as data, which can increasingly occur in today's distributed applications and services. For instance, a task processor with local process information might need to migrate to a new location, in response to a run-time re-configuration of some target system component (notice that such a re-configuration may be the effect of a previous dynamic adaptation activity).

Ideal requirements for the process engine can therefore be summed up as multi-dimensional distribution (including distribution of the process definition, resources, enactment data and enactment architecture), and temporal variability of those distribution dimensions.

Software process, workflow and agent coordination research have produced a number of advanced results in decentralized process technology: among them, multi-agent engines, either peer-to-peer (Juliette [8], Serendipity-II [17], Cougaar [11]), or hierarchical (OPSS [12]); multi-server Web-centered (WebWork [26], Endeavors [4]) or database-centered systems (Opera [2]); federation systems, such as APEL [34] and OzWeb [21]. Those systems and their typologies comply with our requirements at various degrees. An in-depth discussion of those requirements and a synopsis of several process engines in that respect can be found in [32].

3 Technical Description

We are building an infrastructure named KX (*Kinesthetics eXtreme*) to enable the *Continual Validation* of complex distributed software systems, in the context of DARPA's DASADA program [10]. Continual Validation operates on a running system to ensure that critical functioning and assurance factors are constantly preserved, by rapidly and properly adapting the system whenever the modification of field conditions demand it.

KX aims to achieve continual validation by superimposing a minimally intrusive controlling meta-architecture on top of the target system. Such meta-architecture is in charge to introduce an adaptation feedback and feedforward control loop onto the target system, detecting and responding to the occurrence of certain conditions. Generally, such conditions would indicate errors and failures of some sort, or at least undesirable behavior such as degrading performance, and can arise within components, or at inter-components boundaries (i.e., on the connectors of the target architecture).

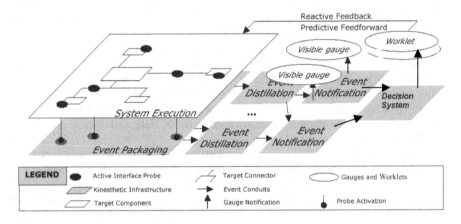

Fig. 1. KX meta-architecture

Compared to the fine-grained level of internal diagnostics and remedies that can be sometimes performed in isolation by a self-assured, fault-tolerant component, the KX meta-architecture aims to handle more global situations, perhaps involving heterogeneous components obtained from multiple sources where it would be difficult if not impossible to retrofit self-assurance. For instance, by monitoring conditions in architectural connectors and correlating them to conditions arising in dependent components, it can correctly interpret and detect mishaps like functional and performance mismatches, breaches of interface contracts and others, which may have far-reaching, domino effects on systems that are built out of a variety of COTS and proprietary components. Notice that, in order to avoid interference to or unnecessary overriding of any self-assurance facilities present within single components, KX must be enabled to reason about some specifications of what those facilities are likely to do under externally observable circumstances.

The major conceptual elements of KX are shown in Fig.1:

- A set of probes, registering and reporting relevant information on the behavior of the target system. An approach to automatically inserting probes into the source code of a target system via *active interfaces* is found in [19]; another approach is to replace dynamic link libraries [3].

- A distributed asynchronous event bus for receiving target system events, including manufactured events such as "heartbeats", from the probes and directing them through packaging, filtering and notification facilities;
- A set of gauges to describe and measure the progress of the target system (and also the work done "behind the scenes" by the meta-architecture. Gauges in their raw form are machine-readable data packets carrying significant monitoring information that is synthesized from the event traffic in the bus via proper matching and filtering. KX renders gauges either as user-friendly visual or textual panels of Web-based consoles dedicated to human system operators and administrators, or directly as data feeds into automated decision support;
- Decision support systems and agents, to respond to the conditions indicated through the gauges by determining appropriate target system adaptations;
- Actuation facilities for the delivery and execution of any adaptation measures decided upon on the basis of gauge readings. As outlined in Section 2, our platform of choice is agent-based and employs Worklets as its actuators.

In the KX context, the process engine coordinating dynamic adaptation is one possible implementation of the decision support component. It can be seen as either complementary or altogether alternative to any decision facilities devoted to the monitoring and administration of the running system on the part of humans. Process- and agent-based dynamic adaptation allows KX to automatically implement a tighter closed control loop compared to human decision-making supports, which typically have longer reaction and response times, and lean towards open loop control. (See for example the DASADA MesoMorph [29] project, which relies on a wealth of design time - architecture, requirements - and run time information - gauge readings - to enable a human role – the *Change Administrator* – to take informed decisions on software variation and reconfiguration.) Furthermore, our approach suggests and supports the codification, materialization, and enforcement of sophisticated and explicit dynamic adaptation processes, which set it apart from other reactive architectures, such as that proposed in [9], in which any process remains implicit.

3.1   Monitoring and Triggering

The enactment of a fragment of the dynamic adaptation process is triggered by the occurrence of significant conditions within the target system, which are detected and reported by the monitoring part of the meta-architecture. Conditions can be simple: for instance, a single event might be sufficient to indicate the raising of a critical exception by a target system component, and require the recovery of the failed computation. Many times, however, conditions are complex, i.e., defined in terms of partially ordered sets - *posets* – of events For instance, only a sequence of events can hint at the progressive degradation of some service parameter, demanding the preventive replication of some bottleneck target system component in order to preserve QoS. Or, the (likely) crash of some other component – calling for its re-instantiation and re-initialization - can be detected by composing timeout events for requests directed to that component, and possibly the lack of a periodic "heartbeat" event originating from the same component.

   A subscription mechanism is a convenient way to declare what posets the dynamic adaptation process is interested into, i.e., what kind of conditions arising in the target system it can handle and what information is sought about them. In practice, however, poset subscription may be complicated or impractical. Therefore, the componentized KX event bus provides *distillers*, which subscribe to those individual events that might appear in a poset, keep notice of what has been seen so far (e.g., via Finite State Automata), and report poset occurrences to *notifiers*. Notifiers then compile other, higher-level events on the basis of the content of the poset, and report them in meaningful forms to the process engine and/or any gauges.

3.2   Instantiation and Dispatching of Dynamic Adaptation Agents

With respect to the monitoring subsystem, the process engine behaves in a completely reactive way. Once it is notified about a condition, the engine may dynamically initiate a complex set of interrelated adaptation operations, which typically require the instantiation of one or more Worklets, their initialization, and finally their dispatching.

Each Worklet can contain one or more mobile code snippets (in our terminology, *worklet junctions*) that are suitable for actuating the required adaptation of the target system. Junctions' data structures can be initialized with data, typically coming from the task definition, the process context, and the information contained in the event(s) that represents the triggering condition. Furthermore, any process-related configuration of Worklets is accounted for by *worklet jackets,* which allow scripting of certain aspects of Worklet behavior in the course of its route. Among them, pre-conditions and timing for junction delivery and activation, repetition of junction execution, exit conditions for the junction's work, directives to supersede, suspend, and reactivate a junction upon delivery of another one, and so on.

One important consideration is that the definition of the dynamic adaptation process must enable the engine to reason about which worklet junctions are applicable to what target components under which conditions. Hence, substantial formalized knowledge about the specifications of the requirements, architecture and dynamics of the target system must be made available to the process. Also, knowledge about the available worklet junctions (or tailorable templates) and their dynamic adaptation capabilities must be characterized accordingly. Formal specifications languages or Architecture Description Languages (ADLs) that allow expressing architectural events and behavior– as well as properties and constraints – may be suitable means to reach these ends. For example, the ABLE project [1] proposes to exploit Acme [15] to define a rule-base that associates "repair strategies" to events (and posets) in the system that signal the violation architectural constraints and properties. Such a rule base can represent a valid basis for defining a dynamic adaptation process. Other languages, like Rapide [23] and Darwin [24], may be equally suitable. (Further discussion of requirements and merits of these and other approaches is out of the scope of this short paper.)

On the basis of the aforementioned knowledge, the process engine requests junctions for the dynamic adaptation task at hand from a Worklet Factory, which has access to a categorized semantic catalogue of junction classes and instantiates them on its behalf. Interfaces exposed by junctions in the catalogue must be matched to the kind of capabilities that are necessary for the task and to descriptions of the target components subject to dynamic adaptation.

Once a Worklet gets to a target component, the interaction between the junction(s) it carries and that component is mediated by a *host adaptor*, which semantically resolves any impedance mismatch between the interface of a junction and that of the component (see Fig. 2). The original purpose of the host adaptor was to provide each worklet junction with a consistent abstract interface to a variety of component types, including COTS or legacy components, that can be subject to forms of dynamic adaptation that are *semantically* equivalent from the worklet junction's perspective.

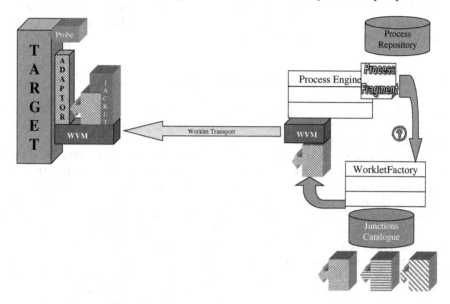

Fig. 2. Selecting junctions and shipping Worklets.

There is a tradeoff, however, between the complexity of the host adaptor and the complexity of the worklet junctions its supports. Our first realization of Worklets used JPython scripts for the entire worklet body, which allowed very simple worklets but required a very heavyweight host adaptor (including, among other facilities, the entire JPython interpreter) – which made it unsuitable for the constrained-resource devices (e.g., PalmOS or PocketPC PDAs) we target for some applications. Requiring the identical abstraction on such devices as on, say, conventional website servers was prohibitive. The current implementation instead uses Java code augmented by our own peculiar jacket scripting, which allows for lightweight/subset JVM implementations (e.g., WABA, see http://www.wabasoft.com/) and relaxed requirements on host adaptors, e.g., in the simplest case to directly expose the local API "as is" - but of course requires more specialized knowledge and advanced capabilities on the part of individual worklet junctions.

The transport services, as well as the worklet junction execution context and the interpretation of jacket scripts, are provided by a generic *Worklet Virtual Machine* (WVM) located at each target component intended to host worklets (generally integrated into the host adaptor). For each dynamic adaptation task, the process engine typically schedules the shipping of multiple Worklets. Each Worklet may traverse various hosts in its route, installing junctions in the corresponding WVMs.

Execution of the procedural code of the junctions is (optionally) governed by jackets and carries out adaptation of the target component through the programmatic interface provided by the adaptor. Junctions' data structures may be modified as a result of those operations. At the end of its route, the Worklet may go back to its origin, for any reporting and housekeeping needs, which are performed by a specialized *origin junction*.

Each stop on a Worklet's route represents thence the finest unit of process granularity, and the traversal of the whole route can be seen in itself as a micro-workflow; in turn, that is only a single schedulable step in the context of a multi-Worklet dynamic adaptation process fragment.

3.3   Process-Based Dynamic Adaptation: A Practical Example

To solidify our technical discussion, we now consider the case of a mission-critical component-based application, which relies on and integrates a number of external third-party data sources to provide its services.

Of course, modifications to one or more data sources may significantly disrupt our application. Imagine that the provider of a data source has decided to extend its reachability, to be able to service greater data volumes to more clients. The primary source has changed its network location, while the original location is still in use, but as a secondary mirror with somewhat inferior service level. Furthermore, during the upgrade the provider has partially modified the data definition schema, to accommodate a new wealth of information for its new clients. However, the data source provider has devised and negotiated with its clients a mechanism to handle this kind of upgrading situation, and a converter (e.g., between the old and new XML Schema, assuming XML-codified data) is made available for download.

This scenario can be resolved on-the-fly by a community of Worklets with appropriate capabilities that execute a well-planned dynamic adaptation process. Our mission-critical application is faced with a composite situation: degradation of service from the original data source site, coupled with partial or total inability to make proper use of that data. Those two conditions can be recognized at different levels: respectively, analysis of network traffic from/to the data source, and alarms raised by the parsing/processing application component that "wraps" the data source. Notice that there is a process granularity issue here: those conditions can either each trigger an autonomous dynamic adaptation reaction, aiming at overcoming that individual situation, or may be recognized (and responded to) together as the signature of a major data source upgrade (perhaps on the basis of accumulated experience and incremental process improvement). In the former case, two process fragments will be enacted autonomously, which will variously overlap and interact. In the latter case, the overall dynamic adaptation plan will integrate both fragments and will schedule them in order, as a single complex dynamic adaptation operation. Below, we take this option for simplicity sake.

At first, bots-like Worklets can be dispatched in parallel by the dynamic adaptation process, with appropriate instructions to retrieve the network location of the new primary data source site and the converter that allows migration to the new data interface. This task – which may be a complex sub-process in itself - represents a pre-requisite for any actual dynamic adaptation of the system, given the necessity to incorporate and employ the retrieved knowledge. The process can then proceed by sending out a Worklet with the converter to the component in charge of wrapping the data source, which will execute it in order to be able to correctly process information again. Once this adaptation is performed and proves correct, another Worklet can be dispatched to the same component, in order to reconfigure its connection to the data source to point to the new primary site. In addition, if the communication performance still remains below the service level that must be assured, another Worklet can instantiate a new component, i.e., a load-balancing proxy for the two mirrors, perhaps with on-board cache; in that case, the connection needs to be again reconfigured to take advantage of the proxy.

3.4   Levels of Application of Dynamic Adaptation

Dynamic adaptation can be carried out at various stages in the life of a target application, from installation (e.g., remedies in case the installation script fails because a component executable is missing), to deployment (e.g., identify alternative hosts for components that fail to deploy on the default host), operation (e.g. maintain critical quality parameters in a desired range), and upgrade (e.g. substitute components on-the-fly with new versions).

Notice also that, in KX, dynamic adaptation can happen not only on the target system but also on the meta-architecture itself, thus enabling flexible monitoring and control modalities that adapt KX functioning parameters to changes in the target. We have identified three major contexts in KX in which dynamic adaptation applies[1]:

- Dynamic adaptation of the target system: this is essential to implement the actuating part of the feedback/feed forward loop of KX;
- Dynamic adaptation of probes and the filtering and pattern matching mechanisms as well as rules: this allows to vary the kind of system information that is sought and exploited by KX, in response to the dynamics of the target system operation;
- Dynamic adaptation of the notification and gauging facilities: this allows to vary the amount and type of information that is reported about the target system, as well as the ways in which it is made available to the decision support components.

4   Related Work

Adaptation of software can be carried out at many degrees: at one extreme, *macro-adaptation* can be achieved only by extensively re-engineering the system; at the other, *micro-adaptation* consists of fine-tuning of running software. Examples of the latter are often found in software (such as drivers) that manages system resources that may have multiple operation modes, and can be optimized on demand or automatically. A more sophisticated flavor of micro-adaptation is implemented in

---

[1]   Additionally, dynamic adaptation of the (process-based) decision support component can be seen as a form of rapid process evolution at enactment time - similar for example to the TCCS approach of C3DS (see the relevant discussion in Section 4). This is for now outside the scope of our work.

fault-tolerant software by internal application-specific diagnostic code that triggers changes involving a single or a few components.

Dynamic adaptation operates at an intermediate level - meso-adaptation [25] - and as an external facility. Limited, specialized forms of dynamic adaptation are enabled by technologies that are in everyday use. Examples are plug-ins for the reconfiguration and enhancement of WWW browsers and other Internet applications; or software update utilities that operate with mixed push/pull modalities over the Internet to propose, install or upgrade software packages, and negotiate any installation and configuration issues, typically with user supervision.

We are interested in investigating more general-purpose and complex dynamic adaptation scenarios, involving a multiplicity of heterogeneous components and a variety of interwoven adaptation procedures. Similar software adaptation granularity is being pursued by a number of other approaches. We focus here – for the sake of brevity – on process and agent-based efforts and their enabling technologies.

Run-time dynamic adaptation can be seen as a specialized case of distributed systems coordination. Research on coordination languages for distributed and more specifically agent-based software has produced a large number of competing approaches and results [5] [28]. Recently, the use of processes as a means for agent coordination has grabbed the attention of researchers [16]. In fact, process formalisms allow describing coordination explicitly and abstractly at the same time. Moreover, they usually combine declarative and imperative connotations; thus, they are feasible for reasoning about the coordination model, as well as implementing it over the distributed software system. Therefore, a number of proposals to employ process enactment facilities as the coordinating core of a distributed system have been put forward.

Coordinating agent applications is one of the goals of Juliette [8]. Juliette is a peer-to-peer distributed process engine, whose agents carry out an overall coordination plan formally defined in the little-JIL visual process language [31], which follows a top-down hierarchical coordination model. Juliette could be seen as an enabler of our dynamic adaptation approach: it can provide "pure" coordination semantics to the dynamic adaptation process – encoded in Little-JIL - and distribute them to its multiple decentralized task processors. The computational mechanics associated to those dynamic adaptation tasks must be however distributed separately, for example, via Worklets that would be pulled as needed by the task processors and would actuate dynamic adaptation procedures onto the target system components. This way, no adaptation functionality needs to be hardcoded into the target system components, nor into the task processors.

Another system that could be similarly employed is Cougaar [11]. Cougaar is a platform for the creation and management of large-scale agent applications, whose centerpiece is a distributed process planning and execution engine. Cougaar's resident process formalism owes much to the domain of military logistics. The timely delivery of the mobile code actuating dynamic adaptation could be approached in this case as a logistics problem, which would allow exploiting some interesting Cougaar features, such as real-time monitoring of the process execution, evaluation of deviations and alternative plans, and selective re-planning. Furthermore, Cougaar supports a plug-in mechanism for the substitution of the default process formalism with others, and composition of applications via process federation. This could lead to process re-use, since fragments of pre-existing software processes dealing with configuration, deployment, validation, etc., could be composed into the dynamic adaptation process.

Our initial experiments with dynamic adaptation indeed regarded the integration of worklets with Juliette. We used our own mockup of the decentralized process enactment facilities of Juliette[2] to request worklets to a worklet factory, dispatch them to Juliette agendas responsible for task scheduling and execution onto target components, and study interaction of worklets with the Little-JIL process paradigm. Our next experiments intend to investigate the use of Cougaar.

While systems like Cougaar and Juliette can be employed for orchestrating a community of agents, which in turn exert control on the target application, other work uses a process engine as a sort of dynamic middleware that directly regulates the intended behavior of the target system. Such an approach aims at defining and enforcing all inter-component interactions as a process. This can enable dynamic adaptation to a certain degree, as far as intended modifications to the system's behavior can be described, either a priori as alternative process courses, or by evolving the process at enactment time.

For example, the TCCS platform delivered by the C3DS project [30] supports on-the-fly composition and reconfiguration of distributed applications. All the operations made available by the interface of each component are described as process tasks. The TCCS process engine defines and automates a *composed service* by sequencing and scheduling some of those operations. The transactionality of the process engine is exploited for run-time evolution of the process, enabling dynamic re-deployment and reconfiguration of the composed service. However, finer-grained dynamic adaptation that affects the internal computational logic of one component, or multiple components in a concerted way, remains inaccessible to this approach. PIE [13.] takes a similar stance, aiming at supporting and managing *federations* of (mostly) COTS components, which together must provide some complex service. PIE provides a middleware, which adds control facilities on top of a range of communication facilities. The control layer implements any process guidance via handlers that react to and manipulate the communications exchanged by federation components. Handlers can be dynamically plugged in the control layer; hence, a specific dynamic adaptation task can be carried out by plugging in an appropriate handler. The granularity of dynamic adaptation is somewhat finer than that of TCCS, since besides influencing inter-component interactions, PIE can also modify on-the-fly the semantics of those interactions.

Finally, we consider the Software Dock [18], which combines process and agents technologies in a way similar to our approach, but limited to the automation of distributed deployment activities. An effort aimed at enabling self-adapting software [27] is now under way, which in part builds upon the experience of the Software Dock. It outlines a variety of agent roles for enacting adaptation processes, a contribution that may be relevant to our work, in order to precisely characterize Worklet types for specific levels of dynamic adaptation (see Section 3.4). Furthermore, it recognizes the need for an "abstract" coordination service to orchestrate those agents, which we propose to implement by exploiting process technology.

---

[2] We were unable to obtain the real Juliette from U. Massachusetts at that time due to licensing difficulties, which are currently being resolved.

5 Conclusions

Dynamic adaptation of complex distributed software systems at run-time is both an opportunity and a challenge. It can benefit development, evolution and operation of software (particularly component-based software) in terms of quality and costs; however, it poses various serious difficulties. It demands considerable formal knowledge about the specifications of the system, and ways to express, reason about and exploit that knowledge to come up with appropriate adaptation procedures. It requires facilities to coordinate the actuation upon system components of those – possibly sophisticated - procedures. It must provide computational mechanisms for interfacing to system components and modifying their functionality on the fly.

We propose a dynamic adaptation approach that incorporates facets of essential software processes such as configuration management, deployment, evolution and validation in an integrated dynamic adaptation process. Such a process allows to explicitly codifying adaptation procedures to be carried out in response to a variety of conditions.

We have conceived a platform based upon decentralized process and software agent technologies for the support and enactment of dynamic adaptation processes. The process engine serves as the coordinator of those agents, which in turn are the actuators of adaptation procedures upon components of the distributed system subject to dynamic adaptation. This approach permits to attack separately the coordination and computational aspects of dynamic adaptation.

The first and second generations of the worklets system have already been released to some external users. We are currently developing the first release of our dynamic adaptation platform, which must integrate our worklets mobile agents with a decentralized process engine. We have carried out experiments with some engines, and are now implementing advanced features such as the worklet factory and jackets (see Section 3.2).

Finally, we are in the process of applying dynamic adaptation to various targets, as diverse as a multimedia-enabled educational groupware platform, a crisis operation planning application, and mobile localization telecommunications services. This variety of case studies is likely to provide us with considerable insights on the feasibility of our approach, and on a set of questions that remain open at this stage. Among them: the level of accuracy and detail of the target system specifications necessary to the dynamic adaptation process; the most appropriate process paradigms and any extensions to them that may be needed for specific dynamic adaptation processes; architectural constraints on the monitoring and control meta-architecture; efficiency issues; responsiveness and real-time requirements.

Acknowledgements. We would like to thank the other members of the Programming Systems Lab as well as Lee Osterweil for their insightful comments. Effort sponsored in part by the Defense Advanced Research Projects Agency, and Air Force Research Laboratory, under agreement numbers F30602-00-2-0611 and F30602-97-2-0022, and in part by NSF CCR-9970790 and EIA-0071954. Government is authorized to reproduce and distribute reprints for Governmental purposes notwithstanding any copyright annotation thereon. The views and conclusions contained in this document are those of the authors and should not be interpreted as representing the official policies or endorsements, either expressed or implied, of the Defense Advanced Research Projects Agency, the Air Force, NSF or the U.S. Government.

References

1. The ABLE Project.
   http://www.cs.cmu.edu/afs/cs.cmu.edu/project/able/www/index.html
2. Alonso, G.: OPERA: A design and programming paradigm for heterogeneous distributed applications. In Proceedings of the International Process Technology Workshop, Villard de Lans – Grenoble, France, September 1-3 1999.
3. Balzer, R., Goldman, N.: Mediating Connectors. In Proceedings the 19th IEEE international Conference on Distributed Computing Systems Workshop, Austin TX, May 31 - June 5, 1999,
   http://www.isi.edu/software-sciences/wrappers/ieeemediatingconnectors.pdf
4. Bolcer. G., Taylor, R.: Endeavors: a Process System Integration Infrastructure. In Proceedings of the 4th International Conference on Software Process (ICSP4), Brighton, U.K., December 2-6, 1996.
5. Brogi, A., Jacquet, J.M.: On the Expressiveness of Coordination Models. In Proceedings of the 3rd International Conference on Coordination Languages and Models (COORDINATION 99), Amsterdam, The Netherlands, April 26-28, 1999.
6. C3DS Home Page. http://www.newcastle.research.ec.org/c3ds/index.html
7. Carriero, N., Gelernter L.: Coordination Languages and their Significance. Communications of the ACM, Vol. 35, no. 2, pages 97-107, February 1992.
8. Cass, A. G., Staudt Lerner B., McCall, E. K., Osterweil, L. J., Wise, A.: Logically Centralized, Physically Distributed Control in a Process Runtime Environment. Technical Report # UM-CS-1999-065, University of Massachusetts, Computer Science Department, November 11, 1999.
9. Ceri, S., Di Nitto, E., Discenza, A., Fuggetta, A., Valetto, G.: DERPA: A Generic Distributed Event-based Reactive Processing Architecture. Technical report, CEFRIEL, Milan, Italy, March 1998.
10. Columbia University Programming Systems Laboratory, DARPA-funded DASADA project. http://www.psl.cs.columbia.edu/dasada/
11. Cougaar Open Source Agent Architecture. http://www.cougaar.org/index.html
12. Cugola, G., Di Nitto, E., Fuggetta, A.: Exploiting an Event-based Infrastructure to Develop Complex Distributed Systems. In Proceedings of the 20th International Conference on Software Engineering, Kyoto, Japan, April 1998.
13. Cugola, G., Cunin, P.Y., Dami, S., Estublier, J., Fuggetta, A., Pacull, F., Riviere, M., Verjus, H.: Support for Software Federations: The Pie Platform. In Proceedings of the 7th European Workshop on Software Process Technology EWSPT-7, Kaprun, Austria, February 2000.
14. DASADA Program Overview.
   http://www.if.afrl.af.mil/tech/programs/dasada/program-overview.html
15. Garlan, D., Monroe, R.T., Wile, D.: Acme: An Architecture Description Interchange Language. In Proceedings of CASCON '97, November 1997.
16. Griss, M.L., Chen, Q., Osterweil, L.J., Bolcer, G.A., Kessler, R.R.: Agents and Workflow – An Intimate Connection or Just Friends?. Panel report in Proceedings of the Technology of Object-Oriented Languages and Systems USA Conference (TOOLS-USA 99), Santa Barbara CA, July 30- August 3, 1999.
17. Grundy, J., Apperley, M., Hosking J., Mugridge, W.: A Decentralized Architecture for Software Process Modeling and Enactment. IEEE Internet Computing: Special Issue on Software Engineering via the Internet, 2(5): 53-62, September/October 1998.

18. Hall R.S., Heimbigner, D.M., Wolf, A.L.: A Cooperative Approach to Support Software Deployment Using the Software Dock. In Proceedings of the International Conference on Software Engineering (ICSE'99), Los Angeles CA, May 1999.

19. Heineman, G.T.: Adaptation and Software Architecture. In Proceedings of the 3rd International Workshop on Software Architecture, November 1998.

20. Holder, O., Ben-Shaul, I., Gazit, H.: Dynamic Layout of Distributed Applications in FarGo. In Proceedings of the 21st International Conference on Software Engineering (ICSE'99), Los Angeles CA, USA, May 1999.

21. Kaiser, G., Dossick, S., Jiang, W., Yang, J.J., Ye, S.X.: WWW-based Collaboration Environments with Distributed Tool Services. World Wide Web Journal, vol. 1, 1998, pages 3-25. http://www.psl.cs.columbia.edu/ftp/psl/CUCS-003-97.ps.gz

22. Kaiser, G., Stone, A., Dossick S.: A Mobile Agent Approach to Lightweight Process Workflow. In Proceedings of the International Process Technology Workshop, Villard de Lans, France, September 1-3 1999. http://www.psl.cs.columbia.edu/ftp/psl/CUCS-021-99.pdf.

23. Luckham, D.C., Vera, J.: An Event-Based Architecture Definition Language. IEEE Transactions on Software Engineering, vol. 21, no. 9, pages 717-734, September 1995.

24. Magee, J., Kramer, J.: Dynamic Structure in Software Architectures. In Proceedings of ACM SIGSOFT'96: Fourth Symposium on the Foundations of Software Engineering (FSE4), San Francisco CA, October 1996.

25. MesoMORPH: Meso-Adaptation of Systems. http://www.cis.gsu.edu/~mmoore/MesoMORPH/

26. Miller, J., Palaniswami, D., Sheth, A., Kochut, K., Singh, H.: WebWork: METEOR2's Web-based Workflow Management System. Journal of Intelligent Information Management Systems, pp. 185-215, 1997.

27. Oreizy, P., Gorlick, M.M., Taylor, R.N., Heimbigner, D.M., Johnson, G., Medvidovic, N., Quilici, A., Rosenblum, D.S., Wolf, A.L.: An Architecture-Based Approach to Self-Adaptive Software. IEEE Intelligent Systems, vol. 14, no. 3, May/June 1999, pp. 54-62.

28. Papadopolous, G. A., Arbab F.: Coordination Models and Languages. Advances in Computers, Vol. 48, Academic-Press, 1998.

29. Rugaber, S.: A Tool Suite for Evolving Legacy Software. In Proceedings of the International Conference on Software Maintenance'99, Oxford, England, August 30 - September 3, 1999.

30. Shirvastava, S.K., Bellissard, L., Feliot, D., Herrmann, M., De Palma, N., Wheater, S.M.: A Workflow and Agent based Platform for Service Provisioning. C3DS Technical Report # 32, 2000.

31. Staudt Lerner, B., Osterweil, L.J., Sutton, Jr., S.M., Wise A,: Programming Process Coordination in Little-JIL. In Proceedings of the 6th European Workshop on Software Process Technology (EWSPT'98), pp. 127-131, September 1998, Weybridge, UK.

32. Valetto, G.: Process-Orchestrated Software: Towards a Workflow Approach to the Coordination of Distributed Systems. Technical Report # CUCS-016-00, Columbia University, Department of Computer Science, May 2000.

33. Wise, A., Cass, A.G., Staudt Lerner, B., McCall, E.K., Osterweil, L.J., Sutton, Jr., S.M.: Using Little-JIL to Coordinate Agents in Software Engineering. In Proceedings of the Automated Software Engineering Conference (ASE 2000), Grenoble, France, September 11-15, 2000.

34. Dami, S., Estublier, J., Amiour, M.: APEL: A Graphical Yet Executable Formalism for Process Modeling. Automated Software Engineering, 5(1):61–96, January 1998.

Process Support for Mobile Work across Heterogeneous Systems

Alf Inge Wang[1] and Liu Chunnian[2]

[1] Department of Computer and Information Science,
Norwegian University of Science and Technology (NTNU),
N-7491 Trondheim, Norway, Phone: +47 73594485, Fax: +47 73594466,
alfw@idi.ntnu.no, http://www.idi.ntnu.no/~alfw
[2] Beijing Polytechnic University (BPU), Beijing,
P.R. China, Email: ai@bjpu.edu.cn ***

Abstract. The emerging field of *mobile computing (MC)* studies systems in which computational components may change locations. In terms of hardware, mobile work is usually across heterogeneous systems in Web extended by novel mobile devices. In terms of software, mobile work technically involves mobile agents and new generation of middleware. However, in general mobile work presents a new challenge and great opportunities to research in software engineering as a whole. In this paper, we focus our attention on process support for mobile work, that is an important aspect of software engineering. We present a classification and characterisation of mobile work mainly from the process point of view, and specify the requirements of process support for mobile work. The last part of the paper compares three process centred environments in regards to mobility support, and identifies their shortcomings.

Keywords: Mobile Computing, Heterogeneous Web-based Systems, Mobile Agents, Middleware, Software Processes

1 Introduction

In the recent years, mobile computing has gained more and more attention. New technology has made it possible for people to move around on different locations while working and parts of the software system change location during execution. Traditionally, portable PCs have been the working environment for mobile work, but smaller computational devices such as personal data assistants (PDAs) and mobile phones are becoming increasingly important as working environments. In this mobile world, it is necessary to identify the new requirements mobility introduces to process support needed in software engineering. This paper classifies and characterises mobile work, identifies some requirements needed to provide

---

*** Chunnian Liu's work was supported in part by the Natural Science Foundation of China (NSFC), Beijing Municipal Natural Science Foundation (BMNSF), and the 863 High-Tech Program of China, as well as by NTNU, Norway.

V. Ambriola (Ed.): EWSPT 2001, LNCS 2077, pp. 117–129, 2001.

process support for mobile computing, and investigates how these requirements are fulfilled in existing process centred environments.

The paper is organised as the following: Section 2 defines and describes mobile work, and discusses different kinds of mobile work. Section 3 identifies requirements to provide process support for mobile work. Section 4 describes briefly three process centred environments and compares their ability to provide support for mobile work requirements. Section 5 summarises and concludes the paper.

2 Classification and Characterisation of Mobile Work

Mobile work refers to systems in which computational components may change locations [2]. Such systems are extensions to more traditional Web-based distributed systems due to the rapid development of component miniaturisation; high-speed wireless communication, as well as mobile software agent technology. Mobile work usually needs information sharing and activity coordination, so it can be also regarded as a novel kind of **computer-supported cooperative work (CSCW)** [3].

In traditional CSCW research community, mobile software agents have received a lot of attention, where agents move along a fixed network structure. The new issues in mobile work are the moving hardware, and hence the moving of software agents in dynamic networks. The new research project MOWAHS at IDI/NTNU [1], as a successor of the CAGIS project on agent-based CSCW [6,9] also conducted at IDI/NTNU, addresses the new research issues raised by mobile work.

There are various kinds of mobile work, and new form of mobile work continues to emerge every day. Here we try to categorise different kinds of mobile work, so that we can proceed in the next section with the process support for each different kind of mobile work.

In [2], physical and logical mobilities are distinguished on a coarse level. From a more practical point of view, we can recognise the following different kinds of mobile work:

- **Hardware Mobility**: Computational hardware moves in physical space. We can further recognise the following sub-categories:
    - *Fixed Network*: Here we have the hardware infrastructure for traditional Web-based CSCW.
    - *Mobile Hardware Attached to Fixed Network*: Here we have a fixed core network and a fringe of mobile hardware. The latter can be connected (via base stations) to the core network, or disconnected (working alone). We can think out a lot of examples of this kind of mobile work: Notebook computers used in travel; Cellular telephone with limited Internet access; PDAs with built-in wireless capabilities; Global positioning systems such as information kiosks connected to a fixed network, providing tourist information to cars over a low power wireless link.

- *Temporary Network*: Here we have a network consisting of mobile hardware exclusively and existing in a short time for a particular task. A good example is that at a conference where every participant has a laptop. These laptops can form a temporary network to facilitate conference discussion via wireless communication. After the conference, such a network will stop existing.
- **Software Mobility on a Fixed Network**: Computational processes migrate inside a fixed network. This kind of mobile work includes code on demand, remote evaluation, and more recently, mobile agents. Software mobility on a fixed network has been studied for years, and the underlying assumption has been the hardware stability. A consequence of this assumption is that the mobility space reflects directly the structure of the underlying network.
- **Combined Mobility**: This represents the current trend of mobility, allowing mobile software to migrate among both mobile and stationary hardware. In this case, the mobility space is more complicated. A good example is the remote access to database (or email server): a mobile agent moving back and forth between a (fixed) email server and a mobile notebook computer that is disconnected and reconnected to the server from time to time. Even when the connection is cut off, the user of the notebook still can issue queries (or send emails), the agent residing on the notebook computer collects the queries (or the sent emails); When the connection is resumed, the agent moves to the database server to execute the queries (or sends the out-going emails and receives the coming emails), while the notebook can be disconnected; Finally, when the connection is reestablished again, the agent will move back to the notebook presenting the query results (or the received emails).

3   The Requirements of Process Support to Mobile Computing

In the previous section, we distinguish hardware mobility from software mobility. Note that from the software engineering point of view, the two kinds of mobility present quite different perspectives. Hardware mobility, being possible due to component miniaturisation and high-speed wireless communication, presents end-users new opportunities, advantages and convenience in their professional work and daily life. But for software engineers of distributed applications, it represents a very challenging, new target execution environment. On the other hand, software mobility may be transparent to end-users, while giving a new design tool for the developers of distributed applications. The aim of the research in software engineering for mobility is to develop models; techniques and tools for this new generation of distributed systems that fulfil the requirements of the changed execution environments posed by hardware mobility. Software mobility can be regarded as the weapon in the research.

Various branches of software engineering are effected by mobility (formal modelling, algorithms, security, etc.). In this paper, we focus on the process aspect of software engineering. We would like to outline the requirements of process support for mobile work.

A *software process* is the total set of software engineering activities needed to transform a user's requirements into functioning software. A *software process model* is a framework providing the definitions, structures, standards, and relationships of the various process elements so that common technology, methods and measurements can be applied by any software project.

In general, all software development projects need process support in terms of process modelling, process architecture, and process support tools. If the development is a cooperative effort (CSCW), the process become more advanced and complicated, involving new issues such as group awareness, multi-user interfaces, concurrency control, communication and coordination within the group, shared information space and the support of a heterogeneous, open environment which integrates existing single-user applications. Finally, Mobile Work can be regarded as a novel type of CSCW: while information sharing and activity coordination are also needed as in general CSCW, it opens a new dimension of mobility of both hardware and software. Thus, the process support for mobile work will be even more complicated.

In the following, we will outline the requirement of process support to mobile work. The process support will be discussed in terms of process modelling, process architecture, and process support tools. For each category, we will first outline the generic requirements for all CSCW, then point out the new challenges concerning mobile work.

1. **Process Modelling**

   1.1 *Generic for all CSCW*: Process models define action flow/events and communication flow/events. We need a process modelling language (PML) to specify the models. Usually the PML allows object-oriented definitions of process elements (activities, artifacts, resources, *etc.*) in a hierarchical manner (through sub-typing and aggregation, *etc.*). Process models are the basis for any systematic process understanding, analysis and enaction. Without models, the process support can only be provided here and there, in an ad-hoc way. Based on the process model, process elicitation, process planning/scheduling/enaction can be done systematically in general or even automatically (for strict process).

   1.2 *Specific for Mobile Work*: Here in addition to the generic process modelling, we need to model mobility. **Mobility Modelling** consists of three main parts:

   1.2.1 **The unit of mobility**: the smallest component in the system that is allowed to move. A natural choice is to make the unit of mobility coincide with the unit of execution. For hardware, a unit of mobility means a physical device, while finer-grained units would be parts of devices and unsuitable to reasonable modelling. For software, a unit of mobility means a mobile agent. Though in practice finer-grained units (such as code on demand) are pervasive, their modelling presents a challenge to research community. Each unit of mobility in the system should have a *state* in mobility modelling.

1.2.2 **The location**: the position of a mobile unit in space. The type of location is affected by the choice of unit of mobility. For example, locations for moving devices can be described by their physical coordinates, for mobile agents by the addresses of their hosts, and for code fragments by the process identifiers. Location can be modelled by a variable belonging to the state of a mobile unit.

1.2.3 **Context changes**: Mobile computing is context-aware computing. Conventional computing fosters a static context with no or small, predictable changes, while in mobile computing changes in location may lead to abrupt and unpredictable changes in the context. Note that the location of a mobile unit cannot solely determine the context that the unit perceives, because the context relies on other factors such as administrative domains. Formulation of context and mechanisms for managing context changes are major challenges.

In order to handle context changes, the model must support some *coordination* mechanism that can specify how the unit of mobility interacts with its context separately from the behaviour of the unit itself. Mobility poses some novel challenges to coordination (*e.g.* context varies with high frequency; traditional naming schemes – such as Internet DNS – cannot be used for mobile agents and fluid network).

2. **Process Architecture**

2.1 *Generic for all CSCW*: Process architecture must possess the following features to support CSCW in general:

2.1.1 **Facilitating the creation of a community memory**
The intra-project memory facilitates important features in CSCW, such as group awareness, and change management to support process evolution.

2.1.2 **Supporting distribution of documents/work/resource/...**
The architecture should provide support for transparently distributed people (stakeholders, product users, and SPEGs – Software Process Engineering Groups), artifacts, process objects and execution behaviour. Each component of the architecture (processes, object state and behaviour, interpreter, user interface, etc.) can be accessed and executed by remote users through a standard *http* server and may be physically located on distributed machines throughout the Internet.

2.1.3 **Supporting integration with external tools**
The architecture should support bi-directional communication between internal objects and external tools and services. API-based integration can be supported by handlers (Java applets), allowing bi-directional calls to internal and external interfaces, tools, and services.

2.1.4 **Being platform independent**
To facilitate the installation and execution of a process support system, the architecture should be designed as a set of highly componentised, lightweight, concurrent elements (as Java applets), to be

used across different platforms, easily transported across the WWW, or embedded in *html* pages. The architecture should also provide an integrated environment for operation and communication.

2.2 *Specific for Mobile Work*: We have seen from the above list that a lot of software mobility has been involved. However, there are some underlying assumptions: uniform type of client devices, on-line work only in a network, and the stability of the network. With drifting away of computing from traditional computers and hardware mobility, these assumptions do not hold any more, so the process architecture should have the following extra supporting features:

2.2.1 Supporting heterogeneity of computing devices: a workflow process framework and a multi-agent architecture that can run on anything from a desktop computer to a mobile phone.

2.2.2 Supporting mobility, especially the following off-line facilities:

2.2.2.1 off-line workflow capacities for PDAs and mobile phones

2.2.2.2 synchronisation between different devices after working off-line

2.2.2.3 handling workflow changes when devices are off-line

3. Process Support Tools

3.1 *Generic for all CSCW*:

The impact of modelling in CSCW is through a set of process support tools including: Tools for group awareness such as a process information system (PIS). With that, individuals can view pending tasks and requests, and find references to supporting information, process forms, *etc.*; Tools for information-sharing and coordination to reduce and solve conflicts occurring in cooperative work; Tools for communication and tools for change management.

3.2 *Specific for Mobile Work*:

The impact of formal modelling in mobile computing is through the development of appropriate middleware that rests above the operating system and provides developers with specialised mechanisms and services in a highly integrated fashion. Middleware specialised for mobility is a new generation of middleware. Hardware mobility and software mobility give rise of different middleware:

3.2.1 **Middleware for hardware mobility**: The tasks for this kind of middleware include: detecting location changes; specifying what belongs to the context of computation; relating location changes to context modifications; determining how the computation itself is affected by the changes in the context.

Note that middleware for hardware mobility should hide its work into the underlying runtime support, so that the hardware mobility can be transparent as much as possible to the developers of distributed application.

3.2.2 **Middleware utilising software mobility**: Middleware was originally invented by the earlier study of software mobility on a fixed network. The more comprehensive concepts of software mobility, as given in this paper, provide higher level of abstraction and flexibility that enable code and state relocation. The next generation of middleware should fully utilise the advantages of software mobility to support varying grains of mobility, different rebinding strategies, and different architectural styles for relocation, all in a single, uniform programming interface.

4   Comparing Three PCE in Regards to Mobility Support

In this section, we will compare three PCE in regards to mobility support. The three environment compared are the Endeavors workflow system, the Process-Web workflow system, and the CAGIS PCE. The next three subsections will briefly describe the three PCEs and they will be compared in regards to the requirements listed in section 3.

4.1   Endeavors

Endeavors is an open, distributed, extensible process execution environment developed at University of California Irvine, and has been licensed by Endeavors Technology Incorporated. It is designed to improve coordination and managerial control of development by allowing flexible definition, modelling, and execution of typical workflow applications. There are five main characteristics for Endeavors:

- **Distribution** Support for transparently distributed people, artifacts, process objects, and execution behaviour (handlers) using web protocols.
- **Integration** Allows bi-directional communication between its internal objects and external tools, objects, and services through its open interfaces across all levels of the architecture. Multiple programming languages are also supported through APIs.
- **Incremental Adoption** Components of the system (user interfaces, interpreters, and editing tools), may be down-loaded as needed, and no explicit system installation is required to view and execute a workflow-style process.
- **Customisation and Reuse** Implemented as a layered virtual machines architecture, and allows object-oriented extensions of the architecture, interfaces, and data formats at each layer.
- **Dynamic Change** Allows dynamic changing of object fields and methods, the ability to dynamically change the object behaviours at runtime, and late binding of resources needed to execute a workflow process. Process interpreters are dynamically created as needed.

The comparison in this paper is based on the University prototype of Endeavors and not the recent commercial tools. More details about the Endeavors can be found in [5].

4.2   ProcessWeb

ProcessWeb [14] is a web-interface based workflow system based on the ProcessWise [8] Integrator (produced by ICL) implemented by Information Process Group, University of Manchester. The web-interface is provided through the ProcessWise Integrator application interface. ProcessWise Integrator creates an environment enabling the activities of people in an enterprise to be coordinated and integrated with the organisation's computing facilities. A process management system built using the ProcessWise Integrator has a client/server structure and consist of four main components as shown in figure 1: User Interface, Process Control Manager, Process description in PML, and an Application Interface. The most important component of ProcessWise Integrator is the Process Control Manager (process engine), which acts as the central server. Its main function is to interpret the PML description of the process. To ensure that processes may continue indefinitely, the Process Control Manager has been implemented using a persistent store technology.

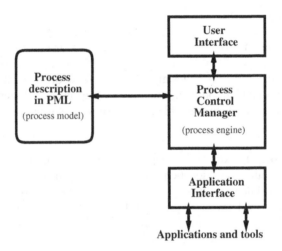

Fig. 1. Structure of ProcessWise Integrator

4.3   CAGIS PCE

The CAGIS PCE is designed to model and enact cooperative and individual activities that can be distributed over several workspaces, and consists of three subsystems:

- **CAGIS SimpleProcess** is a workflow tool with a web-interface, used to model processes consisting of networks of activities executed by individuals. For users of CAGIS SimpleProcess, the activities will be shown as webpages that can contain a work description, links to relevant document or tools, HTML-forms for entering necessary information, or a Java applet. A process in CAGIS SimpleProcess can consist of several autonomous *process fragments* that can be distributed over several workspaces. A process fragment can be anything from one single activity to several related activities. Hierarchical workspaces (i.e., a tree structure) are used model the organisation executing the process, and CAGIS SimpleProcess has support for moving process fragments between workspaces (between users) and between sites. A more detailed description of this workflow tool is found in [10].

- **CAGIS Distributed Intelligent Agent System (DIAS)** takes care of cooperative activities between workspaces in the CAGIS PCE framework [13,7,4]. The software agents in CAGIS DIAS can be used to coordinate artifacts and resources, negotiate about artifacts and resources, monitor the working environment for changes or events, provide infrastructure for brainstorming, electronic meetings, trading services etc. CAGIS DIAS provides the infrastructure for creating cooperating agents, and consists of four main components: Agents, Agent Meeting Places (AMPs), Workspaces, and Repositories.
- **CAGIS GlueServer** To enable CAGIS SimpleProcess to interact with the CAGIS DIAS, we have built a CAGIS GlueServer. The CAGIS GlueServer is a middleware that uses a so-called GlueModel, where relations between process fragments and software agents are defined. The GlueModel can be seen as a part of the process model defining rules for interaction between people or groups of people, but also as a meta-model since it can specify changes of the process model. By using a *separate model* to describe the interconnection between agents and process fragments, it is possible to use other workflow tools (e.g. than CAGIS SimpleProcess) as well as other agent systems. This makes the CAGIS PCE more open-ended, and ready to meet future challenges. The GlueServer and the GlueModel are described in further detail in [12].

A typical interaction between the three main components in the CAGIS PCE is illustrated in figure 2 and can have the following sequence:

1. The workflow tool, *CAGIS SimpleProcess*, will report its process state to the *CAGIS GlueServer*.
2. The *CAGIS GlueSever* then looks for cooperative rules defining relationships between process fragments and software agents. If a relationship that maps the current process state is found, the *CAGIS GlueServer* will initiate one or more software agents in the *CAGIS DIAS*.
3. The software agents will typically execute cooperative activities where several roles are involved. When the cooperative effort has terminated, a result will be reported to the *CAGIS GlueServer* (e.g. successful negotiation).
4. The *CAGIS GlueServer* will then activate a reaction defined in the Glue-Model specified for the result. Reactions can be executed in the *CAGIS SimpleProcess* workflow tool, the *CAGIS DIAS* or in the *CAGIS GlueServer* itself.

A more detailed description of the CAGIS PCE is presented in [11].

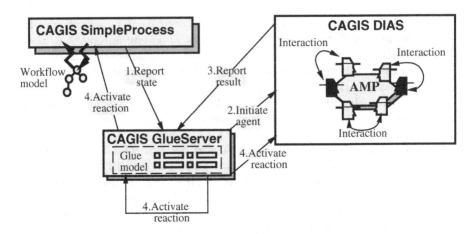

Fig. 2. The CAGIS PCE architecture

4.4   Comparison of Mobility Support

The comparison of mobility support in the three PCEs described above is based on the requirements listed in section 3. Since none of the PCEs we have compared has been designed initially to support mobile work, and we have investigated what is lacking in this respect. Table 1 presents the results from comparing the three PCEs with regards to mobility requirements.

Process Modelling. From the table, we can see that all PCEs have support for defining models for generic processes as expected. The way the processes are modelled in the three PCEs however varies. In Endeavors, processes are modelled as network of activities combined with artifacts and resources. The process models in ProcessWeb are represented as a set of roles with interactions. The interactions represent data- and control-flow between roles. CAGIS PCE uses a combined process modelling approach where individual activities are modelled as activities with pre-order dependencies and cooperative activities are represented by several cooperative agents. In addition, a GlueModel is used to model the dependencies between activities and agents.

The abilities to model mobile work are not so well supported as for general processes. In ProcessWeb, the process modelling language does not facilitate specific support for mobile work. Endeavors and CAGIS PCE both give some support for mobile work by allowing parts of the process model to move between sites and expressing the location of the mobile unit. In Endeavors, the execution of an activity represented as an applet can be moved to be executed locally. In CAGIS PCE, both process fragments (representing one or more activities) and software agents can be moved between workspaces. The location for the mobile unit is represented as an URL for both Endeavors and CAGIS PCE. None of the PCEs has extensive support for context changes for mobile units.

Table 1. Comparison of three PCEs in regards to mobility support

Requirement	Endeavors	ProcessWeb	CAGIS PCE
1.1 Generic Process Modelling	Yes	Yes	Yes
1.2.1 Unit of mobility	Applet	No	Proc. frag. / Mob. agent
1.2.2 Location	URL	No	URL
1.2.3 Context changes	No	No	No
2.1.1 Facilitating Comm. Mem.	Yes	Yes	Yes
2.1.2 Distrib. of artifacts	Yes	Yes	Yes
2.1.3 Integr. external tools	Yes	On server	Only Java-appl./plug-ins
2.1.4 a) Platform indep. server	Yes	No	No
2.1.4 b) Platform indep. client	Yes	Yes	Yes
2.2.1 Hardware indep.	Partly	Partly	Partly
2.2.2.1 Off-Line support	No	No	No
2.2.2.2 Sync off-line	No	No	No
2.2.2.3 WF changes off-line	No	No	No
3.1 Process Support Tools	Yes	Yes	Yes
3.2.1 Middleware HW comp	No	No	No
3.2.2 Middleware SW mobile	No	No	Partly

Process Architecture. All PCEs provide the most necessary features needed to provide a generic process architecture for cooperative work such as facilitating the creation of a community memory, supporting distribution of artifacts, supporting integration with external tools, and being platform independent. Integration of external tools for clients are rather limited in ProcessWeb and CAGIS PCE where most of the user interaction is provided through a Web-browser. Endeavors is also the only PCE that is completely platform independent (also the server), since it is entirely implemented in Java.

Requirements needed for the process architecture for mobile work is rather poorly supported by the three PCEs. All the PCEs supports workflow clients that can run on different platforms, but smaller mobile devices such as PDAs and mobile phones are not supported. Support for handling off-line workflow, synchronisation between devices after being off-line, and handling workflow changes when devices are off-line are not support by any of the PCEs. The commercial version of Endeavors has however capabilities to deal with such problems.

Process Support Tools. All the PCEs provide a set of process tools or building blocks for implementing tools for group awareness, for sharing information, cooperative activities, change management, etc. Middleware for hardware mobility used e.g., to detect location changes are not present. CAGIS PCE has some limited support for middleware utilising software mobility in the Glue-Server component. The GlueServer makes it possible to specify that at certain events, parts of the process model (process fragments) should be moved from one workspace to another. In addition, this GlueServer can initiate mobile agents.

5   Conclusions and Future Work

This paper has identified some requirements to support mobile work. We have further compared three existing PCEs in regards to mobility support and found that they do not provide the needed facilities to support such work. In a new project called MObile Work Across Heterogeneous Systems (MOWAHS), we will use CAGIS PCE as a starting point to a PCE that is able to support mobile work. We will also look at other existing technology enabling mobile work. Only future experiments will show how useful a PCE for mobile work is, and realistic scenarios should be used to evaluate our approach.

References

1. Reidar Conradi (ed.). MOWAHS: Mobile Work Across Heterogeneous Systems, 2000. Research Project supported by the Research Council of Norway 2001-2004, IDI/NTNU.
2. A.L. Murphy G-C. Roman, G.P. Picco. Software Engineering for Mobility: A Roadmap. In *The future of Software Engineering (ed. by A. Finkelstein), ACM Press, p.243-258*, 2000.
3. Jonathan Grudin. Computer-Supported Cooperative Work: Its History and Participation. *IEEE Computer*, 27(5):19–26, 1994.
4. Anders Aas Hanssen and Bård Smidsrød Nymoen. DIAS II - Distributed Intelligent Agent System II. Technical report, Norwegian University of Science and Technology (NTNU), January 2000. Technical Report, Dept. of Computer and Information Science.
5. Arthur S. Hitomi and Dong Le. Endeavours and Component Reuse in Web-Driven Process Workflow. In *Proceedings of the California Software Symposium*, Irvine, California, USA, 23 October 1998.
6. IDI NTNU. CAGIS - Cooperating Agents in the Global Information Space, 1996. in http://www.idi.ntnu.no/IDT/f-plan/prosjekter/cagis.html.
7. Geir Prestegård, Anders Aas Hanssen, Snorre Brandstadmoen, and Bård Smidsrød Nymoen. DIAS - Distributed Intelligent Agent System, April 1999. EPOS TR 359 (pre-diploma project thesis), 396 p. + CD, Dept. of Computer and Information Science, NTNU, Trondheim.
8. ICL Enterprises Process Management Centre, Enterprise Technology. *ProcessWise Integrator, PML Reference*. Staffordshire, UK, first edition, April 1996.
9. Heri Ramampiaro, Terje Brasethvik, and Alf Inge Wang. Supporting Distributed Cooperative Work in CAGIS. In *4th IASTED International Conference on Software Engineering and Applications (SEA'2000)*, Las Vegas, Nevada, USA, 6-9 November 2000.
10. Alf Inge Wang. Support for Mobile Software Processes in CAGIS. In Reidar Conradi, editor, *Seventh European Workshop on Software Process Technology*, Kaprun near Salzburg, Austria, 22-25 February 2000.
11. Alf Inge Wang. *Using a Mobile, Agent-based Environment to support Cooperative Software Processes*. PhD thesis, Norwegian University of Science and Technology, Dept. of Computer and Information Science, NTNU, Trondheim, Norway, February 5th 2001.

12. Alf Inge Wang, Reidar Conradi, and Chunnian Liu. Integrating Workflow with Interacting Agents to support Cooperative Software Engineering. In *Proc. IASTED Internation Conference Software Engineering and Applications*, Las Vegas, Nevada, USA, 6-9 November 2000.
13. Alf Inge Wang, Chunnian Liu, and Reidar Conradi. A Multi-Agent Architecture for Cooperative Software Engineering. In *Proc. The Eleventh International Conference on Software Engineering and Knowledge Engineering (SEKE'99)*, pages 1–22, Kaiserslautern, Germany, 17-19 June 1999.
14. Benjamin Yeomans. Enhancing the world wide web. Technical report, Computer Science Dept., University of Manchester, 1996. Supervisor: Prof. Brian Warboys.

A Delegation Based Model for Distributed Software Process Management

Simon Becker, Dirk Jäger, Ansgar Schleicher, Bernhard Westfechtel

Aachen University of Technology
Department of Computer Science III
D-52056 Aachen, Germany
{sbecker|jaeger|schleich|bernhard}@i3.informatik.rwth-aachen.de

Abstract. Complex development processes which cross organizational boundaries require specialized support by process management systems. Such processes are planned in a top-down manner. A suitable cooperation model for these processes is the delegation of process parts. Because the client and the contractor of a delegation may be independent organizations they may have diverging interest concerning autonomy of process execution, information-hiding, control, etc. We propose a concept for delegating process parts which takes these interests into account and describe how delegation is implemented in the process management system AHEAD.
Keywords: process modeling, process management, interorganization cooperation, delegation, distributed processes

1 Introduction

Developing complex technical products has become a challenging task which can only be handled by the cooperation of many individuals. A process management system (PMS) supports the manager to control such a development process which involves a large number of developers. The skills required for developing a product can be quite diverse and thus the employees involved in the development processes can belong to different organizational units. Those can be different branches of a company or even different companies which may be geographically dispersed. Each organization conducts its part of the process, which is guided by the organizations' local PMS. These local PMS must be integrated to establish the interorganizational processes.

Integration of processes can follow different models [19, 1]. Which of these is appropriate depends on the application domain. For companies that e.g. aim at integrating processes along a supply chain, chained execution is a good model. In contrast to this, we regard a top-down approach more suitable for modeling development processes in which one organization acts as a supervisor and delegates parts of the process to other organizations.

Again, several models can be applied here. Taking a black-box approach, the process at the delegating organization simply triggers the execution of a process at the contractor organization without having knowledge about the internals

V. Ambriola (Ed.): EWSPT 2001, LNCS 2077, pp. 130–144, 2001.

of this process or receiving feedback on its progress. This approach is hardly applicable because it has been recognized, that the client-contractor relationship is more complex in reality. The delegation of a task should also include guidelines how the task has to be performed, milestones to monitor the progress of the project, etc. An adequate model for the delegation of processes must take into account additional requirements like security, information-hiding, and autonomy of process execution [18, 14].

In this paper we present an approach that allows for the delegation of parts of development processes which are modeled as process nets in a PMS. The parts can be selected on the fly which gives the manager a great flexibility in deciding which tasks he wants to delegate. The manager can monitor the execution of the delegated parts without seeing the details of their realization. In this way, the approach satisfies the needs of the client as well as of the contractor of a delegation. Moreover, the system automatically ensures the integration of the process parts and the consistency of the overall model which results in a tighter coupling of the participating PMSs than it is usually realized in federated process centered software engineering environments (PSEE) [1].

The rest of this paper is structured as follows: In Section 2 we will introduce the scenario of delegation in development processes and discuss the requirements which have to be fulfilled by a PMS to support delegation. Section 3 briefly introduces the process modeling language of dynamic task nets. In Section 4 we describe how delegation is supported by the AHEAD management system which uses dynamic task nets as process modeling language. Section 5 discusses related work and Section 6 concludes the paper.

2   A Concept of Delegation

Interorganizational processes emerge whenever organizations agree to cooperate. The subject of the cooperation and the relationship between the cooperating organizations determine the nature of the interorganizational process and how it should be supported by a PMS. Therefore, we will start with a short discussion of possible cooperation scenarios and point out in which of these delegation is a suitable cooperation model.

Our approach does not focus on routine *business processes*. Organizations which want to cooperate by integrating their business processes, e.g. along a supply chain, usually do not delegate process parts. The processes to be integrated already exist and have to be chained. Most of the work on interorganizational workflows deals with the chaining of existing workflows.

In contrast to this, we are interested in supporting *development processes* which are highly dynamic and can not be planned in advance in every detail but only on a coarse-grained level. Which activities have to be performed in detail depends on the results of previous activities. For example, which coding activities are needed in a software project depends on the design document which is the result of a design activity.

This kind of planning can only be done in a top-down manner. Therefore, one of the cooperating organizations is responsible for it and acts as a supervisor of the interorganizational process. Such a situation naturally arises when an organization is the initiator of a development process and acts as the *client* of other organizations which are hired as *contractors*. The client organization delegates parts of the process to its contractors, which enact these process parts. We will use the terms *client* and *contractor* in the following to refer to the roles involved in a delegation. An organization may participate in more than one delegation in different roles. A contractor can delegate parts of its process to subcontractors. In this case the contractor acts as a client of his subcontractors.

In the most general case, the client and the contractor are independent organizations which are only connected by the delegation. Both may have different interests, e.g. the client wants the contractor to produce a product as good as possible while the contractor tries to produce a product which meets but not exceeds the agreed specification. Likewise, the client is interested in the overall result of the process while the contractor does not care about it, etc. Our goal was to create a model of delegation which takes into account the interests of client and contractor. This proved to be hard because these interests are in some cases conflicting. As a result, we have defined the following set of requirements along which we constructed our system:

- *Delegation of processes fragments.* The system should be able to delegate process fragments consisting of several tasks including their relationships. This means that the client should be able to specify the steps of the processes on a coarse-grained level. For example, software development projects for German government organizations have to use the V-Model. A client can enforce this by specifying the phases of this model as top-level activities of a delegated process.
- *Delegation as a contract.* The delegation of a part of a process should be viewed as a contract. Once the client and the contractor have agreed to it, none of them is entitled to change the delegated process independently.
- *Control of process execution.* The client should be able to monitor the execution of the delegated tasks in his own PMS. The delegated tasks are milestones of the project and their states provide the client with feedback concerning the progress of the delegated part of the process.
- *Refinement by contractor.* The contractor can refine each of the delegated tasks as long as the delegated coarse-grained process remains unchanged. This requirement reflects that each organization has its specific standards and processes to realize certain tasks.
- *Autonomous execution.* The contractor should autonomously execute the delegated process fragment. This requirement is to be understood in two ways. Firstly, on the conceptual level it means that the contractor has full control over the execution of the delegated part of the process. The client PMS merely provides a read only view on it but cannot be used to influence it (e.g. by performing operations on the delegated tasks). Secondly, with regard to the coupling of the management tools involved, it means that the

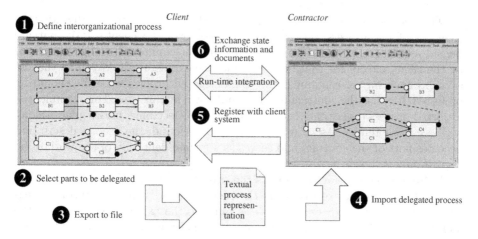

Fig. 1. Steps of delegation

contractor PMS should be able to execute its part of the process without contacting the client PMS.

- *Information hiding.* While the client wishes to monitor the delegated process part, the contractor usually does not want him to see all the details of process refinement. Therefore, the contractor PMS should be able to hide levels of process refinement and, in the extreme case, provide the client PMS only with information concerning the coarse-grained tasks of the original delegation process.

- *Preservation of execution semantics.* An important requirement of delegation is that in the contractor PMS the delegated process should be executed exactly as it would be in the client PMS. This requirement is naturally fulfilled if both systems use the same PML. However, there are many different process modeling formalisms around, and in general, systems may cooperate which use different PMLs. In this case, a translation step is required. However, the translation usually is not trivial. Though each net-based PML has modeling elements for activities, documents, control flow, etc. their semantics may be different. A naive and direct translation between two PMLs might result in a translated net having the same topology as the original one but exhibiting a completely different behavior. Thus, our approach as far as it is presented in this paper is restricted to the homogeneous case in which client and contractor use the same PML.

Figure 1 shows the steps in which a delegation is performed. At first, the process manager of the client specifies the interorganizational process including the parts to be delegated to contractors in the following. In Step 2, parts which are suitable for delegation are selected. Here, suitable is to be understood with regard to the real-world process. In addition, the selected parts have to satisfy some conditions with regard to the semantics of the employed modeling formalism, e.g connectedness, which will be discussed in Section 4.

The selected part of the process is exported to a file in Step 3. The exported elements of the process net are not removed form the client's PMS but are tagged as being exported. These parts of the net cannot be changed anymore by the client, except for that he can revoke the export at all. We think that an asynchronous way of communicating the delegated process via a file should be preferred, because the contractor can be unknown at this time. For example, the exported process description can be published at electronic market places along with a call for tender. As soon as a contractor is found, the process description becomes part of the contract and serves as a formal definition of the work to be carried out.

In Step 4 the contractor imports the process definition. The process model created there is a copy of the net in the client system. Next, the contractor registers with the client (Step 5). For this purpose the exported net includes the address of the client. A direct communication is established and the interorganizational process is ready for enactment.

At runtime, the contractor is responsible for executing the exported activities. The state of the execution is reported to the client which updates his copy of the exported net. Likewise, input and output documents of the delegated activities have to be propagated over the network as well.

3   Dynamic Task Nets

The concept of process delegation which is presented in this paper was developed for dynamic task nets. Dynamic task nets are a visual language for modeling development processes [9]. The concept is implemented within the PMS AHEAD (Adaptable Human-centered Environment for the Administration of Development processes) which uses dynamic task nets as process modeling formalism [12, 11]. In AHEAD there are basically two user roles: the *process manager* who is responsible for planning and the *developers* who are guided by the PMS. A process manager uses the *management tool* of AHEAD which displays a view on the complete process net. All screenshots throughout this paper show the main window of the management tool. The developers interact with the system via the *developer front ends*. The front ends provide each developer with an agenda which contains those tasks currently assigned to him.

The language of dynamic task nets is formally specified as a graph-based meta model in the executable specification language PROGRES [13, 16]. The specification includes the types of modeling elements and their possible relationships as well as complex commands for constructing, analyzing and enacting a task net.

Figure 2 shows a sample task net instance. Tasks are shown as boxes. They have *input parameters* (empty circles) and *output parameters* (filled circles). A task's parameters are placeholders for the documents the task is working on. Tasks are connected by control flow relationships, denoted by arrows, which describe the order of execution. Data flow relationships, denoted by dashed arrows, can be viewed as a refinement of control flow relationships. Data flows specify

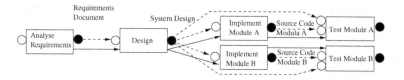

Fig. 2. Sample task net

which output document of one task is consumed as an input document by another task. The actual flow of documents is model by passing tokens which are produced by output parameters and consumed by input parameters.

Another important feature of dynamic task nets is the distinction between *complex tasks* and *atomic tasks*. Complex tasks can be refined by a net of subtasks. A complex tasks can have two kinds of parameters: *external parameters* are used for passing documents between tasks on the same hierarchy level while *internal parameters* serve to pass documents between a task and its refining subtasks.

To make process models executable, not only the structure but also the behavior of tasks has to be defined. This is achieved by assigning a state to each task, e.g. `Waiting`, `Active` or `Done`. State transitions are either triggered by certain events within the task net or are requested by the user, e.g. a developer changes a task's state from `Waiting` to `Active` when he starts working at this task, later he may have successfully finished the tasks and changes the state to `Done`. Whether the developer may perform these state changes depends, among others, on how the task is embedded in the net. For example, if there is an incoming control flow edge specifying that the task and its predecessor have to be executed sequentially, the task can only be started if the predecessor is in state `Done`.

Because development processes cannot be fully planned in advance, dynamic task nets allow for the intertwined execution and modification of process models. Operations changing the net structure can be applied to a task net in execution. The formal definition of all these operations ensures that the consistency of the net is always maintained.

In general, the executability of a certain operation at one task depends on the state of its predecessor, successor, parent and child tasks, and their parameters. We refer to these model elements as the *context* of the task.

4   Delegation in Dynamic Task Nets

So far, we have presented the concept of delegation on a rather abstract level and we have pointed out in which situations it can be applied. In this section we will present the implementation of delegation in the process management system AHEAD. For this purpose we will refer to Figure 1 and describe each step in detail from a technical point of view with help of a small example process.

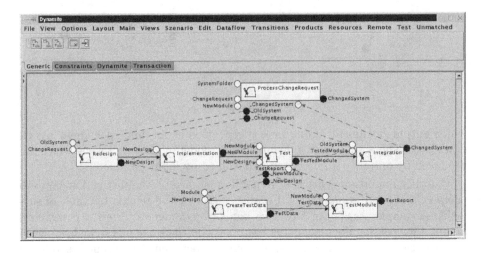

Fig. 3. Definition of the interorganizational process

4.1   Definition of the Interorganizational Process

The definition of an interorganizational process (Step 1 of Figure 1) does not differ from the definition of a local process at this stage. Figure 3 shows a screen shot of AHEAD's manager view. The process manager has constructed a model of a process for processing a change request. We can see three levels of refinement. The task `ProcessChangeRequest` at the top represents the process as a whole. It is refined into the sequence of `Redesign`, `Implementation`, `Test` and `Integration`. The task `Test` is again refined into `CreateTestData` and `PerformTest`. At this point, the manager decides that it may be a good idea to hire a contractor for doing the implementation and the subsequent test, while the redesign of the system remains with his own organization.

4.2   Selecting the Tasks to be Delegated

To start a delegation, the manager has to select the tasks to be delegated and invokes a command on these which prepares them for export (Step 2 of Figure 1). In terms of our graph-based process model, preparation for export means that a special node of type `ExportLink` is introduced into the net which connects the delegated tasks. The command also enforces a number of conditions which ensure the consistency of the model:

- The delegated top-level tasks have to be connected by control flows. Unconnected nets should not really cause problems from a technical point of view but we think they should be treated a two seperate delegations.
- Each element of the net may only be exported once, because a task can only be delegated to one contractor.
- The refining subnet of each task has to be exported as well if it exists. Defining a subnet means to specify how the contractor should perform the delegated task. Therefore, the subnet must be part of the delegation.

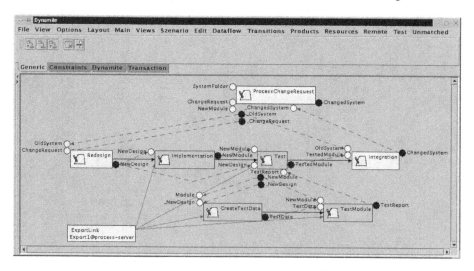

Fig. 4. Selecting the tasks to be delegated

The status of the net after preparation for export is shown in Figure 4. Normally, the node of type `ExportLink` in the window's lower left is an internal node of the model and not shown to the tool's user. Rather, the now prepared and later exported tasks are visualized by a different, here darker color. The export link also serves as the data structure in which all information concerning the delegation is stored, including the URL which identifies the client system and the delegation. Through this URL the contractor can contact the client after having imported the delegated net and establish a connecting for coupling the parts of the interorganizational process.

4.3   Exporting the Delegated Net

After having selected the delegated tasks, the manager invokes the command for the actual export (Step 3 of Figure 1). This command at first retrieves the parameters of the exported tasks. Then, by adding an export edge to each parameter, they are marked for export as well (Figure 5). Though parameters are modeled as nodes of the net, they are subordinated model elements which are only meaningful together with their tasks.

Next, the command retrieves the context of the delegated net. The context is the set of those nodes which are connected by edges to the nodes marked for export. These nodes are added to the exported net via edges of type `context` (dashed edges originating from the node `ExportLink` in Figure 5). By including the context of the exported net, the enactment of the process in the contractor's PMS is greatly simplified as we will point out in Section 4.5.

After these preparing steps, a textual representation of the exported net is written to a file. The task net is represented as an attributed graph according to GXL [10], a graph-based exchange format based on XML. The textual rep-

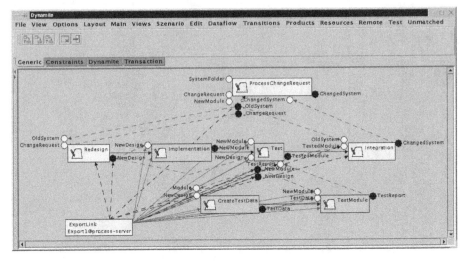

Fig. 5. Exporting the selected tasks

resentation also includes the export link of this delegation through which the contractor can identify the client system.

As soon as the export is finished the PMS rejects all changes to the exported net by the client process manager. The execution of the other parts of the net may continue normally. The PMS now waits for being contacted by a contractor which has imported the task and claims to be responsible for them. However, the client process manager can call a command which revokes the export, removes the export link and thus invalidates the file containing the process description. After the connection between client and contractor has been established, net changes are possible if both agree to them (see Section 4.6).

4.4   Importing the Delegated Net at the Contractor

To import the delegated net (Step 4 of Figure 1), the contractor reads the textual representation and constructs a task net accordingly (see Figure 6). This net also contains the tasks and parameters of the context. Just as the delegated net is in a read-only state in the client PMS, the context of the delegation is read-only in the contractor PMS, which is shown to the user by a different color of the tasks. Internally, there is an import link node (not shown here) which corresponds to the export link node in the client PMS. The contractor system now contacts and registers with the client (Step 5 of Figure 1). In the following, each system reports changes of the execution state of model elements on which the remote system contains a read-only view.

Note that the context of the net in Figure 6 is really limited to those nodes which are directly connected to the delegated net by an edge[1]. The predecessor task Redesign and its output parameter NewDesign are part of the context

---

[1] Not all edges of the internal model are shown to the user. The edges connecting tasks and their subtasks are e.g. visualized by the arrangement of tasks in different layers.

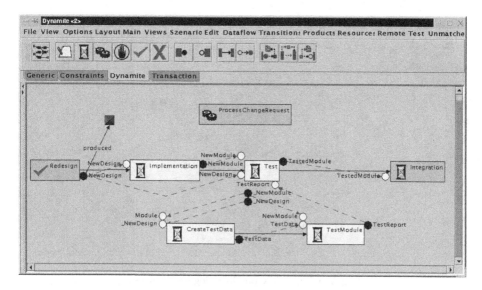

Fig. 6. Contractor PMS executes the delegated process

but its input parameters `OldDesign` and `ChangeRequest` are not. From the contractors point of view, the context is the interface to the client process. The executability of the task `Implementation` in the contractor system depends on the execution state of its predecessor task and the availability of the input document passed through the parameter `NewDesign`. The contractor does not have to know what inputs are required for `Redesign`.

However, the parameters of the delegated task net are not suited as the only specification of the deliverables of a delegation. There have to be accompanying specification documents, which are outside the scope of the process model just as the transfer of the process description itself can naturally not be part of the process description.

4.5   Executing the Interorganizational Process

The presence of the delegated net's context at the contractor greatly simplifies the realization of the integration mechanism between the systems (Step 6 of Figure 1). From the enacting process engine's point of view, read only tasks are handled like odinary tasks. The difference is that no local user of the system, developer or process manager, has the permission to change these tasks. Instead, a component of the PMS, the *link manager*, acts as a user of these tasks by invoking the same operations on them as normal users invoke on local tasks.

Unlike a human user, the link manager does not call operations on the process model to reflect the progress of the real-world process. It merely reacts on messages sent by a peer system concerning changes in its part of the model. Likewise, the link manager monitors the local process model. If it detects a change

---

Therefore, the parent task of a delegated net, in this case `ProcessChangeRequest`, is always part of the context, though the user does not see an edge.

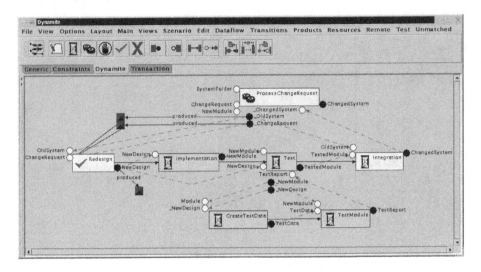

Fig. 7. Client view on the delegated process

at a tasks that is part of the context of a delegation, it sends a message to the contractor PMS.

Figure 7 shows the task net in execution at the client. By looking at the icon of the task `ProcessChangeRequest` we can tell that the task's state is `Active`, i.e. the task is executed right now. Through its internal output parameters `OldSystem` and `ChangeRequest` the task has passed the respective documents to its subtask `Redesign`. The task `Redesign` has read the documents, and it has produced a new design, denoted by the token which is attached to the output parameter `NewDesign`. After this, the task was finished and the developer to whom the task was assigned has switched its state to `Done`.

Now let us have a look at the contractor PMS as it is shown in Figure 6. The contractor sees the state of the parent task `ProcessChangeRequest` and of the predecessor task `Redesign` which are part of its context. He does not see the tokens passed between them. The token produced by the output parameter of `Redesign` is also present in the contractor PMS. It was created by the link manager after the client system informed it about this change in the context of the delegation. Through the connection between the link managers, the actual design document, let us e.g. assume some UML model, was transferred from the client's document repository to the contractor's repository.

The developer to whom the task `Implementation` is assigned can now see in his front end that the design document is available. He can invoke the command for consuming the token which causes the actual document to be transferred to his local workspace where he can work on it.

4.6   Changing an Exported Net

Throughout this paper, we have emphasized that the delegation of a process net is a contract. Neither the client nor the contractor is therefore entitled to change the delegated net. The parts of the net to be delegated should thus be chosen very carefully. However, due to the unpredictability of development processes changes to delegated nets might become necessary. The PML of dynamic task nets allows for changes at process enactment time. They are performed by the process manager and they are not unusual.

But in case of a delegation, there are two process managers and, because client and contractor are independent organizations, both have to agree to change the delegated part of the net. How this agreement is reached is beyond the scope of our management system. As soon as an agreement is reached, the manager at the contractor can switch the state of the delegated tasks to `Planning`. In that state, the client PMS permits the manager at the client to modify the delegated net. Each change is propagated by the link manager to the contractor where it is executed first, because the complete information, especially concerning the refinement of delegated tasks, is only available at the contractor. Therefore, attempts to change the net may as well fail and in this case the contractor's manager has to do some preparing modifications at first. Only if the change succeeds in the contractor system, it is also performed in the client system. Altogether, one can say that changing a delegation during enactment is difficult not only with regard to the process model, but also in real-life. It certainly requires frequent interaction of the involved people.

5   Related Work

Distribution and distributed enactment of processes and workflows have been studied to some extent and implemented in several systems, e.g. Oz [3], PROSYT [6] or FUNSOFT Nets [7]. Most of these approaches focus on connecting already existing processes. With regard to interorganizational cooperations this means that each organization's part of a process is modeled separately including the connection points to the other parts. These systems neglect the requirements of interorganizational cooperations, which are formulated in [18, 14, 1, 20], and have their strength in supporting a distributed team of developers who are members of the same organization. The loose coupling is typical of federated PSEEs where the overall process which is established through the federation remains implicit. In contrast to this, Tiako proposes in [17] to explicitly model the federation process instead and introduces the notion of delegation.

In [8] Dowson reports on the IStar environment in which single tasks can be delegated to contractors. For each delegation, a contract specification describes the contractor's obligations. It is in the contractors responsibility to decide how these obligations are fulfilled. The approach does not allow for the delegation of a whole subnet. Therefore, guidelines how to perform a delegated task can only be given as an annotation to the task and do not integrate with the process model as they do in our system.

Research by van der Aalst [20, 19] provides valuable insight into the interoperability of workflow management systems. He identifies several forms of interaction among which we can find *subcontracting*. Again, subcontracting is limited to single activities of the workflow. There are other WfMS which offer distribution of workflows, e.g. ADEPT [2] or Mentor [15]. In these systems, distribution is used to cope with a huge number of workflows as it might occur in a large enterprise. Critical issues are the migration of workflow execution between different workflow servers and the reduction of communication overhead. Organizational boundaries and the requirements resulting from them are not considered.

Delegation requires the transfer of process descriptions and their subsequent enactment by the target PMS. In the area of workflow management the Workflow Management Coalition has specified the Workflow Process Definition Language (WPDL) [5] and an API for connecting workflow servers at runtime [4]. The interfaces defined by the WfMC do not support delegation as introduced in this paper but merely provide low-level support for system integration. We did not use the WPDL for process exchange in our system because it is confined to the workflow domain, and mapping dynamic task nets to WPDL would result in a loss of semantics.

6   Conclusion

In this paper, we have presented a concept by which a client in an interorganizational development process can delegate parts of net-based process models to contractors. The approach takes into account the special circumstances which arise when different organizations agree to cooperate in a development project. The achieved integration of the process parts is tighter than it is in comparable approaches for distributed process enactment. Nevertheless, client and contractor may autonomously execute their process parts as long as the delegated net, which is part of the contract between them, remains unchanged.

We have implemented the concept of delegation within the process management system AHEAD for the modeling language of dynamic task nets. To perform an operation at one model element, the context of this element has to be known. The realized export and integration mechanism therefore includes the context of the delegated net. This greatly simplifies the implementation of the coupling because the underlying process engine can treat delegated or imported tasks just like ordinary local tasks. To update the read-only copies of tasks the process link managers have been introduced which monitor the process execution and inform their remote counterparts if changes at relevant parts of the process occur.

The system, as it is implemented so far, does not take into account issues like authentification and security. Moreover, it has to be ensured that no conflicting update messages cross each other on the network and thus the interorganizational process gets into an inconsistent state. And finally, the requirement of autonomous execution means that PMSs which participate in a cooperation may be temporarily down without affecting the other systems. If a system is down, its local process state cannot change and therefore there is no need to update the read-only view which is maintained by other systems on that process. But a PMS must be able to distinguish between a broken network connection and a peer system that is currently inactive, so a more elaborated communication protocol is needed here. It is not our aim to solve all these problems. Distributed system research has dealt with these problems and came up with a number of well known solutions for them. In our work, we have concentrated on elaborating the requirements which a PMS should meet to support delegation, and we have shown how delegation mechanisms can be implemented.

References

1. C. Basile, S. Calanna, E. Di Nitto, A. Fuggetta, and M. Gemo. Mechanisms and policies for federated PSEEs: Basic concepts and open issues. In Carlo Montagnero, editor, *Proceedings of the 5th European Workshop on Software Process Technology*, LNCS 1149, pages 86–91, Nancy, France, October 1996. Springer.
2. Thomas Bauer and Peter Dadam. A distributed execution environment for large-scale workflow management systems with subnets and server migration. In *Proceedings of the second IFCIS conference on Cooperative Information Systems (CoopIS'97)*, pages 99–108, Kiawah Island, South Caroline, USA, June 1997.
3. Israel Ben-Shaul and Gail E. Kaiser. Federating process-centered environments: the OZ experience. *Automated Software Engineering*, 5:97–132, 1998.
4. Workflow Management Coalition. Workflow client API specification. Technical report, Workflow Management Coalition, http://www.aiim.org/wfmc/standards, July 1998.
5. Workflow Management Coalition. Process definition interchange. Technical report, Workflow Management Coalition, http://www.aiim.org/wfmc/standards, October 1999.
6. Gianpaolo Cugola and Carlo Ghezzi. Design and implementation of PROSYT: a distributed process support system. In *Proceedings of the 8th International Workshop on Enabling Technologies: Infrastructure for Collaborative Enterprises*, California, USA, June 1999. Stanford University.
7. Wolfgang Deiters and Volker Gruhn. Process management in practice, applying the FUNSOFT net approach to large-scale processes. *Automated Software Engineering*, 5:7–25, 1998.
8. Mark Dowson. Integrated project support with IStar. *IEEE Software*, 4:6–15, November 1987.
9. Peter Heimann, Gregor Joeris, Carl-Arndt Krapp, and Bernhard Westfechtel. DYNAMITE: Dynamic task nets for software process management. In *Proceedings of the 18th ICSE*, pages 331–341, Berlin, March 1996. IEEE Computer Society Press.
10. Ric Holt, Andreas Winter, and Andreas Schürr. GXL: Toward a standard exchange format. In *Proceedings of the 7th Working Conference on Reverse Engineering (WCRE 2000)*, Brisbane, Australia, November 2000.
11. Dirk Jäger. Generating tools from graph-based specifications. *Information and Software Technology*, 42:129–139, 2000.
12. Dirk Jäger, Ansgar Schleicher, and Bernhard Westfechtel. AHEAD: A graph-based system for modeling and managing development processes. In Manfred Nagl and Andy Schürr, editors, *AGTIVE — Applications of Graph Transformations with Industrial Relevance*, LNCS 1779, Castle Rolduc, The Netherlands, September 1999. Springer-Verlag.
13. Carl-Arndt Krapp. *An Adaptable Environment for the Management of Development Processes*. PhD thesis, RWTH Aachen, Aachen, Germany, 1998.

14. Heiko Ludwig and Keith Whittingham.   Virtual enterprise co-ordinator: Agreement-driven gateways for cross-organisational workflow management. In Dimitros Georgakopoulos, Wolfgang Prinz, and Alexander L. Wolf, editors, *Proceedings of the International Joint Conference on Work Activities, Coordination and Collaboration (WAC-99)*, pages 29–38, N.Y., February 22–25 1999. ACM Press.

15. P. Muth, D. Wodtke, J. Weissenfels, A. Kotz Dittrich, and G. Weikum. From centralized workflow specification to distributed workflow execution. *JIIS – special issue on workflow management*, 10(2), March 1998.

16. Andy Schürr. Introduction to the specification language PROGRES. In Manfred Nagl, editor, *Building Tightly-Integrated Software Development Environments: The IPSEN Approach*, LNCS 1170, pages 248–279, Berlin, Heidelberg, New York, 1996. Springer Verlag.

17. Pierre F. Tiako. Modelling the federation of process sensitive engineering environments: Basic concepts and perspectives. In *Proceedings of the 6th European Workshop on Software Process Technology (EWSPT'98)*, Weybridge, UK, September 1998.

18. Pierre F. Tiako and Jean-Claude Derniame. Modelling trusted process components for distributed software development. In *Proceedings of the International Process Technology Workshop (IPTW)*, Grenoble, France, September 1999.

19. Wil M. P. van der Aalst. Interorganizational workflows – an approach based on message sequence charts and Petri nets. *Systems Analysis, Modeling and Simulation*, 34(3):335 – 367, 1999.

20. Wil M. P. van der Aalst. Process-oriented architectures for electronic commerce and interorganizational workflow. *Information Systems*, 24(8):639–671, 1999.

Applying Real-Time Scheduling Techniques to Software Processes: A Position Paper

Aaron G. Cass and Leon J. Osterweil

Department of Computer Science
University of Massachusetts
Amherst, MA 01003-4610
{acass, ljo}@cs.umass.edu

Abstract. Process and workflow technology have traditionally not allowed for the specification of, nor run-time enforcement of, real-time requirements, despite the fact that time-to-market and other real-time constraints are more stringent than ever. Without specification of timing constraints, process designers cannot effectively reason about real-time constraints on process programs and the efficacy of their process programs in satisfying those constraints. Furthermore, without executable semantics for those timing specifications, such reasoning might not be applicable to the process as actually executed. We seek to support reasoning about the real-time requirements of software processes. In this paper, we describe work in which we have added real-time specifications to a process programming language, and in which we have added deadline timers and task scheduling to enforce the real-time requirements of processes.

1 Introduction

Software process research is based on the notion, borrowed from manufacturing, that the way to build a good product is to have a good process by which that product is developed. Process programming languages were developed to help describe and make more repeatable the good processes of software development. These processes mostly involve human agents that do the bulk of the work. However, at specified points in the process, an automated agent might be introduced to perform some portion of the task, such as compiling the source code or executing a test. Software development processes, consisting of both automated and human-executed tasks, have real-time requirements. Phases of development must be done in timely fashion in order to allow enough time for later phases before the ship date arrives. At a finer-grained level, automated tasks can and should be done quickly to avoid delaying the overall progress of the development effort and to keep the human engineers from needlessly waiting.

In this work, we have extended an existing process programming language to provide deadline timers and dynamic scheduling to ensure that tasks will be completed within specified timing constraints.

V. Ambriola (Ed.): EWSPT 2001, LNCS 2077, pp. 145–151, 2001.

As part of our ongoing research in process programming, we have developed Little-JIL [9,10], a hierarchical, graphical, executable, and semantically rich process programming language. We are interested in applying scheduling techniques to process programs written in Little-JIL. As an example, consider a software design process. Clearly, a software design for a large software system requires human efforts on a scale of many designers working together for days, weeks, and months. However, there are points in the process where tasks are carried out that need to be done automatically and quickly, and as software engineering becomes better understood, the percentage of the process that can be done automatically and should be done quickly will increase. One area that can and should be automated is the periodic checking of the conformance of the design with respect to various design rules. If the conformance checking is not done in a timely fashion, the next design iteration will be delayed, the fixing of conformance errors will be delayed, and the project with either lack desired features or fail to meet time-to-market goals. This tension between tasks with loose, long deadlines and tasks with tight, short deadlines represents the key real-time characteristic of the kind of tasks we are trying to solve in this work.

A portion of a software design process program, including design conformance checking, is shown in Figure 1. The Add Component step at the root of the tree is a sequential step (indicated by the arrow), which means that the substeps must execute in left to right order without overlap. Therefore, the designer must first define a component and then integrate it in the overall design. After that, design conformance checking is performed, in this case by automated checkers.

We seek an approach that will allow the flexible specification of real-time requirements in a variety of scenarios. One scenario of interest is one in which overall design phase timing constraints are specified in addition to the real-time requirements of conformance checking. Another common scenario my be one in which we can't precisely estimate the time it takes to define and integrate a component, but yet we can give fairly accurate and precise estimates of the conformance checking activities because they are performed by automated checkers. Furthermore, these estimates will improve on each iteration through the recorded experience of past checks.

We therefore seek an approach that allows the enforcement of real-time schedules for all or part of a process program. In the rest of this paper, we further study the scenario in which the conformance checking sub-process is the only part of the process that has real-time requirements.

In this conformance checking sub-process, we would like to get as much useful conformance checking done as is possible in the time given. There are different categories of checks which can be done in parallel (as indicated by the two horizontal lines in the Perform All Checks step), each with current estimates of how long they will take to perform (perhaps based on previously recorded experience). If possible, we would like to perform all checks as the process specifies. However, there are real-time failures that might preclude this. In this work, we aim to deal with at least two kinds of real-time failure:

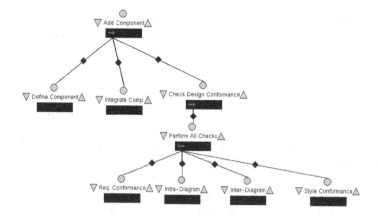

Fig. 1. An example Little-JIL process program

- Scheduling failure – If we can determine, based on current estimates of how much time each task will take, that it is impossible to complete all the conformance checks in the alloted time, then we must choose a different set of checks to perform.
- Deadline expiration – Once scheduled, tasks might overrun their deadlines if the timing estimates were inaccurate, or if the agents involved are busy with other tasks. In this case, we need to choose a different set of checks to perform, based on how many we have performed and how much time we have left to perform checks.

1.1 Differences from Traditional Real-Time Problem Domain

The kinds of problems that can be expressed in Little-JIL are different from the traditional real-time problems in many ways. Primary among these is the fact that some tasks are done by humans, while others are done by software tools and therefore some tasks have tighter deadlines than others. Many tasks might take hours, days, or weeks while others expect a response time of seconds or less. In fact, because of the looseness of some of the deadlines, it may be desirable to not even include some tasks in a real-time schedule, choosing only to schedule those tasks that have tight deadlines. We seek a flexible approach that allows the mixing of coarse timing constraints with fine-grained ones. We seek an approach that allows for not scheduling some tasks (perhaps human-executed tasks) with coarse timing constraints while still scheduling the time-critical tasks.

2 Related Work

Other workflow and process languages have included timing notions. For example, the workflow language WIDE [2,3] allows the specification of a delayed start to a task, which can be used to check to see if another activity was accomplished during the delay. Their approach integrates the real-time failure handling with the normal control flow instead of separating this exceptional behavior.

There is a similar mechanism in SLANG [1]. A timeout duration can be specified between two transitions, called the start transition and the end transition, in the Petri-Net. If the end transition is reached, the current time is checked to ensure that it is within the specified duration after the firing of the start transition. If it is not, the end transition's TO (timeout) half is fired. This mechanism requires that transitions must be modified in order to be allowable end transitions for the timeout duration – thus the specification of timeouts is not separated from the specification of normal flow and task decomposition.

Our work is also related to work in real-time scheduling. For example, Liestman and Campbell [6] introduce primary and alternate algorithms for computing solutions of differing quality and timing characteristics. They then attempt to schedule the primary alternative, but if no valid schedule can be constructed, they attempt the alternate algorithm. Liu et al. [7] provide dynamic approaches to scheduling calculations that are logically broken into mandatory and optional subtasks.

3   Our Approach

Our approach has been two-fold. We first provide a simple deadline timer mechanism for the specification of maximum durations of leaf steps and then we use this information to produce schedules of complex structures.

3.1   Deadline Timers

Our approach has been to allow the specification of maximum durations on step specifications in Little-JIL processes, as shown in Figure 2, in which the leaf conformance checking steps are assigned durations of 150 time units. At runtime, the duration, if specified, is used to initialize a timer. Then, if the agent for the step executes the step within the duration, the step completes normally. However, if the timer expires before the step is done, the Little-JIL run-time system [4] causes a Little-JIL exception to be thrown.

This exception is handled in the same way as other exceptions are handled according to the language semantics [9]. The exception mechanism takes advantage of the hierarchical structure of Little-JIL programs to provide natural scopes for exception handling. When a step throws an exception, the parent step has the first opportunity to react to the exception. It can do so by executing a handler, which is a potentially complex Little-JIL step, or it can throw the exception further up the hierarchy. In this way, the exception can be handled at the scope at which it is most naturally handled.

Because we have treated deadline expiration as an exception like any other, we can provide some real-time assurances with relatively little additional language or run-time complexity. As an example, consider the Little-JIL program shown in Figure 2, an extension of the one shown in Figure 1. In this program,

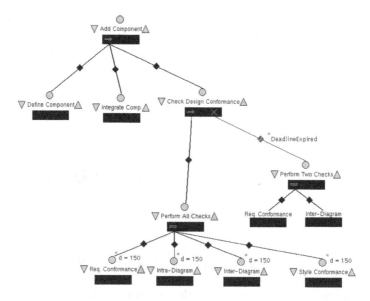

Fig. 2. A Little-JIL process program with a deadline expiration exception handler.

the DeadlineExpired exception is handled by performing the two most important checks instead of all four that are specified in the normal process description.

3.2   Real-Time Scheduling

As we have detailed in [5], we have integrated real-time scheduling techniques into Little-JIL. We have adapted a real-time heuristic-search based dynamic scheduling algorithm [8] to work with the hierarchical structures of Little-JIL programs. The scheduler we have developed takes both timing estimates and resource requirements into account to determine when steps can be executed. Where there is no resource contention, the scheduler allows two steps to be scheduled to execute in parallel. Once this scheduler was adapted to work with Little-JIL structures, we updated the Little-JIL run-time to call the scheduler at appropriate times. When the Little-JIL run-time attempts to execute a step, if that step has a timing specification, the scheduler is called to determine if the estimates of the running-times of the substeps are consistent with the timing specification of this newly executing root step.

The scheduler uses a heuristic-search approach to arrive at a schedule, a set of starting times for the steps in a Little-JIL process. If no such schedule is possible, the scheduler can cause a SchedulingFailure exception to be thrown. Just as any other Little-JIL exception, this exception can be handled at any higher scope. We have shown an example process in Figure 3 that shows the use of a handler for this type of exception to perform a different set of conformance checks. This is much like the deadline expiration example except that in the case

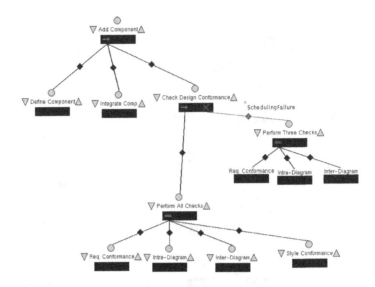

Fig. 3. A Little-JIL process program with a scheduling failure exception handler.

of scheduling failure, the exception occurs before the substeps are executed and so there is more time to execute an effective fix.

4   Conclusion

Because real-world software development processes have timing requirements about which process designers need to reason and provide assurances, we have added the ability to specify and enforce real-time constraints in Little-JIL. Our approach provides flexibility in the specification of real-time requirements, and allows for the handling of two different kinds of real-time failures. The approach uses the exception handling mechanisms of Little-JIL to keep the specification of the handling of real-time failures separate from the specification of normal process flow.

Acknowledgements. This research was partially supported by the Air Force Research Laboratory/IFTD and the Defense Advanced Research Projects Agency under Contract F30602-97-2-0032 and by the U.S. Department of Defense/Army and the Defense Advance Research Projects Agency under Contract DAAH01-00-C-R231. The U.S. Government is authorized to reproduce and distribute reprints for Governmental purposes notwithstanding any copyright annotation thereon.

The views and conclusions contained herein are those of the authors and should not be interpreted as necessarily representing the official policies or endorsements, either expressed or implied of the Defense Advanced Research

Projects Agency, the Air Force Research Laboratory/IFTD, the U.S. Dept. of Defense, the U. S. Army, or the U.S. Government.

References

1. S. Bandinelli, A. Fuggetta, and S. Grigolli. Process modeling in-the-large with SLANG. In *Proc. of the Second Int. Conf. on the Soft. Process*, pages 75–83. IEEE Computer Society Press, 1993.
2. L. Baresi, F. Casati, S. Castano, M. G. Fugini, I. Mirbel, and B. Pernici. WIDE workflow development methodology. In *Proc. of the Int. Joint Conf. on Work Activities, Coordination, and Collaboration*, 1999. San Francisco, CA.
3. F. Casati, S. Ceri, S. Paraboschi, and G. Pozzi. Specification and implementation of exceptions in workflow management systems. *ACM Trans. on Database Systems*, 24(3):405–451, Sept. 1999.
4. A. G. Cass, B. S. Lerner, E. K. McCall, L. J. Osterweil, and A. Wise. Logically central, physically distributed control in a process runtime environment. Technical Report 99-65, U. of Massachusetts, Dept. of Comp. Sci., Nov. 1999.
5. A. G. Cass, K. Ramamritham, and L. J. Osterweil. Exploiting hierarchy for planning and scheduling. Technical Report 2000-064, U. of Massachusetts, Dept. of Comp. Sci., Dec. 2000.
6. A. L. Liestman and R. H. Campbell. A fault-tolerant scheduling problem. *IEEE Trans. on Soft. Eng.*, 12(11):1089–95, Nov. 1986.
7. J. W. Liu, K. Lin, W. Shih, A. C. Yu, J. Chung, and W. Zhao. Algorithms for scheduling imprecise computations. *IEEE Computer*, 24(5):58–68, May 1991.
8. K. Ramamritham, J. A. Stankovic, and P. Shiah. Efficient scheduling algorithms for real-time multiprocessor systems. *IEEE Transactions on Parallel and Distributed Systems*, 1(2):184–194, Apr. 1990.
9. A. Wise. Little-JIL 1.0 Language Report. Technical Report 98-24, U. of Massachusetts, Dept. of Comp. Sci., Apr. 1998.
10. A. Wise, A. G. Cass, B. S. Lerner, E. K. McCall, L. J. Osterweil, and S. M. Sutton, Jr. Using Little-JIL to coordinate agents in software engineering. In *Proc. of the Automated Software Engineering Conf.*, Sept. 2000. Grenoble, France.

Building Expressive and Flexible Process Models Using a UML-Based Approach

Josep M. Ribó[1] and Xavier Franch[2]

[1] Universitat de Lleida
C. Jaume II, 69 E-25001 Lleida (Catalunya, Spain)
josepma@eup.udl.es
[2] Universitat Politècnica de Catalunya (UPC),
c/ Jordi Girona 1-3 (Campus Nord, C6) E-08034 Barcelona (Catalunya, Spain)
franch@lsi.upc.es

Abstract. Some limitations have been identified in current software process modelling languages concerning *expressiveness, standardization* and *flexibility*. We outline the main features of a software process modelling language called PROMENADE which aims at improving the above-mentioned issues. Expressiveness is enhanced in PROMENADE by the combination of proactive and reactive control, using precedence relationships between tasks and ECA-rules, respectively. Standardization is achieved by the mapping of PROMENADE features into a slightly extended UML. PROMENADE also supports the definition of flexible models by leaving some parts undefined until enactment time. We illustrate the use of PROMENADE by presenting in some detail a case study consisting in the modelling of the process of construction of a software component library.

1   Introduction

In the last few years, a second generation of process modelling languages (PML) has emerged to solve some of the problems that were detected in the previous ones [6, 14, 17]. However, there subsist several features that have not been completely solved: expressive power of the language; use of notations and semantics widely accepted by the software engineering community; ability to build models from existing pieces and flexibility of process enactment are some of them.

1.1 Expressiveness

The need for a flexible and expressive modelling of process control-flow, together with the ability to define new control-flow dependencies, has been recognized in the field of workflow management [8, 10, 13] but, in our opinion, equivalent results have not been obtained in the related area of SPM.

The very nature of software processes involve a loose control and a high degree of collaboration. In spite of this, most of existing approaches lead to very prescriptive

V. Ambriola (Ed.): EWSPT 2001, LNCS 2077, pp. 152–172, 2001.

models which do not conform to the way in which software is actually developed. Even the most recent ones (APEL, E3, Little JIL, Peace+, etc.), which provide some higher level mechanisms to improve comprehensibility, still fail in achieving the level of expressiveness needed for a realistic SPM (i.e. in most cases the control flow constructs are very basic and unable to model complex dependencies).

1.2 Standardization

The intensive SPM research has stimulated progress in the field but, on the other hand, it has lead to a proliferation of languages and notations that has hampered the wide use of the software process technology within the software engineering community. To cope with these limitations, some UML-based proposals do exist to extend its application range to the modelling of processes [1, 9, 18]. The extent of these UML-based proposals is usually limited to the definition of several stereotypes, which is clearly not enough to provide rich SPM capabilities (e.g., no new typed-attributes or operations can be incorporated to a stereotyped metaclass and the resulting metamodel is not completely comprehensible).

1.3 Flexibility

Most initial approaches to SPM (specially the activity-oriented ones) tended to be too prescriptive and did not deal with the inherent evolutionary nature of both software and software processes. Two general, non-exclusive solutions to this problem have been provided by different systems, namely (1) to allow *changes on-the-fly* of the enacting process and (2) to provide means to refine parts of the model during enactment.

1.4 The PROMENADE Approach

PROMENADE (**PRO**cess-oriented **M**odelling and **ENA**ctment of software **DE**velopments) is part of the *second generation of PMLs* intended to make some contributions to the improvement of the referred issues (expressiveness, standardization and flexibility).

Expressiveness is enhanced in PROMENADE by providing both proactive and reactive controls, as recommended in [17].

- Proactive control. Software processes are modelled by stating in a declarative way the precedence relationships existing between the different activities taking part in them. PROMENADE provides a predefined set of such precedence relationships and it supports also the definition of new ones.
- Reactive control. PROMENADE also allows the modelling of the behaviour of a task by describing how it reacts to certain events. This reaction is encapsulated in ECA-rules associated to tasks or other entities.

With respect to standardization, PROMENADE is based on the UML notation, making it more attractive for software engineers (not yet another formalism to be learned). Our UML-based proposal is twofold.

- On the one hand, we build the PROMENADE metamodel by derivation of the UML metamodel [18] while keeping it as an instance of the MOF model [12].

This approach allows the addition of new metaclasses to the UML metamodel (by subclasifying the existing ones) while relying on the semantics of UML.

- On the other hand, we provide a mapping from this extension to an alternative one which uses only the UML extension mechanisms (stereotypes, tagged values, etc.), obtaining thus a full UML-compatible model.

Flexibility is achieved in PROMENADE through the definition of hierarchies of task and document refinements (i.e., different ways to carry out activities and to give contents to documents). This is different from other approaches that consider only one level of activity realization [7]. At enactment time, one of those refinements is to be selected (even a new refinement can be created). Sometimes, dependencies between different alternative refinements are also taken into account.

The main objective of this article is to model a software process case study with PROMENADE; namely, the construction of a library of software components. To do this, we organise the paper as follows. Section 2 presents the main features of PROMENADE. Section 3 develops the library construction case study with this PML and section 4 gives the conclusions.

2   The Process Modelling Language PROMENADE

In this section we outline those aspects of PROMENADE that are used in the example developed in section 3. Interested readers are referred to our previous works [5, 15, 16] for a more detailed explanation of these topics.

2.1 Static Model

The part of the PROMENADE metamodel intended to deal with the static (structural) part of a SPM is built as an extension of the UML metamodel [18], adding a metaelement for each one of the core elements that take part in any PROMENADE model (e.g., *MetaTask* for tasks, *MetaDocument* for documents, *SPMetamod* for the model itself, etc.) and some generalization and association relationships linking the added metaelements. The model elements are seen as instances of the metaelements (e.g., the class *BuildComponent* as instance of *MetaTask*) whose (meta)features (metaattributes and metaoperations) have been given a value. Therefore the process of building a model in PROMENADE will consist mainly in creating instances of the metamodel classes and give values to its metafeatures.

PROMENADE defines a universal or *reference model* that constitutes the basis on which any other process model will be built. Thus, it contains the core elements that will be a part of any model described in PROMENADE (see table 1). The features associated to these elements are the ones needed to characterize any instance of them. The static model of PROMENADE is presented in more detail in [5].

The reference model is defined as an instance of the PROMENADE metamodel.

Table 1. Predefined classes in the PROMENADE reference model

Class	Description	Some instances	Attributes	Some methods
Docu-ment	Any container of information involved in the software development process	A specification; a test plan; an e-mail	Link to contents; relevant dates; version; status	Document updating with or without new version creation; document edition
Commu-nication	Any document used for people communication; can be stored in a computer or not	A fax; an e-mail; human voice	Link (if any) to contents; transmission date; status	*Send* and *Read*; many others inherited from *Document*
Task	Any action performed during the software process	Specification; component testing; error-reporting	Precondition; status; success condition; deadline (if any)	Changes of task status
Agent	Any entity playing an active part in the software process	Myself; my workstation; a compiler	Profile; location; humans skills	Just structural ones
Tool	Any agent implemented through a software tool	A compiler; a navigator	Root directory for the tool; binary file location	Just structural ones
Resource	Any help to be used during software process	An online tutorial on Java; a Web site	Platform requirements; location	*Access*
Role	Any part to be played during the software process	Programmer; manager	Tasks for which the role is responsible	Just structural ones

2.2 Dynamic Model: Proactive Control

PROMENADE defines both atomic and composite tasks. The proactive view of the dynamic model describes the behaviour of the composite ones by means of precedence relationships (*precedences* for short) between their subtasks. PROMENADE distinguishes among several types of precedences.

Basic Precedences

Basic precedences state the requirements that are necessary for a task to start and/or finish its enactment. Unlike other approaches, they are not limited to relate two activities with an "end-start" transition condition. Instead, they provide additional information: type of the precedence; kind of connection among its origin tasks; parameter binding between its origin and destination tasks (parameters represent documents managed by the tasks); and a predicate (condition), whose fulfilment is necessary for a precedence to be applicable. Fig. 1 shows the graphical representation of basic precedences (p's and q's are the parameters).

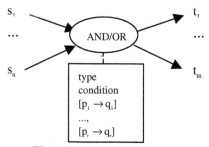

Fig. 1: Representation of precedences

PROMENADE predefines a catalogue of basic precedence types (see table 2). Although it is complete enough to cope with basic process models, more complex or detailed ones may need new basic precedences (e.g., to deal with dates). Because of this, PROMENADE also supports the definition of new types of basic precedences by stating a start condition and an end condition for their target tasks by means of OCL-constraints.

Table 2: Different types of basic precedences

Type	Notation	Meaning
start	$s \rightarrow_{start} t$	*t* may start only if *s* has started previously
end	$s \rightarrow_{end} t$	*t* may finish only if *s* has finished previously
strong	$s \rightarrow_{strong} t$	*t* may start only if *s* has finished successfully previously
feedback	$s \rightarrow_{fbk} t$	*t* may be reexecuted after the unsuccessful end of *s*

PROMENADE precedences are modelled subclassifying UML dependencies. The details of this modelling are presented in [26].

Derived Precedences

Some precedences that arise in the modelling of more sophisticated processes may be described in terms of other existing ones. Although these precedences are not strictly necessary to model a process, they are convenient in order to make the resulting models more comprehensible and the language itself user-friendly.

Let us consider, for instance, the following situation in a SPM for component-based software development: *the implementation of a component should begin some time after the starting point of its specification and should finish after the end of its specification*. This can be easily modelled by a combination of a *start* and an *end* basic precedences . The situation is then an instance of a new type of precedence (the *weak* type, defined in fig. 2) that arises often in other contexts. Weak precedence relationships and other derived ones are predefined in PROMENADE; also, new types of derived precedences can be introduced using the notation shown in fig. 2.

```
precedence weak
    is_noted_as  <"weak", S, T, combi, pb>
            with:
                S, T: set(Task)
                combi: enum{AND, OR, NULL}
                pb: set(Binding)
    is_defined_as
            precedences:
                <"start", S, T, combi, pb>
                <"end", S, T, pb>
end precedence
```

Fig. 2: Definition of the weak precedence

Dynamic Precedences

Precedences are a part of the model, hence they must be introduced at model definition time. Some of them, however, may only be determined precisely at enactment time, when the model is instantiated.

An example is the precedence: *in order to validate an implementation of a software component, it is required to test every individual operation of that component*, because the set of operations of a specific component is not known in advance.

PROMENADE dynamic precedence relationships face that limitation. A dynamic precedence stands for an unknown number of "normal" (i.e., non-dynamic) ones; the concrete number will be fixed during enactment, depending on the value of an expression defined in terms of one or more parameters of the tasks involved in the precedence. Section 3 gives an example of dynamic precedence.

2.3 Dynamic Model: Reactive Control

We define *reactive control* in PROMENADE as the control described by means of *actions* performed on an *entity* as a response (reaction) to an *event*. The specific action that is triggered by a particular event is described by an ECA-rule associated to the entity.

- The *action* has the same meaning as in UML (i.e., performing operations on objects or modifying links and values of attributes). The most typical reactive action consists in starting or finishing the enactment of a task *t* when a specific event occurs. In order to maintain correctness, actions must keep model invariants.
- An *entity* is any subclass of *Type* (*Document, Task, Role*, etc.), being in fact a *Task* in most cases.
- An *event* is a specific occurrence that takes place during model enactment. Events are described below.

Notice that, while in proactive control tasks are initiated and finished explicitly by their responsible (when they are ready), in reactive control, this starting and ending may be carried out automatically on the occurrence of a certain event. Notice also that automatic tasks provide a reactive behaviour; they start and finish automatically on the occurrence of state-change events (see below).

Events

PROMENADE defines three kinds of events that are modelled by subclassifying the event class hierarchy of UML, as shown in fig. 3.
1. The reception of a communication (by either a task or a role). The signal associated to the event must be of type *Communication*.
2. The change of state of an entity (usually a task or a document). It supports reaction to enactment and ending of tasks, among others.
3. A time event.

- Absolute time event To represent events of the sort: *currentDate>10.01.2001*. They are modelled as UML change events (since they model the satisfaction of a certain condition).
- Duration event. To state conditions on duration, such as *It has passed more than 2 days since the starting point of a task*. These may be naturally modelled as UML time events (which also refer to time elapsed).

Events are broadcast to all the entities of the model.

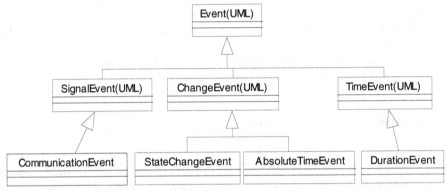

Fig. 3: Modelling of events in PROMENADE

ECA-Rules

ECA-rules are a common way for representing reactive control [3]. They specify which action must be executed on the occurrence of an event if a certain condition holds.

As attributes and operations, ECA-rules are associated to entities. A specific ECA-rule is activated when the entity to which it is associated receives an instance of the event that triggers it.

ECA-rules may be modelled as UML transitions[1]. On the other hand, ECA-rules are to be considered features of entities. For these reasons we have modelled ECA-rules as subtypes of both *BehaviouralFeature* and *Transition* (both UML metaclasses). The *source* and *target* associations for a specific ECA-rule are implemented by means of a virtual state.

2.4 Communications

A PROMENADE communication represents a high-level transmission of information between several *communication-ends* (tasks or roles). Communications may act as events. Therefore, the reception of a communication may activate a reactive response on the receiver entity.

---

[1] Although UML transitions connect a source vertex with a target one in a statechart diagram, which is not the case of ECA-rules.

A communication-end may send *out-communications* and receive *in-commmunications* (see fig. 15). The sending of an out-communication of type *C* by a communication-end is broadcast along the model and it is caught by any communication-end which has an in-communication of type *C* defined. In- and out- communications are represented by means of UML compartments.

In order to make communications compatible with events, we model PROMENADE communications as UML signals. This leads to the extension of the UML metamodel in the way presented in figure 4.

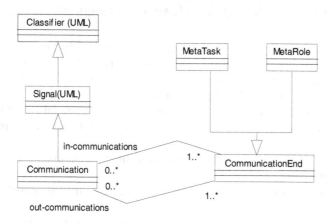

Fig. 4: Modelling of Communications as UML-signals (extension to the UML metamodel).

With this extension, any PROMENADE model is able to define its own hierarchy of communications in the same way as a hierarchy of signals can be defined in UML. The hierarchy of communications shown in figure 5 has been predefined and incorporated to the PROMENADE reference model. Each specific model will define its own hierarchy of communications by subclassifying the predefined ones (multiple inheri-

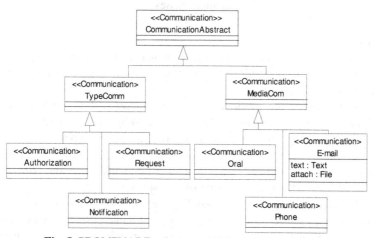

Fig. 5: PROMENADE reference model concerning communications

tance may be used as is shown in section 3). Notice that the definition of communication classes is similar to the definition of *Signal* classes in UML.

We use UML dependencies to represent in a graphical way that a communication *C* sent by an origin communication-end to a destination communication-end. In particular, we define a new stereotype <<*comsent*>> based on the *Dependency* metaclass. We refer to section 3 for examples.

3   A Case Study: A Library of Software Components

The purpose of the process we are going to model is the construction of a software component to be added to the internal library of components of a software company. To be more concrete, we focus on components as encapsulations of data structures, as thus in libraries as LEDA [11], Booch Components [2] and others.

The modelling of this process must take into account several special requirements:
- It should be possible to carry out many component-building activities in different ways.
- The non-functional aspects of the component implementation are to be taken into account.
- Models for task behaviour should come up naturally, either in proactive or reactive way.
- All kind of existing communications should be included in the model.
- The resulting model should be detailed and as less prescriptive as possible.

3.1 Static Model

In this section we define in standard UML the main structural elements that are involved in the process: documents, tasks, roles and communications, all of them defined as instances of the corresponding metaclasses.

Documents
The most important types of documents that are managed in the process are:
- *Component*: The whole result of the process, defined as a (multi-level) aggregation of the other documents.
- *SpecDoc*: It contains the specification of the component, built up from the functional and non-functional parts (*FSpecDoc* and *NFSpecDoc* respectively). These component documents may take different forms, as discussed below.
- *ImplDoc*: The implementation document contains the code of the component and also documents with the description of its non-functional behaviour (*BehDoc*), its test plan (*ImplTestPlan)* and the result of its test (*ImplEvalDoc*).
- *Sched*: Document containing the scheduling plan (deadlines, responsibilities, etc.).

These general classes can be refined in many ways in a concrete software process. Fig. 6 shows an excerpt of the whole document class hierarchy with several alternative document refinements, complemented with the fig. 7 that includes aggregation relationships for representing composition of documents. It is worth noting that multiple levels of refinements are allowed. As examples, let us consider two particular refinements:

- *FSpecDoc*: Three different strategies are shown, including two formal specification strategies and a general concept (*InformalFSpecDoc*). One of the formal frameworks (model oriented specifications) has been refined into more concrete documents, using particular specification languages; this could also be done for the other classes, with as many levels as required. Documents for test plans in formal specification approaches also appear; this is an example of how a particular refinement strategy may impact on refinements of other documents.

- *NFSpecDoc*: We show just the NoFun particular approach developed in [4]. This strategy requires the existence of a new type of document, *PropertyModule*, used to define non-functional attributes of software in a systematic way. This is an example of how a particular refinement strategy may impact on higher levels of the document specialisation hierarchy.

Notice that the hierarchy root (*Document*) belongs to the PROMENADE reference model and hence, it is common to any model written with this PML.

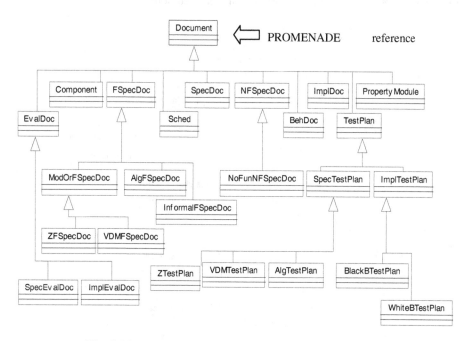

Fig. 6: Hierarchy of documents for the Component library example

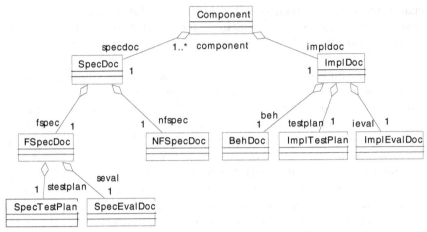

Fig. 7: Aggregation of documents for the Component library example.

Notice that the diagrams provided so far are not enough, since some elements of the static model are linked by associations relationships. We provide then a third diagram. Figure 8 shows the most relevant associations for documents.

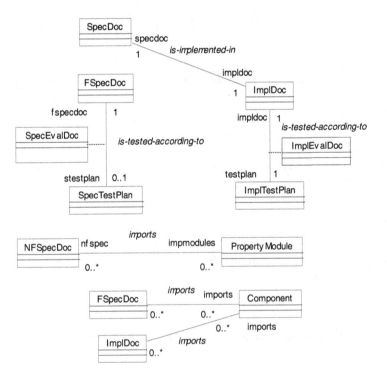

Fig. 8: Association relationships between documents.

Tasks

We describe below the tasks that conform the first level of process decomposition. Figure 9 shows a UML graphical representation of them along with their parameters, using a *parameter* compartment that keeps track of the documents that are involved in the task.

- *BuildComponent*: This is the main task of the model. It is the supertask of all the following tasks..
- *SuperviseProcess:* It grants the main authorizations which are necessary to develop the process (authorization to init, to reschedule tasks and to abort). It defines three subtasks in order to do this: *sendInit, evaluateRescheduling, evaluateAbortion.*

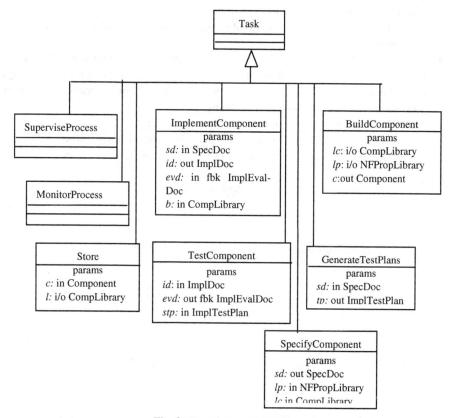

Fig. 9: The first level of tasks

- *MonitorProcess*: It controls the development of the process: (1) it receives the communications that inform about the ending of the process activities; (2) it receives many tasks' result evaluation; (3) it communicates the approaching of their deadlines. It also recommends actions like reescheduling or abortion to *SuperviseProcess* (i.e. these actions must be authorized by *SuperviseProcess*). It performs its functionality by means of two subtasks: (1) *CollectCommsMakeProp*, which is in charge of collecting communications from other tasks, making abort or schedule recommendations to *SuperviseProcess* and also sending abort communications to the rest of the tasks (it is a reactive task); (2) *ScheduleTasks*, responsible for providing the initial task schedule and subsequent reschedules, if any.

- *SpecifyComponent*: It performs the specification of the component. We distinguish between functional and non-functional specifications (subtasks *FSpecifyComponent* and *NFSpecifyComponent*). As in the case of documents, these tasks can be refined following different strategies.
- *ImplementComponent*: It carries out the implementation of the component. Again, many refinements are possible. In our case (data-structure components), it involves the statement of an internal representation for the component and the implementation of each one of its operations.
- *GenerateTestPlans*: It is in charge of developing the plans for testing the component implementation.
- *TestComponent*: It performs the test of the component implementation. Two kinds of test are provided as predefined alternative refinements for this task, although other estrategies can be introduced. One task result is the evaluation document, which is sent as a communication to *MonitorProcess*.
- *Store*: It stores the component into a component library.

MonitorProcess and *SuperviseProcess* conform the administrative tasks, while the others are the technical ones. All technical tasks send a notification to *MonitorProcess* upon completion.

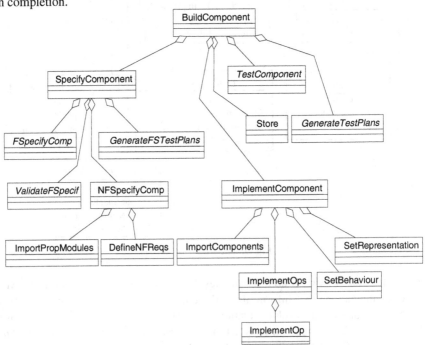

Fig. 10: Aggregation relationships for some task classes

In a similar way to documents, tasks may be organized in PROMENADE according to many axes: aggregation (how composite tasks are decomposed into simpler ones, leading to a task-subtasks relationship), generalization (keeping track of various strategies to implement tasks, thus following different *task refinements*) and associations. We show here the first two ones.

Task aggregation for this case study is shown in figure 10. Notice that several task-subtask decomposition levels are allowed. Notice also that we have modelled the process to a quite detailed level.

Figure 11 shows an excerpt of the hierarchies of possible refinements for the tasks *TestComponent* and *GenerateTestPlans*. A specific task refinement may be selected at enactment time; the documents that act as parameters of the task refinements of a task *t* must be, in their turn, refinements of the parameters of *t*.

There may be some dependencies between task refinement choices. For example, if the task refinement *BlackBTestComponent* is chosen as a strategy to test a component implementation, then the choice of *GenerateBlackBTestPlans* as a refinement for *GenerateTestPlans* is required. These dependencies between task refinements are represented in PROMENADE by means of UML dependencies stereotyped as <<refinementDep>>. An example is shown in figure 11. Notice that this kind of dependencies may also occur between document refinements. On the other hand, the link between tasks and document refinements is established by means of task parameters.

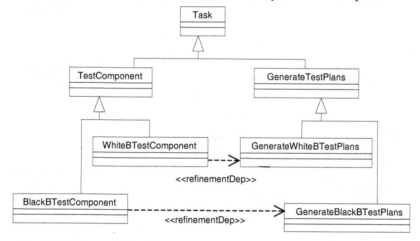

Fig. 11: Refinement hierarchy for the task *TestComponent* and *GenerateTestPlans*

Communications

Table 3 shows the meaning of each communication class while figure 12 shows the hierarchy of communications that is used in this example. As a managerial decision, all the communications are sent by e-mail. The communication classes *Authorisation, Request, Notification* and *E-mail* are defined in the PROMENADE reference model (see fig. 12); in fact, the different kinds of communications are defined by multiple inheritance from *E-mail* and one of the other three classes.

The behaviour of these communications is shown in section 3.3.

Table 3: Meaning of communications

Communication (source→destination)	Meaning
Abort (MonitorProcess → all technical tasks)	Notification to abort immediately the process
AbortA (SuperviseProcess→MonitorProcess)	Authorization to abort the process. Response to *AbortQ*
AbortQ (MonitorProcess→SuperviseProcess)	Request to abort the whole process.
CompleNot (all tech. tasks→MonitorProcess)	Notification concerning the completion of a task (parameter: the completed task).
DeadlineNot (all tech. tasks→MonitorProcess)	Approaching deadline of a task or deadline reached. (parameter: task).
Eval (TestComponent →MonitorProcess)	Document with the component evaluation. (parameter evd: *ImplEvalDoc*)
InitA (SuperviseProcess→MonitorProcess)	Authorization to init the development process.
ReeschA (SuperviseProcess→MonitorProcess)	Authorization to generate a new proc. schedule.
ReeschQ (MonitorProcess→SuperviseProcess)	Request to generate a new process schedule.
Reesched (MonitorProcess→all tech. tasks)	The notification of the new reeschedule. (parameter s: Sched)

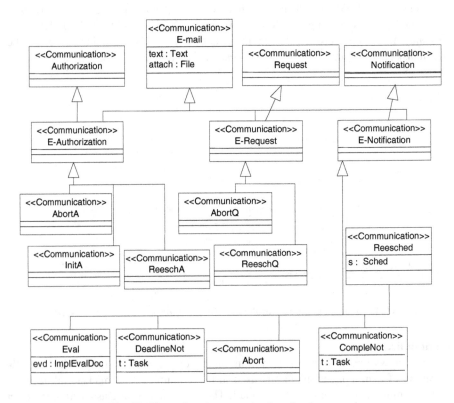

Fig. 12: Hierarchy of communications for the example

3.2   Dynamic Model. Proactive View

The proactive view of the dynamic model describes the behaviour of the composite tasks of the model by means of precedence relationships between their subtasks. In order to have a global view of the PROMENADE features in this respect we present the behaviour of tasks *BuildComponent* (the main task of the process), *Implement-Component* (a subtask of *BuildComponent*) and *ImplementOps* (a subtask of *ImplementComponent*) in figures 13 and 14, respectively (see next pages).

The following aspects are worth mentioning:

- The behaviour of the administrative tasks, *SuperviseProcess* and *MonitorProcess*, is mostly reactive (its behaviour is driven by reactive constraints), thus it will be presented in section 3.3.
- Each composite task has its own precedence diagram associated. This diagram is not standard UML. Recall that we have extended the UML metamodel with precedences and we have provided a representation for them (see fig. 1). However, an alternative modelling using the extension mechanisms of UML (thus, keeping standardization completely) is given in [16].
- The process behaviour has been modelled in an expressive and non-prescriptive way, due to the declarative behaviour modelling achieved using precedences (vs. transitions) and to the various precedence relationships defined by PROMENADE (including derived ones like *weak*). Notice, for instance, that there may be a certain degree of concurrence between *SpecifyComponent* and *ImplementComponent* (i.e. although they do not need to be executed sequentially one after the other, *SpecifyComponent* must start and finish before *ImplementComponent*). Some other precedence requirements are stricter; for instance, a component can be stored only if its test has finished successfully, thus the *strong* precedence relationship between *TestComponent* and *Store*. Last, the supertask *BuildComponent* cannot finish until the rest of the tasks have finished and that they cannot start either until *BuildComponent* has started.
- A parameter of a task *t* can be bound to a component of a parameter of another task *s* with which *t* is linked (by means of a precedence relationship). Consider the example of the link between *BuildComponent* and *SpecifyComponent* (fig. 13). To state that the result of *SpecifyComponent* will be precisely the specification document of the component being built, the output parameter *sd* of *SpecifyComponent* is linked with a part of the built component *c.specdoc*.
- Dynamic precedence allow the construction of an expressive model in an elegant way. Consider the task *ImplementOps* (fig. 14) which is decomposed into several subtasks *ImplementOp*, one for each of the component operations. This dynamic precedence will generate dynamically (i.e., at enactment time) several instances of *ImplementOp*, which will be linked with *ImplementOps* with a pair of normal *start* and *end* precedences. Notice that we are really improving the expressive power of the language, since this situation could not be modelled with normal, static precedences defined at modelling time.

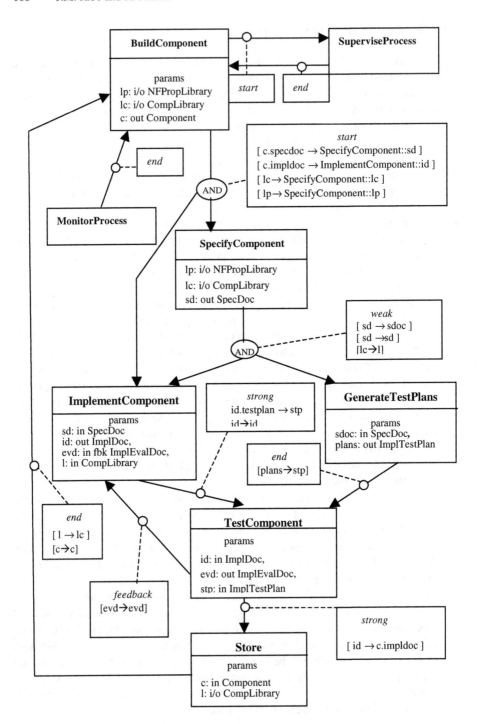

Fig. 13: Precedence diagram for BuildComponent

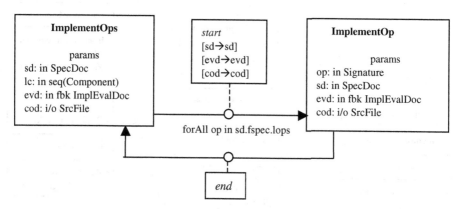

Fig. 14: Precedence diagram for ImplementOps

3.3   Dynamic Model. Reactive View and Communications

The reactive view of the dynamic model describes the behaviour of the composite tasks of the model by means of ECA rules and communications sent between them.
Figure 15 depicts the diagrams containing the reactive view of the global process and figure 16 shows some ECA rules involved in the description of the reactive behaviour. The following aspects are remarkable concerning the reactive issues of this example:

- The administrative task *SuperviseProcess* has two subtasks, namely *EvaluateReescheduling* and *EvaluateAbortion*, which are activated reactively on the reception of the communications of type *ReeschQ* and *AbortQ* (respectively) from *MonitorProcess* (this is controled by means of the ECA-rules *evaluateR* and *evaluateA*). These two subtasks are responsible for sending an answer to *Monitor-Process* concerning its abortion/reescheduling suggestion. Its third subtask (*SendInit*) is activated proactively and is responsible for initiating the whole process (which is done by sending the communication *inita* to *MonitorProcess*).
- The task *MonitorProcess* is activated reactively on the reception of the communication of type *InitA* from *SuperviseProcess* (the ECA-rule *initProcess* is responsible for that). One of its subtasks, namely (*ReescheduleTasks*) is activated on the reception of a communication of type *ReeschA* from *SuperviseProcess*.
- The communications informing *MonitorProcess* about the completion of technical tasks (*Comple*) or their approaching to the deadline (*DeadlineNot*) are sent automatically to *MonitorProcess* at the end of the corresponding tasks by means of the ECA-rules *complete* and *approachingDeadline*.
- The sending of the evaluation document from *TestComponent* to *MonitorProcess* is done automatically at the end of *TestComponent* by means of the ECA-rule *sendEval*.
- The ECA-rule *abortProcess* (attached to all technical tasks) is responsible for starting the abortion process on the reception of the communication *abort* from *MonitorProcess*.

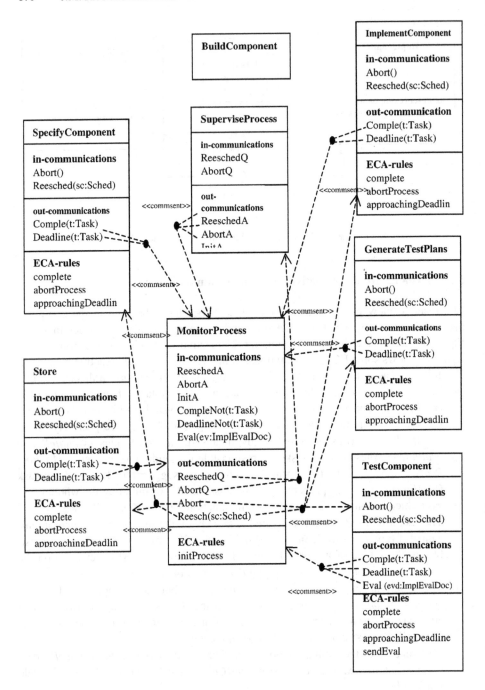

Fig. 15: Reactive and communication view for the whole model

```
Task: MonitorProcess (supertask: BuildComponent):
ECA-rule initProcess
              triggering event: initEv: CommunicationEvent
              with initEv.signal=InitA
              condition: true
              action: status:=active
  Task: EvaluateReescheduling (supertask: SuperviseProcess):
  ECA-rule evaluateR
              triggering event: reeschQEv: CommunicationEvent
              with reeschQEv.signal=ReeschQ
              condition: true
              action: status:=active
                             ECA-rule reinit
              triggering event: complEv: StateChangeEvent
              with complEv.changeExpression=
                 (status=completeSucc)
              condition: true
              action: status:=idle
  Task: All technical tasks (supertask: BuildComponent):
  ECA-rule approachingDeadline
         triggering event: deadEv: AbsoluteTimeEvent
                          with changeExpression=
                             (time=finishBefore-K or time=finishBefore)
         condition: true
         action: DeadlineNot(self).send()
  ECA-rule complete...
  ECA-rule abortProcess...
```

Fig. 16: ECA-rules that control the reactive behaviour of the process

4   Conclusions

Some limitations have been identified in current software PML, concerning *expressiveness*, *standardization* and *flexibility* of most of current approaches. We have outlined the most significant aspects of a PML called PROMENADE which aims at improving the above-mentioned features. Among these aspects we have highlighted the achievement of expressiveness by means of defining a rich proactive and reactive controls; the intensive use of UML to keep standardization (both by extending explicitly its metamodel and by defining a UML profile) and the flexibility achieved by defining hierarchies of document and task refinements. We have illustrated them with a case study consisting in the construction of a library of software components.

References

1.   Allweyer, T; Loos, P: Process Orientation in UML through Integration of Event-Driven Process Chains. Proceedings of UML 98' Workshop, Ecole Superioeure des Sciences Appliquées pour l'Ingénieur-Mulhouse Université de Haute-Alsace (1998), 183-193.

2. Booch, G.; Weller, D.G.; Wright, S.: The Booch Library for ADA95 (1999 version). Available at http://www.pogner.demon.co.uk/components.bc

3. Finkelstein, A.; Kramer, J.; Nuseibeh, B. (eds.): Software Process Modelling and Technology. Advanced Software Development Series, Vol. 3. John Wiley & Sons Inc., New York Chichester Toronto Brisbane Singapore (1994).

4. Franch, X.: Systematic Formulation of Non-Functional Characteristics of Software. In Procs. 3rd IEEE International Conference on Requirements Engineering (ICRE), Colorado Springs (Colorado, USA), April 1998, pp. 174-181.

5. Franch, X.; Ribó, J.M. Using UML for Modelling the Static Part of a Software Process. In Proceedings of UML '99, Forth Collins CO (USA). Lecture Notes in Computer Science (LNCS), Vol. 1723, pp. 292-307. Springer-Verlag (1999).

6. Franch, X.; Ribó, J.M. Some Reflexions in the Modelling of Software Processes. In Proceedings of the International Process Technology Workshop (IPTW-99) (Villard de Lans, France). January 1999.

7. Heimann, P.; Joeris, G.; Krapp, C. A.; Westfechtel, B. DYNAMITE: Dynamic Task Nets for Software Process Management. In Proc. of the 18th. Int. Conf. on Software Engineering. Berlin, Germany, 1996 pp. 331-341.

8. Jablonski, S.; Bussler, C.: *Workflow Management. Modelling Concepts, Architecture and Implementation.* ISBN 1-85032-222-8 International Thomson Computer Press (1996).

9. Jäger, D.; Schleicher, A.; Westfechtel, B.: Object-Oriented Software Process Modelling. Proceedings of the 7th European Software Engineering Conference (ESEC), LNCS 1687 Toulouse (France), September 1999.

10. Joeris, G.; Herzog, O.: Towards a Flexible and High-Level Modelling and Enacting of Processes. Proceedings of the 11th. Conference on Advanced Information System Engineering (CAiSE), LNCS 1626, pp. 88-102, 1999.

11. Mehlhorn, K., Näher, St.: The LEDA Platform of Combinatorial and Geometric Computing. Cambridge University Press, 1999.

12. Meta Object Facility Specification. (MOF). Version 1.3 OMG document formal/00-04-03. March, 2000

13. Reichert M, Dadam P: ADEPT-flex Supporting Dynamic Changes of Workflows Without Losing Control. Journal Of Intelligent Information Systems, 10, 93-129 (1998). Kluwer Academic Publishers.

14. Ribó, J.M.; Franch, X. Searching for Expressiveness, Modularity, Flexibility and Standarisation in Software Process Modeling. In proceedings of the Brazilian Symposium on Software Engineering (SBES-00). Joao Pessoa , Brazil, pp. 259-276

15. Ribó J.M; Franch X.: PROMENADE, a PML intended to enhance standardization, expressiveness and modularity in SPM. Research Report LSI-00-34-R, Dept. LSI, Politechnical University of Catalonia (2000).

16. Ribó J.M., Franch, X.: Using UML for Process Technology Modelling. Submitted to European Software Engineering Conference (ESEC '01).

17. Sutton, S.M.; Osterweil, L.J.: The Design of a Next-Generation Process Language. Proceedings of ESEC/FSE '97, Lecture Notes in Computer Science, Vol. 1301, M. Jazayeri and H. Schaure (eds.). Springer-Verlag, Berlin Heidelberg New York (1997), 142-158.

18. Unified Modelling Language (UML) 1.3 specification. OMG document formal/00-03-01. March, 2000

Describing Process Patterns with UML
(Position Paper)

Harald Störrle

Ludwig-Maximilians-Universität München
stoerrle@informatik.uni-muenchen.de

Abstract. Patterns are widely used for describing software designs, i.e., product structures—but they may also be used to describe *process* structure, by adapting the well known pattern description schemes to the software process domain. But patterns may also be applied useful to describe *process* structures. This paper describes, how process patterns may be described using UML.

1 Introduction

1.1 Motivation

Workflows concerning software processes have been described in a variety of formalisms and styles (see e.g. [11] for a survey). Today, some essential requirements are still not adequately addressed by many of them.

Understandability. Practitioners explicitly ask for *"well-structured"* process models that are *"easy to understand and easy to apply"* (cf. requirements 2 and 3 in [13]). The vast majority of traditional processes, however, are monolithic and have a steep learning curve.

Flexibility. Many developers feel that their creativity is stifled by too rigid a development process. In fact, some would argue, that this is exactly the purpose. Anyway, enforcing a process is sometimes a difficult managerial task, and there are circumstances where traditional (large scale) processes just aren't appropriate, as is shown by the recently soaring interest in so called lightweight processes like *"extreme programming"*.

Precision. On the other hand, a development process must be formal enough to allow for automatic enactment and formal analysis, at least in selected places. Ideally, this would be combined with the previous requirement to achieve a kind of controlled and graded formality of the process.

Fractal structure. Finally, the componentware paradigm has manifest implications on the overall structure of the development process: if the product structure is fractal, the process structure better be fractal as well. Otherwise the mapping between process and product alone becomes a major challenge. This is a weakness of iterative process models like the *"Unified Process"* (UP, cf. [9]).

V. Ambriola (Ed.): EWSPT 2001, LNCS 2077, pp. 173–181, 2001.

1.2 Benefits of Approach

I believe, that process patterns using UML are a novel way for dealing with these issues which is superior to traditional approaches for the following reasons. First, consider the contribution of the UML. On the one hand, the UML is (and will be) *"the lingua franca of the software engineering community"* (cf. [18, p. v]). This means that almost every professional understands UML now and in the future. This results in network effects, so that, by using the UML, the understandability of process models is increased dramatically.

On the other hand, UML is now rapidly being developed into a body of mathematically precise formalisms (cf. [17,12,19]), opening up the road to enactment and formal analysis, not only of process models, but also of the product models, requiring even more process support to handle the added complexity.

Secondly, consider the contributions of process patterns. The notion of (design) pattern is widely accepted among practitioners. Patterns capture small, coherent, and self-sufficient pieces of knowledge, thus allowing their application in different contexts, and in particular, on different scales. Using (design) patterns is a form of reuse of (design) knowledge.

Process patterns are exactly like design patterns, except that they exist in the *process* domain. Actually, the term "design pattern" is a bit misleading: what classical design patterns like Model-View-Controller etc. really talk about is (only) the *product*, that is, the *result* of the design, not the *process* of designing it. So, I shall speak of result patterns vs. process patterns to make clear the difference.

The benefits of design patterns may be transferred to the process domain: by using the same pattern in different contexts, pattern-oriented process-descriptions are less redundant, and thus easier to understand and apply than traditional ones. Also, each pattern may be formulated with its own degree of formality (e.g. strictness of applicability criteria), allowing for flexible control of formality. Patterns may be used both to guide the development process, and to document a development after-the-fact. Patching-in ad-hoc steps into a process becomes trivial.

Finally, patterns are scale-invariant, that is, they may be applied on any scale of granularity or abstraction. Using a language of process patterns this way, a component-oriented discipline of software construction is easily accommodated: building systems from components results in a hierarchical and self-similar (i.e.: fractal) product structure (cf. e.g. [2,8,5,14]). This is probably *the* single most important advantage process patterns have over traditional processes.

2 Using UML to Describe Software Processes

Today, the UML is the most widely understood design notation in software engineering. Obviously, it would be helpful to use it for the description of processes.

However, describing workflows is still not very well catered for by the UML (cf. [10,1]). The standard proper contains only activity graphs (and a few comments in one of the "*UML Standard Profiles*", see [15, part 4]). The UP offers a little more in terms of notations and concepts, and, while technically not part of the standard itself, is a kind of quasi-standard in this area.

The UP extends the UML notation by two elements: a twin cog wheel-symbol for SubactivityStates[1] (a syntactic stereotype), and symbols for workers and resources (see [9, pp. 25, 145]).

I add a further element: an icon that looks like a rectangle with a dog's ear that denotes documents (see e.g. Figure 1). The document type may be displayed as text or graphically. The semantics of such documents may be defined in different ways: document types representing a particular UML diagram type or ModelElement are completely specified by this fact alone. Documents representing programs are specified by the programming language grammar. Other kinds of document types may or may not be be specified explicitly. Conceptually, a document icon maps to a Document which is assumed to be a kind of Classifier, e.g. such as may be associated as the type of an ObjectFlowState (see Section 3.5). In order to distinguish diagrams using these symbols from ordinary UML activity diagrams, I call them workflow diagrams. Note that, syntactically, workflow diagrams are just UML activity diagrams with special PresentationElements for SubactivityState and Document. A very similar type of diagram (see Figure 1, left) is also used informally in the UP, but not properly defined there.

Observe that workflow diagrams may be presented in a coarse version, where all SubactivityStates are presented by the UP's twin cog wheel icon. Conceptually, they may be refined by an arbitrary ActivityGraph. Resolving this refinement would result in a graph like in Figure 2. Observe that, again, syntactically this is an activity diagram. Similarly, the document types could be refined if that were desired.

3   Describing Process Patterns

Process patterns can be described by a schema similar to that known from result patterns. The overall descriptive scheme for process patterns and the terminology are taken from [6, p. 5f]. In the following subsections I will first describe the overall schema, and then the modifications resulting from transferring it to the process domain (see [2] for a discussion of the requirements of process vs. result structure patterns).

---

[1] When talking about UML in detail, referring to its metamodel is inevitable. In order to be very clear about what I refer to, metaclasses will always be printed in the font used here.

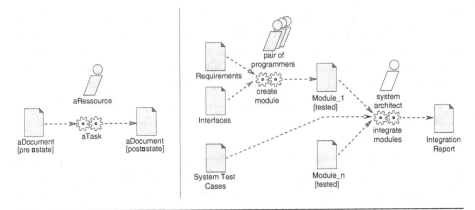

Fig. 1. Describing workflows: the process pattern description schema, abridged from RUP (left); a sample workflow (right). Note how sets of patterns may be joined together into a workflow by merging Documents.

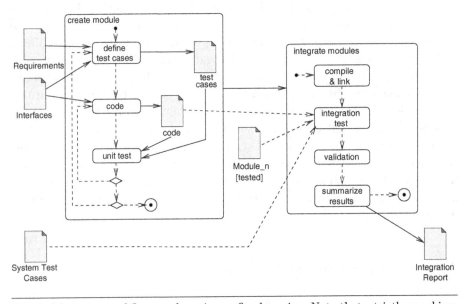

Fig. 2. The same workflow as above in a refined version. Note that, strictly speaking, this is not proper UML since in UML, SubActivityStates may not be refined graphically.

3.1   Overall Description Schema

The two best known books on design patterns [3,6] propose very similar description schemas. I adopt their terminology as far as possible (see Table 1 for a comparison).

Table 1. Comparison of pattern schemas.

POSA [3]	GOF [6]	this paper
Name	Pattern Name	Name
n.a.	Classification	Classification
Problem	Intent	Intent
Also known as	Also known as	Also known as
Example	Motivation	Motivation
Context	Applicability	Applicability
Structure	Structure	Process
Dynamic Aspects	Collaborations	n.a.
n.a.	Participants	Participants
Implications	Consequences	Consequences
Implementation	Implementation	Implementation
Sample Solution	Sample Code	Sample Execution
Applications	Known Uses	Known Uses
References	Related Patterns	Related Patterns

Name. First, each pattern has a name, usually identical to the name of the task that is supported by this pattern.

Classification. As pattern catalogs may grow rather large, there must be a systematic way of retrieving them. This aspect is not present in [3], and appears as part of the name aspect in [6]. See Section 3.2.

Intent. A intuitive account of the rationale of the pattern, its benefits and application area.

Also known as. Sometimes, there is not a unique best name of a patterns, but a number of equally adequate names, which are given here.

Motivation. A scenario that illustrates the problem, applicability conditions and purpose of the pattern.

Applicability. The prerequisites for applying a pattern, the context where it may be applied. In the scope Capsule, this may be specified by the required Views and possibly consistency conditions established. includes preconditions

Process. In design patterns, this aspect is called "structure" and contains a OMT class diagram. For a process pattern, the equivalent of "structure" is the process, that is the causal structure of activities. See Section 3.3 below.

Participants. In result patterns, this aspect refers to the classes involved. In process patterns, the participants are the documents and resources (including people) that play a role in the pattern. See Section 3.4 below.

Consequences. Discussion of the advantages and disadvantages of using the pattern, e.g. some goal that is achieved, or a property that is established by this pattern (e.g. a postcondition).

Sample Execution. The implementation of a design patterns is a program, that is, an expression of a programming language. The implementation of a process pattern is not a program for some computer, but a procedure in an organization, involving people, tools, organizational facilities and so on.

So, the process pattern analog of sample code is a sample execution, giving an example of how the respective process pattern might be realized by an organization.

Implementation. Discussion of implementation-specific problems, i.e. problems related to the realization of the pattern. As process patterns are realized by organizations, this aspect refers to problems related to organizational and tool problems.

Known Uses. Applying a pattern may be easier when guided by concrete examples where the pattern has been applied to general acclaim.

Related Patterns. Relationships to other patterns, i.e. alternatives, companions, or prerequisites and discussion of differences. Unlike design patterns, process patterns may refer to any kind of patterns, including result, process, and organizational patterns (cf. [7,4]).

This schema does not contain the aspect Collaborations of [6] (called "Dynamic Aspects" in [3]): it is used to represent the behavior (and dynamic structure) of the Structure. This is already catered for by the new aspect Process.

3.2   Classification Aspect

Patterns always exist only as part of a *language* of patterns—this is one defining criterion. These pattern languages may become rather large, and so cataloging and retrieval, and thus classification become important practical problems. For software reuse, the notions "facette" and "simple class" have been introduced for the dimensions of classification, and their respective values (see e.g. [16]). I have identified four classification facettes for process patterns: abstraction level, phase, purpose and scope.

Abstraction level. In [3], the three abstraction levels of idioms, design patterns, and architectural patterns are distinguished. Analogously, process patterns may be classified as techniques, process patterns proper, and development styles.

Phase. Design patterns are attributed to a problem category. The analog for process patterns is the development phase, like specification, design and so on.

Purpose. In [6], result patterns are classified as creational, structural, or behavioral. For processes, there are other purposes, such as the administration, the construction proper, and quality assurance.

Scope. Finally, design patterns may be distinguished according to whether their scope is an object or a class. Since this is a bias towards object-oriented technology which is soundly out of place in the context of processes, these simple classes are replaced by ones that refer to the entities occurring in traditional processes, e.g. architectural style, module, or test case, say.

Note that there is no hard and fast dividing line between the simple classes of the respective facettes.

3.3   Process Aspect

The structure aspect of design patterns is usually expressed as a class diagram. Process patterns obviously do not have a structure in this sense: they specify a (part of a) process. Consequently, this aspect has been renamed to "process", and it consists of a workflow diagram rather than a static structure diagram.

Instead, any of the other UML dynamic notations could be used. In fact, *any* other notation for the description of software processes could be used—none of these, however, reaches the degree of acceptance the UML has.

3.4   Participants Aspect

There are two kinds of participants of a process pattern, documents and resources. In the terminology of the UP, resource refers to tools and machines as well as to people ("workers", see Figure 1).

A Document (i.e. the type of an ObjectFlowState) may be either a prerequisite or a deliverable of a process pattern, or both. It may have a state, possibly expressed as an OCL-constraint.

3.5   Applicability Aspect

Apart from the traditional contents of these aspects (i.e. natural language descriptions of the applicability conditions of using a pattern), in our approach, this aspects may be refined by formal preconditions on participants (e.g. on their state). This is particularly relevant for Documents, of course, but may also be applied to other resources. This opens the road to formal analysis of software processes and automatic enactment.

At this point, a little digression into the UML metamodel is called for. First observe that the notational elements of the UML correspond to concepts in the metamodel, e.g. an activity diagram to an ActivityGraph, an action state node to an ActionState, an object flow node to an ObjectFlowState and so on. I have introduced Document as a special kind of Classifier, and thus it may have a StateMachine to describe its lifecycle. ObjectFlowState has a type, that is, an association to a Classifier such as a ClassifierInState. This may be used to represent the current state of the Document.

Or, in other words (and ending the digression), in workflow diagrams, documents and other resources have lifecycles a particular state of which may be used to inscribe document (or resource) icons in workflow diagrams. So, this state may be used in the specification of a pre- or postcondition of a resource.

Remark. This paper is the shortened version of [20], which includes a discussion of related work, and a more detailed pattern description schema. Also, applying process patterns is explained there.

References

1. Thomas Allweyer and Peter Loos. Process Orientation in UML through Integration of Event-Driven Process Chains. In Pierre-Alain Muller and Jean Bézivin, editors, *International Workshop ≪UML≫'98: Beyond the Notation*, pages 183–193. Ecole Supérieure des Sciences Appliquées pour l'Ingénieur—Mulhouse, Université de Haute-Alsace, 1998.
2. Klaus Bergner, Andreas Rausch, Marc Sihling, and Alexander Vilbig. A Componentware Development Methodology based on Process Patterns. In Joseph Yoder, editor, *Proc. 5th Annual Conf. on the Pattern Languages of Programs (PLoP)*, 1998.
3. Frank Buschmann, Regine Meunier, Hans Rohnert, Peter Sommerlad, and Michael Stal. *Pattern-Oriented Software Architecture. A System of Patterns*. John Wiley & Sons Ltd., 1998.
4. James O. Coplien. A Generative Development-Process Pattern. In James O. Coplien and Douglas C. Schmidt, editors, *Pattern Languages of Program Design*, pages 183–238. Addison-Wesley, 1995.
5. Brian Foote. A Fractal Model of the Lifecycle of Reusable Objects. In James O. Coplien, Russel Winder, and Susan Hutz, editors, *OOPLSA'93 Workshop on Process Standards and Iteration*, 1993.
6. Erich Gamma, Richard Helm, Ralph Johnson, and John Vlissides. *Design Patterns: Elements of Reusable Object-Oriented Software*. Addison-Wesley, 1995.
7. Neil B. Harrison. Organizational Patterns for Teams. Monticello, Illinois, 1995.
8. Wolfgang Hesse. From WOON to EOS: New development methods require a new software process model. In A. Smolyaninov and A. Shestialtynow, editors, *Proc. 1st and 2nd Intl. Ws. on OO Technology (WOON'96/WOON'97)*, pages 88–101, 1997.
9. Ivar Jacobson, Grady Booch, and James Rumbaugh. *The Unified Software Development Process*. Addison-Wesley, 1999.
10. Dirk Jäger, Ansgar Schleicher, and Bernhard Westfechtel. Using UML for Software Process Modeling. Number 1687 in LNCS, pages 91–108, 1998.
11. Marc I. Keller and H. Dieter Rombach. Comparison of Software Process Descriptions. pages 7–18, Hakodate, Japan, October 1990. IEEE Computer Society Press.
12. Alexander Knapp. *A Formal Approach to Object-Oriented Software Engineering*. PhD thesis, Ludwig-Maximilians-Universität München, Institut für Informatik, May 2000.

13. Ralf Kneuper. Requirements on Software Process Technology from the Viewpoint of Commercial Software Development. Number 1487 in LNCS, pages 111–115. Springer Verlag, 1998.
14. Meir M. Lehman. Programs, life cycles, and laws of software evolution. *IEEE Transactions on Software Engineering*, 68(9), September 1980.
15. OMG Unified Modeling Language Specification (version 1.3). Technical report, Object Management Group, June 1998. Available at uml.shl.com.
16. Ruben Prieto-Diaz. *Classification of Reusable Modules*, volume I - Concepts and Models, pages 99–124. ACM Press, 1989.
17. Gianna Reggio, Alexander Knapp, Bernhard Rumpe, Bran Selic, and Roel Wieringa, editors. *Dynamic Behavior in UML Models: Semantic Questions. Workshop Proceedings*, Oktober 2000.
18. Bran Selic, Stuart Kent, and Andy Evans, editors. *Proc. 3rd Intl. Conf. ≪UML≫ 2000—Advancing the Standard*, number 1939 in LNCS. Springer Verlag, October 2000.
19. Harald Störrle. *Models of Software Architecture. Design and Analysis with UML and Petri-nets*. PhD thesis, Ludwig-Maximilians-Universität München, Institut für Informatik, December 2000. in print, ISBN 3-8311-1330-0.
20. Harald Störrle. Describing Process Patterns with UML. Technical report, Institut für Informatik, Universität München, 2001.

Towards a Living Software Development Process Based on Process Patterns [1]

Michael Gnatz, Frank Marschall, Gerhard Popp,
Andreas Rausch, and Wolfgang Schwerin

Technische Universität München, Institut für Informatik,
Lehrstuhl Professor Dr. Manfred Broy,
D-80290 München, Germany
{gnatzm, marschal, popp, rausch, schwerin}@in.tum.de

Abstract. A Software Development Process for a certain enterprise and/or a certain project will usually integrate elements from a variety of existing process models, comprising generic standards as well as specific development methods. Besides that, change and evolution of business and technology imply change and evolution of development processes. In this paper we propose a Process Framework, which is modularly structured, and define the concept of process patterns. This framework allows us to describe development processes in such a way that integration, change and evolution of processes are facilitated. An example illustrates our approach.

1 Introduction

Nowadays, many different process models exist. These models range from generic ones, like the waterfall model [21] or the spiral model [6], to detailed models defining not only major activities and their order of execution but also proposing specific notations and techniques of application. Examples of the latter kind are the Objectory Process [13], the Unified Software Development Process [15], the Catalysis Approach [11], the V-Modell 97 [12], or eXtrem Programming [4] – just to name some of them.

All these process models have their individual assets and drawbacks. Hence, one would wish to take all the different assets and benefits of the various process models as a basic construction kit for an integrated development process tailored to the specific needs of the individual team, project, company, and customer. Jacobson, for example, talks about the unified process as a "strawman" serving only for explanatory purposes and probably never applied exactly as proposed [14].

To assemble a specific development process from existing models we have to identify and characterize explicitly the building blocks and their relations of a process

---

[1] This work originates form the research project *ZEN – Center for Technology, Methodology and Management of Software & Systems Development* – a part of *Bayerischer Forschungsverbund Software-Engineering (FORSOFT)*, supported by the *Bayerische Forschungsstiftung*.

V. Ambriola (Ed.): EWSPT 2001, LNCS 2077, pp. 182–202, 2001.

model in general. Therefore we need a set of basic notions and definitions common for all process models – the Process Framework. This Process Framework must allow us to integrate the various existing process models. The Process Framework can serve as a common basis for the definition of a development process that incorporates the assets and benefits of the different existing process models and that can be flexibly adapted to different kinds of project requirements and situations.

Once you have defined your standardized development process in terms of the Process Framework, you still have to adapt this development process to different projects and project situations. This is often referred to as static tailoring. But, our business is changing almost every day: the requirements of our customers change, new technology has to be adopted, and finally the way we work together evolves. To be successful in a changing environment we not only need static adaptation but also a more flexible way of adaptation - the dynamic adaptation.

Tom DeMarco even mentioned about the nature of process models and methodologies in [10]: „It doesn't reside in a fat book, but rather inside the heads of people carrying out the work." Thus, our Process Framework must additionally offer the ability to incorporate the process knowledge of the whole company. It must provide a platform for a learning organization recording the evolution steps of a living software development process.

Therefore the Process Framework must be open for the integration of new process elements, for the extension and adaptation to new technologies and fields of application. Besides static adaptation – support of different kinds of projects and project situations – there is a need of dynamic adaptation.

In this paper we propose a Process Framework that is sufficiently powerful to fulfill these requirements. First, in Section 2 we give an overview over different modeling levels of development processes. We present the requirements on and user views of a living process model. In the next section, Section 3, we define our Process Framework. In Section 4 we discuss the work product related parts of our framework in more detail, and in Section 5 we present the concept of process patterns, providing guidelines about the organization of the actual development process. A conclusion is given at the end of the paper in Section 6.

2   Basic Concepts of the Living Software Development Process

Various people and groups get into touch with process models and metamodels. In the next section, we discuss the different levels of a software development process. Then, in the following two sections, we present the two main views on process models - the project view and the method view. We will discuss their specific way of interaction with the living software development process we are going to propose in this work. Thus, we can show the needs and benefits of the two different user groups mentioned above.

2.1 Process Models and Metamodels: From a Bird's Eye View

Developing and maintaining software has become one of the most challenging tasks a company can do. Following some kind of process model, such as the Rational Unified Process [17] or the V-Modell 97 [12], promises to provide guidance facilitating the development task. Usually there are different people involved with different views on the development process itself.

Developers and project leaders are concerned about the development process of their individual projects. They concentrate on concrete tasks and results of their actual project, like the development of an analysis model of the system under consideration applying UML use-case diagrams. Accordingly to [28, 29] we can divide the software development process into the *production process*, that is the process in charge of developing and maintaining the products to be delivered, and the *meta process*, that is the process in charge of maintaining and evolving the whole software process. Using this terminology, we see the focus of developers on the production process.

Another group of people being concerned with development processes – especially in large organizations – might be a methodology group which is concerned with the meta process (cf. [28, 29]). Companies, which are on Capability Maturity Model (CMM) level 3 or higher, have a standardized process model [20]. This standard process model provides guidelines and support for organization's projects in general.

If a company is on CMM level 5 a continuous process improvement is enabled by quantitative feedback from the process and from piloting innovative ideas and technologies [20]. The organization as a whole and the projects themselves must address continuous realization of measurable software process improvement, like for instance defect prevention, technology change management, and process change management. Thus, the companies' methodology group must be able to improve and evolve the standard software process. Therefore this group needs a common Process Framework capturing the basic concepts of software development process models. Figure 1 illustrates three levels of an overall model for software development processes where all the different aforementioned views can be mapped on.

The Instance Level captures those elements that belong to a certain project, such as an analysis document of a concrete project.

The Model Level describes a certain software development process. This process definition contains an outline of an analysis document or a description and guidelines of how to organize and hold a workshop with customers to elicit the requirements. This level offers the guideline and information for project managers as well as team members. A specific *Process Model*, as defined in [28], expressed in a suitable process modeling language, would be an element in our Model Level.

The Metamodel Level provides the basic framework to establish a living process model. It offers clear definitions for terms like „Work Product" or „Activity". The Metamodel Level represents the common conceptual base of a companie's methodology group to improve and evolve the underlying standard software development process of the company[2]. It is on this level where (the concepts of) process modeling languages, such as EPOS SPELL and SOCCA (cf. [9, 28]) are to be found.

Metamodel Level

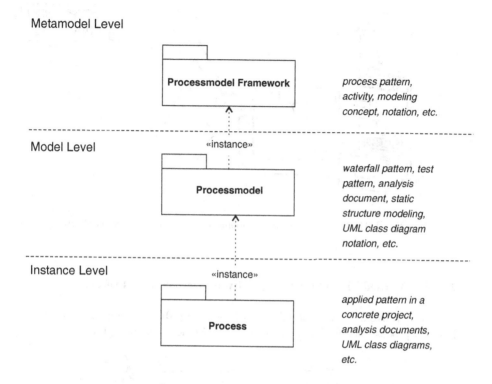

Fig. 1. The Layers of an Overall Process Model

2.2 The Project View of the Living Software Development Process

Project managers and project team members follow the concepts, guidelines, and help that is provided by a specific software development process defined on the Model Level in Figure 1. While performing their daily tasks they are creating instances on the Instance Level in Figure 1. This project view is shown in Figure 2.

Managing a concrete project implies selection of a suitable process from a set of existing, possibly standardized alternatives. Then the chosen process has to be tailored accordingly to the project's characteristics. This tailored process represents the guidelines, which are to be followed in the project. In terms of our Process Framework, given in section 3, the tailored process defines which work products are to be

---

[2] Note, this metamodel structure follows the guidelines provided by the Meta Object Facility (MOF) specification of the Object Management Group (OMG) [19].

produced, and which modeling concepts, notations, and patterns may be applied in the project.

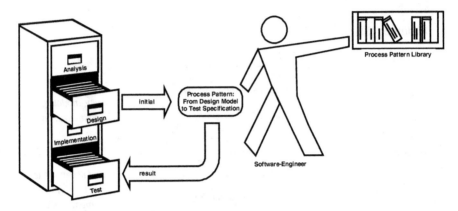

Fig. 2. The Living Software Development Process from the Project View

2.3   The Method View of the Living Software Development Process

Process improvement, as required on CMM level 5 [20] for example, means the evolution of process models, i.e. of elements on the Model Level in Figure 1.

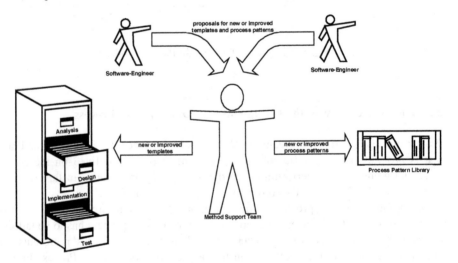

Fig. 3. The Living Software Development Process from the Method View

The formulation of process models on the basis of a well-defined ontology facilitates comprehension and hence changes of development processes. The elements of the

Metamodel Level in Figure 1 are supposed to play the role of such an ontology defining terms like "Activity", "Process Pattern", "Work Product" and their inter-relations. In [9, 28] a set of process modeling languages is discussed, and a basic ontology common for these languages is given.

An ontology for development processes provides both, developers and the methodology group, with a common vocabulary. On the one hand a methodology group can use such an ontology for the definition of standardized processes. On the other hand developers can use this vocabulary for the description of proposals for changes or additional process elements, which reflect their experience made with former process elements. On the basis of these proposals redefinitions by the methodology group can be done. Figure 3 shows this method view on a living software development process.

In our ontology, which we call the Process Framework, given in section 3, we follow the principle of separation of concerns so that changes are facilitated because of having minimal and localized effects.

3   Framework of a Living Software Development Process

In the previous section we have shown how developers and methodology group may interact for elaborating and improving the standard software development process establishing a living software development process. The basic ontology is defined in the Process Framework, which is the Metamodel Level in Figure 1.

The Process Framework must provide the ability to define and maintain a process model, which integrates elements of all the various existing process models, like for instance the Rational Unified Process [17] or the V-Modell 97 [12]. Thus, the framework must enable the methodology group to state clearly the correlations between the elements of the different process models. Additionally, the Process Framework must support static as well as dynamic adaptation of the process model with respect to the evolution and learning of a living organization (c.f. Section 1).

To come up with the model of our Process Framework, we can either develop a brand new model or we can take one of the existing models that is almost well suited for our needs and enhance it. The new, upcoming concept of process patterns seems to be an approach which basically follows our ideas and which may fulfill our requirements. Process patterns are a very general approach allowing us to integrate existing process models without having to develop a brand new model [7], [8], [2], [3]. For example in [1] we have already shown the integration of the V-Modell in the process pattern approach.

The basic idea of the concept of process patterns is to enable us to describe and document process knowledge in a structured, well defined, and modular way. Conform with most authors, patterns in our approach consist mainly of an initial context, a result context, a problem description and a solution. The initial context is an overall situation giving rise to a certain recurring problem that may be solved by a general and proven solution. The solution leads to the result context [5].

We show how the process pattern approach from [7], [8] can be re-used and enhanced to model a sophisticated Process Framework which is powerful enough to integrate different process models, and which is dynamically adaptable. The new, enhanced model is based on a clear separation of concerns between the overall result structure, the consistency criteria, and the process patterns themselves.

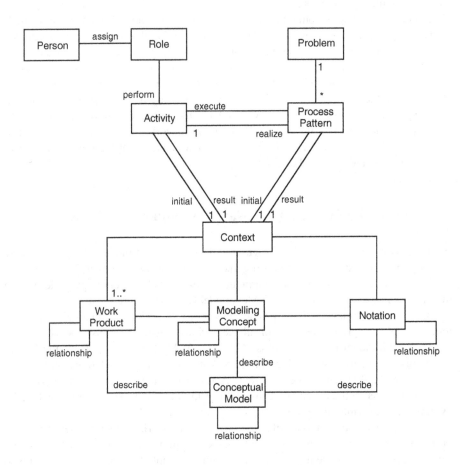

Fig. 4. The Process Framework

Figure 4 illustrates the basic concepts of the proposed Process Framework. It is based on the process pattern approach in [7], [8], and integrates it with an enhanced variant of a widely accepted process model framework (cf. [9]).

A Process Pattern defines a general solution to a certain recurring problem. The problem mentions a concrete situation that may arise during the system development. It mentions internal and external forces, namely influences of customers, competitors, component vendors, time and money constraints and requirements. A process pattern suggests an execution of a possibly temporally ordered set of activities. Activities themselves may be carried out following the guidelines of other, subordinated process patterns realizing the activity in question. Therefore process patterns and activities in our framework may be structured hierarchically, but iterative activities like the application of the spiral model [6] may also result in more complex structures that contain loops.

Process Patterns in our framework represent strategies to solve certain problems. Activities represent development steps and are executed by process patterns. An activity does only describe what is to be done but not how it is to be done. In contrast to that a process pattern provides a solution for realizing an activity. Hence generally one activity might be realized by different process patterns. Activities are performed by definite roles. In turn roles are assigned to corresponding persons.

Each process pattern as well as each activity needs an initial context to produce a result context. The initial context describes the required project situation to perform an activity or pattern, respectively. The result context describes the situation we reach when performing an activity or pattern, respectively. The context captures the internal state of the development project and can be characterized by constraints over the set of work products. Simple constraints are that certain work products have to exist.

A process model assigns certain process patterns, as for instance the pattern "Planning the Project", to certain work products, as for example the "Project Schedule". These work products are described by means of modeling concepts, as for instance "Time Flow Modeling". The modeling concepts are represented by certain notations, such as "UML Sequence Diagrams".

The initial and result context of a process pattern may not only require the existence of certain work products, but also that certain modeling concepts and notations are to be applied for these work products. This is important when a pattern proposes the application of notation specific techniques. For instance in [18] methodical guidelines for the refinement of specifications are introduced. These refinement techniques require the modeling concept "Interaction Modeling" based on the notation "Message Sequence Charts".

Note that the initial and result context of an activity have to be consistent with the initial and result context of a realizing process pattern. Whereas the activity may apply to a set of work products a process pattern realizing the activity must refer to the same set of work products but might furthermore fix notations and modeling concepts for these work products.

Initial and result contexts allow us also to identify activities, which use the same work products. This helps us to identify potentially conflicting activities that cannot be executed simultaneously. However a discussion about work product sharing of concurrent activities is not within the scope of this paper.

The precise definition of the meaning of and context conditions between work products can be achieved by the use of a so-called conceptual model. Work products that are based on sound description techniques have not only a well-defined notation, but also a possibly even formal semantics in form of a mapping from the set of work products into the set of systems (cf. [16, 23, 25]). The conceptual model characterizes, for instance, the set of all systems that might ever exist. This integrated semantics provides the basis for the specification of a semantic preserving translation from specification work products to program code. This can serve as a basis for correct and comprehensive code generation.

The circular relationship associations assigned to various elements, such as work product and conceptual model, in Figure 4 cover the general idea of structuring these elements, for example hierarchically.

4 Model of Work Products

In this section we take a closer look at the work product related part of our Process Framework. First of all, in section 4.1 we discuss the role of work products as part of a process model. For the representation of the information covered by work products we apply modeling concepts and according notations. In section 4.2 we discuss how these framework elements are related.

4.1 Work Product Part of the Process Framework

When we intend to set up a concrete process model (located in the Model Level of Figure 1) one of the first and most important steps is the definition of work products and their relationships. This step has to be taken before the definition of activities, because activities refer to initial and result contexts consisting of work products. Samples for instances of work products are business process model, project contract, or Java class file. Note that these instances are located on the Model Level in Figure 1.

Concerning work product associations of the Process Framework in Figure 4 we modeled a general Relationship association between work products. For setting up a concrete process model we need a more detailed framework where we refine this general relationship between work products to more specific ones, such as

- cartesian product and union to build composite work products, and
- refinement to relate work products representing information on different levels of detail.

Work products and their relations define a structure like a filing cabinet that has to be filled during a development project.

Figure 5 shows an instance diagram illustrating the composition structure of the work product instances Initial Customer Specification and Business Process Model together with the associations Refinement and Simple Binary Undirected Relationship between some of its sub-work products.

An Initial Customer Specification is a work product, which expresses roughly what the customer expects the system to do. It consists of three different parts. Firstly there is a short statement about the goals of the project, the System Vision. Secondly it contains short descriptions of entities the system must handle, the Business Entities. Thirdly there is a set of informally described Business Scenarios, which represent an exemplary specification of business processes.

A Business Process Model provides a more complete and precise representation of the business processes of an organization than the one documented in the Initial Customer Specification. A Task Chain defines the business activities a business process consists of. Moreover it describes the transitions between the activities. A Task Description is a complete definition of all the elements of a business process. In addition to the information covered in a Task Chain, a Task Description contains the effects of the task and information about its performers. The Organizational Structure documents an organization's different departments and the roles, which may perform tasks.

Since a business process model is supposed to consist of task chains, task descriptions, and a documentation of organizational structures (cf. [24]) we composed the business process model by means of according Cartesian Product relations. The fact that a task description is a more detailed specification of a business process than a task chain is reflected by the Refinement relationship between the two work product instances.

The work product instance Business Scenario, which is part of the work product Initial Customer Specification, is also related to the Task Description. Generally a business scenario is an exemplary description of a business process that may be described in full detail in a task description. In order to cover the information about which task description and business scenarios are related we use a Simple Binary Undirected Relationship being an refinement of the general Relationship association in the Process Framework. We refer from this relationship to an additional consistency criterion. This criterion requires a business scenario to denote one of all the possible variants of a business process described in the related task description.

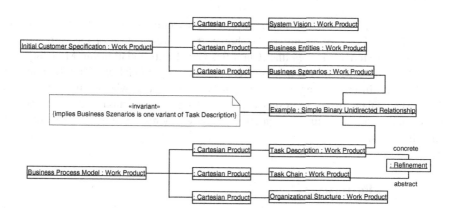

Fig. 5. Instance Diagram of the Work Product 'Business Process Model'

In our process model framework in Figure 4 we proposed a Conceptual Model, which is supposed to play the role of a "semantic" model that helps us express the purpose or meaning of work products in terms of an explicit and precise model resp. ontology. The model given in [27] for business processes would be a suitable conceptual model for the work product instances discussed in this section. However, the Conceptual Model and the mapping of work products to this model is not a topic of this paper. More information about this subject can be found in [25].

4.2 From Work Products to Notations

Most traditional process models (cf. e.g. [9]) do not distinguish between work products, modelling concepts, and notations. However, in our view this distinction is important. In general there are complex relations between these elements of a process model. Thus, following the principle of separation of concerns, we have to make a clear distinction between these concepts and model relationships explicitly. For instance, we can use different Modeling Concepts to describe the contents of Work Products. Besides that, we can represent a given Modeling Concept by different Notations, and vice versa.

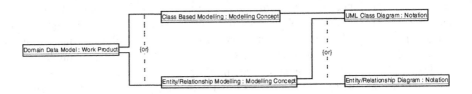

Fig. 6. Instance Diagram of a Work Product, applied Modeling Concepts and Notations.

In Figure 6 we show an instance diagram representing a part of the process model located Model Level of Figure 1. As shown, the representation of the work product Domain Data Model can either Class Based or Entity/Relationship Modeling concepts. Moreover, the process model offers different representations for certain modeling concepts. In this example a system analyst can decide, whether he wants to use UML Class Diagrams to represent concepts of class based modeling, or in case of entity/relationship modeling he can chose either entity/relationship diagrams or UML class diagrams.

5 Process Patterns

A process pattern enables us to describe and document process knowledge in a structured and well-defined way. As already discussed in Section 3 and illustrated in Figure 4 process patterns consist mainly of a problem solved by a proven solution applied through certain activities, and an initial as well as a result context. The activities play important roles in process patterns, because they reflect the tasks, which have to be carried out as described by the solution.

Process patterns, as well as all kinds of patterns, must be presented in an appropriate form to make them easy to understand and discussable. In this section, we first present a uniform pattern description template for process patterns. As already mentioned above, activities are rather important in the context of patterns. For this reason, we present a template for activities, too. Then we provide a sample process pattern to illustrate the basic concepts of process patterns. Once you start filling your pattern library with those patterns you will sooner or later have a huge number of process patterns. For that reason you need some kind of index or guideline to select the patterns concerning your context and problem in your specific project situation.

5.1 Pattern Description Template

A good description helps us grasp the essence of a pattern immediately – what is the problem the pattern addresses, and what is the proposed solution. A good description also provides us with all the details necessary to apply the pattern and to consider the consequences of its application. Moreover a uniform, standardized description template for process patterns is needed. This helps us compare one pattern with another, especially when we are looking for alternative solutions. Furthermore, we are interested in details of the activities, which represent the tasks to be done, by using the solution of a pattern. For these activities we need a uniform, standardized pattern, too.

The basic structure of process pattern, problem, solution, activity and context, we already have mentioned, provides us with a good starting point for a description that meets our requirements. However, a pattern must be named, we want to use diagrams and scenarios to illustrate the solution, and we want to include guidelines for the application of the pattern. Hence, we have to refine the basic structure.

Table 1 shows the enhanced process pattern description template.

Table 1. Process Pattern Description Template

Entry	Process Pattern Description
Name	The name of the pattern.
Author	The name of the creator of the pattern.
Version	The current version number of the pattern. Important during evolution of a pattern.
Also Known As	Other possible names of the pattern, if any available.
Keywords	Some important words describing the context and the intent of the pattern.
Intent	A concise summary of the pattern's rationale and intent. It mentions the particular development issue or problem that is addressed by the pattern.
Problem	The problem the pattern addresses, including a discussion of the specific development task, i.e. the realized activity, and its associated forces.
	Moreover the problem description may contain information with respect to consumers, competitors, and the market situation.
Solution	A solution may suggest certain activities to be applied to solve a certain problem. Possibly an order may be given in which to perform these activities, or alternatives may be proposed. Besides that the solution comprises methodical guidelines and concrete recommendations. A solution shows a possible answer to balance the various forces that drove the project into the current situation.

The solution includes a list of activities for execution. In contrast to these activities, the activity realized by the process pattern is referenced below.

Moreover the solution depicts the relationships of the initial and result contexts of the executed activities and shows how the activities are combined.

Realized Activity	The name of the activity for which the pattern provides a strategy of how to execute it. Every process pattern realizes one activity.
Initial Context	The internal state of the development project, i.e. the state of the corresponding work products, that allows the application of this process pattern.
Result Context	The expected situation after the process pattern has been applied, i.e. the resulting state of the work products.
Pros and Cons	A short discussion of the results, consequences, and trade-offs associated with the pattern. It supports an evaluation of the pattern's usefulness in a concrete project situation. The problem description together with the pros and cons of a pattern helps us in choosing from alternatives, that is static and dynamic tailoring. Thereby these two pattern elements have a purpose similar to selection guidelines in [22].
Example	Known uses of the pattern in practical development projects. These application examples illustrate the acceptance and usefulness of the pattern, but also mention counter-examples and failures.
Related Patterns	A list of related patterns that are either alternatives or useful in conjunction with the described pattern.

Moreover, we need a description template for activities. For a named activity we want to know the belonging development issue and both contexts, the initial and the result. The contexts are summed up in the realized process pattern as described above. Table 2 shows the activity description template.

Table 2. Activity Description Template

Entry	Activity Description
Name	The name of the activity.
Role	A list and description of the roles that may have to perform the activity.
Development Issue	It mentions the particular development issue that is addressed by the activity.
Initial Context	The situation in which the activity may be applied, i.e. the required internal state of the development project. The internal state is particularly given by the state and consistency of the work products the activity needs as input.

Result Context	The expected situation after the activity has been applied. This is the state and consistency of the work products affected by the application of the activity.

5.2 A Process Pattern – From Initial Customer Specification to Business Model

In this section a sample Activity and a corresponding Process Pattern are given to illustrate the basic concepts of process patterns. A detailed discussion of a wider range of process patterns is not in the scope of this paper and can be found in [7], [8]. Please note, that the sample Process Pattern of this section resides in the Instance Level of the Overall Process Model shown in Figure 1.

We show how a certain activity and a certain process pattern realizing this activity can be described in detail following the description template from the previous section. We chose the activity Business Process Modeling and a process pattern called Business Process Modeling Task Analysis with Activity Diagrams. This process pattern provides project team members with a strategy for developing a Business Process Model from an Initial Customer Specification.

Table 3 gives the description of the Business Process Modeling Activity:

Table 3. Activity Description: Business Process Modeling

Entry	Activity Description
Name	Business Process Modeling (BPM)
Role	Business Expert, Software Architect
Development Issue	The goal of performing this activity is to develop a (complete) business process model, which covers all the business scenarios and business entities described by example in the Initial Customer Specification serving as input. Thereby the project goals, system vision, and constraints specified in the initial customer specification are to be taken into account.
Initial Context	Initial Customer Specification[3]
Result Context	Initial Customer Specification, Business Process Model

Table 4 gives the description of the pattern BPM Task Analysis with Activity Diagrams, which realizes the Business Process Modeling activity:

Table 4. Process Pattern Description: BPM Task Analysis with Activity Diagrams

Entry	Process Pattern Description
Name	BPM Task Analysis with Activity Diagrams
Keywords	Business Process Modeling, Task Analysis, UML Activity Diagrams, Stepwise Refinement, Iterated Modeling with Reviews

---

[3] The related work products have already been introduced in section 4.

Intent	Development of

Intent   Development of
- a precise and unambiguous documentation of a BPM
- documentation of BPM on different levels of abstraction cover not only all details but also provide an overview of relevant business processes.
- documentation of BPM such that it can be understood by business experts as well as software developers
- ensured adequacy of BPM (validated model)

Problem   Business experts are available but a precise documentation of as-is and to-be business processes being relevant for the system to be developed does not exist.
High complexity of business processes.
The system vision of the initial customer specification hints at a strong relationship between the system to be developed and the business processes (e.g. support of large parts of business processes by the intended software system).

Solution   In order to achieve a precise and unambiguous documentation of business processes use UML activity diagrams [26] with its formal syntax to describe business processes.
In order to achieve a documentation of different layers of abstraction apply the principle of stepwise refinement (cf. pattern's activity diagram). Start with the definition of major tasks and refine them iteratively.
Ensure adequacy of the business process model by reviewing each iteration of the model with (third party) experts.
Involve business and software architecture experts being fluent with activity diagrams.
The pattern's workflow is illustrated in Figure 7[4].
After having identified major tasks and user classes assign user classes as actors to tasks. Refine task characteristics of major tasks, and define a first version of the tasks' task chains by decomposing it into sub-tasks, and defining their causal dependencies. Consider alternative chains.
Review this first model involving persons representing the identified user classes in the review.
Perform the refinement steps of tasks iteratively and review each iteration (apply pattern Refinement of Activity Diagrams).

Realized Activity   Business Process Modeling
Initial Context   Initial Customer Specification with arbitrary modeling concepts and notations

---

[4] Please note, that this decomposition in activities serves as an illustration of the concept and therefore is not complete. There is also no detailed description of these executed activities provided in this paper.

Result Context	Business Process Model with UML activity diagrams as notation for task chains and a pre- and post-condition style specification of tasks.
Pros and Cons	Pros: – UML Activity Diagrams provide a standardized, concise and unambiguous notation to document business processes (Task Chains). The applied modeling concepts are widely used by business experts (e.g. similarity with Event Driven Process Chains) [24] as well as software developers (e.g. similarity with Petri nets). – This precise way of description supports detailed and precise review. – Iterative modeling and review increases understanding and quality of the business model. Cons: – Usage of specific notations, namely UML activity diagrams, may require training of involved persons. A common understanding of the notation must be ensured. – Stepwise refinement is a pure top down approach so that consideration of existing parts may be difficult.
Related Patterns	See also: BPM Informal Task Analysis

Figure 7 shows the temporal ordering of the activities, which are executed by the BPM Task Analysis with Activity Diagrams Process Pattern. Additionally the input and output work products of the executed activities are given.

Except from BPM Task Analysis with Activity Diagrams, as mentioned in Table 4, the activity Business Process Modeling might be performed in a different way. For example the process pattern BPM Informal Task Analysis represents an alternative strategy for business modeling proposing an informal documentation of business processes. This might be suitable when business processes are simple and the software system does not play a major role in these processes. The pattern map given in Figure 8 shows these two alternative performance strategies for the business modeling activity.

How we perform activities proposed in a process pattern might again be described by further patterns. For example a pattern providing a strategy for the activity Review Business Model might be called Check Coverage of Business Scenarios.

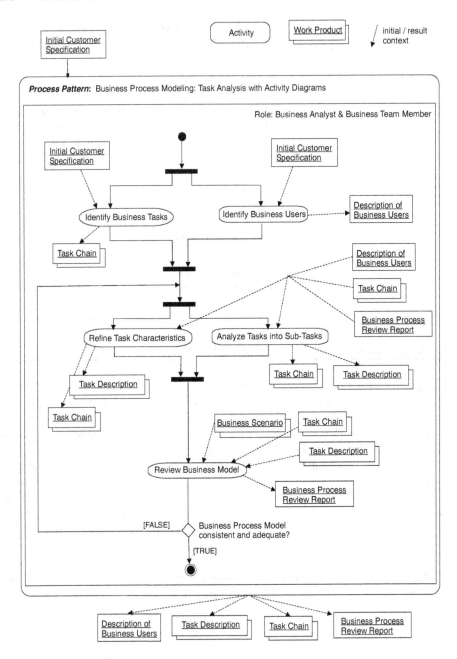

Fig. 7. UML Activity Diagram of the BPM Task Analysis Pattern

5.3 Managing the Process Lifecycle – Process Pattern Maps

As already mentioned process patterns will exist on several levels of detail. Like in other pattern-based approaches, the single patterns may also be combined with each other, forming a multi-level system of patterns. The combination of those patterns forms the lifecycle of a development process. This lifecycle will not be fixed, but will vary from project to project and from situation to situation, according to the specific problems of the projects.

The selection of a process pattern may be outlined as follows: Based on the project's current situation, as partly represented by the state and consistency of work products, the project leader tries to identify the next activities he wants to be executed. This information leads to the selection of one or more alternative process patterns with initial contexts and problem descriptions matching the current situation. After a careful consideration of the alternatives' pros and cons and their problem descriptions one pattern is chosen. This pattern recommends a number of development activities and their temporal order. For each of its activities the solution may require or propose the application of certain process patterns.

By choosing process patterns the project manager forms the process lifecycle. Usually a process pattern library will contain a large number of patterns. We introduce two kinds of pattern maps providing an overview over a set of patterns by structuring them from different points of view.

One possibility is to structure process patterns accordingly to the activities they realize. We call this activity process pattern map. Activity process pattern maps are directed graphs. These graphs have two kinds of nodes, namely activities and process patterns. A process pattern node has edges to all the activities that have to be performed by applying the pattern and exactly one edge to the activity it realizes. Each activity may be performed following the solution provided by a process pattern. Hence each activity node has edges to process pattern nodes that provide guidelines to perform the activity. Figure 8 illustrates such an activity process pattern map that builds a tree. However, as already mentioned there may also exist patterns and activities that deal with refinement and iteration, that introduce loops in the graph.

A second viewpoint on a set of pattern maps is the so-called context process pattern map. This kind of map is a directed graph with contexts as nodes and patterns as arcs. This way we can easily see alternative ways, i.e. process patterns, from one context to another. These maps are similar to the maps presented in [22].

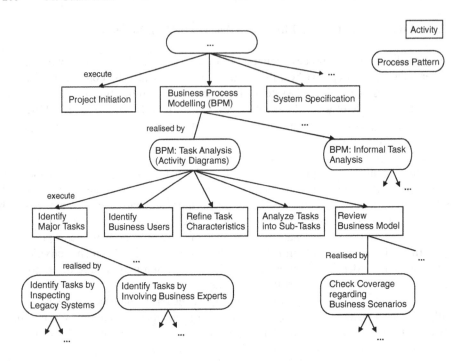

Fig. 8. An Activity Process Pattern Map

6   Conclusion and Further Work

In this paper we introduced a process pattern based approach, which allows software developers to implement a very flexible and tailored development process. According to the best of breed idea a company can combine the most appropriate solutions from different established methods and best practices to form a perfectly tailored process for this company and for all types of projects within the company. Therefore we introduced a Process Framework that facilitates integration, tailoring, and evolution of process models. Further questions concerning the application of a pattern based development process, like the concurrent use of work products through different activities, do not belong to the scope of this work.

We enhanced existing Process Frameworks comprising elements, such as work product, activity, and role, by introducing the notion of process pattern as a modular way for the documentation of development knowledge. Similar to approaches, such as [22], by stating the tackled problem as well as discussing pros and cons, patterns support selection of adequate strategies during process enactment that is problem-driven dynamic process tailoring.

A further difference to existing approaches is the explicit modeling of relationships between work products, modeling concepts, and notations, allowing us to describe and integrate generic processes, referring to work products only in general, with specific development processes providing concrete modeling concepts and notations.

To realize a process pattern approach within a company software developers need some guidance to find their way through the vast number of process patterns that may have been developed at their company. A possible way to store and manage process patterns is a book or folder, where patterns are written down in accordance with a fixed scheme as presented in section 5. However searching for the right pattern for a certain situation within a given context in a book is not very comfortable. Further process patterns evolve and establish dynamically, so it doesn't seem a good idea to document the living process in the form of an unalterable book. Thus a tool to store, present and manage process patterns and work product definitions within an organization dynamically would be very desirable. Due to the continuous evolution and change of a living development process, we work on a tool supporting process model maintenance. Moreover by realizing the presented pattern maps this tool is supposed to provide guidance for software developers in finding their way through the jungle of process patterns.

To sum up the application of a process pattern approach seems to be very promising, as it provides a flexible way to define a tailored development process that can be easily adapted to new requirements. Combined with a reasonable tool support for the management and development of process patterns this approach may help organizations to create and evolve their custom development process.

References

1. Dirk Ansorge, Klaus Bergner, Bernd Deifel, N. Hawlitzky, C. Maier, Barbara Paech, Andras Rausch, Marc Sihling, Veronika Thurner, Sascha Vogel. Managing Componentware Development - Software Reuse and the V-Modell Process. In Lecture Notes in Computer Science 1626, Advanced Information Systems Engineering, Page 134-148, Editors Matthias Jarke, Andreas Oberweis. Springer Verlag. 1999.
2. Scott W. Ambler. Process Patterns: Building Large-Scale Systems Using Object Technology. Cambridge University Press. 1998.
3. Scott W. Ambler. More Process Patterns: Delivering Large-Scale Systems Using Object Technology. Cambridge University Press. 1999.
4. Kent Beck. Extreme Programming Explained: Embrace Change. Addison-Wesley. 1999.
5. Frank Buschmann, Regine Meunier, Hans Rohnert, Peter Sommerlad, Michael Stal. Pattern-Oriented Software Architecture, A System of Patterns. John Wiley & Sons.. 1996.
6. Barry Boehm. A Spiral Model of Software Development and Enhancement. ACM Sigsoft Software Engineering Notes, Vol. 11, No. 4. 1986.
7. Klaus Bergner, Andreas Rausch, Marc Sihling, Alexander Vilbig. A Componentware Development Methodology based on Process Patterns. Proceedings of the 5th Annual Conference on the Pattern Languages of Programs. 1998.
8. Klaus Bergner, Andreas Rausch, Marc Sihling, Alexander Vilbig. A Componentware Methodology based on Process Patterns. Technical Report TUM-I9823, Technische Universität München. 1998.
9. J.-C. Derniame, B. Ali Kaba, D. Wastell (eds.): Software Process, Principles, Methodology, and Technology. Lecture Notes in Computer Science 1500, Springer, 1999.

10. Tom DeMarco, Timothy Lister. Peopleware, Productive Projects and Teams, Second Edition Featuring Eight All-New Chapters. Dorset House Publishing Corporation. 1999.
11. Desmond Francis D'Souza, Alan Cameron Wills. Objects, Components, and Frameworks With Uml: The Catalysis Approach. Addison Wesley Publishing Company. 1998.
12. Wolfgang Dröschel, Manuela Wiemers. Das V-Modell 97. Oldenbourg. 1999.
13. Ivar Jacobson. Object-Oriented Software Engineering: A Use Case Driven Approach. Addison Wesley Publishing Company. 1992.
14. Ivar Jacobson. Component-Based Development Using UML. Invited Talk at SE:E&P'98, Dunedin, Newzealand. 1998.
15. Ivar Jacobson, Grady Booch, James Rumbaugh. Unified Software Development Process. Addison Wesley Publishing Company. 1999.
16. C. Klein, B. Rumpe, M. Broy: A stream-based mathematical model for distributed information processing systems - SysLab system model. In Proceedings of the first International Workshop on Formal Methods for Open Object-based Distributed Systems, Chapmann & Hall, 1996.
17. Philippe Kruchten. The Rational Unified Process, An Introduction, Second Edition. Addison Wesley Longman Inc. 2000.
18. Ingolf Krüger. Distributed System Design with Message Sequence Charts. Dissertation, Technische Universität München. 2000.
19. Object Management Group (OMG). Meta Object Facility (MOF) Specification. http://www.omg.org, document number: 99-06-05.pdf. 1999.
20. Mark C. Paulk, Bill Curtis, Mary Beth Chrissis, and Charles V. Weber. Capability Maturity Model for Software, Version 1.1. Software Engineering Institute, CMU/SEI-93-TR-24, DTIC Number ADA263403. 1993.
21. Winston W. Royce. Managing the Development of Large Software Systems: Concepts and Techniques. In WESCON Technical Papers, Western Electronic Show and Convention, Los Angeles, Aug. 25-28, number 14. 1970.Reprinted in Proceedings of the Ninth International Conference on Software Engineering, Pittsburgh, PA, USA, ACM Press, 1989, pp. 328-338.
22. C. Rolland, N. Prakash. A. Benjamen: A multi-Model View of Process Modelling. Requirements Engineering Journal, to appear.
23. Bernhard Rumpe: Formale Methodik des Entwurfs verteilter objektorientierter Systeme. Herbert Utz Verlag Wissenschaft, 1996.
24. A.-W. Scheer: ARIS, Modellierungsmethoden, Metamodelle, Anwendungen. Springer Verlag, 1998.
25. B. Schätz, F. Huber: Integrating Formal Description Techniques. In: FM'99 - Formal Methods, Proceedings of the World Congress on Formal Methods in the Development of Computing Systems, Volume II. J. M. Wing, J. Woodcock, J. Davies (eds.), Springer Verlag, 1999.
26. OMG: Unified Modeling Language Specification, Version 1.3 alpha R5, March 1999, http://www.omg.org/.
27. Workflow Management Coalition: Terminology & Glossary. Document Number WFMC-TC-1011, Status 3, www.wfmc.org, February 1999.
28. A. Finkelstein, J. Kramer, B. Nuseibeh: Software Process Modelling and Technology. Research Studies Press Ltd, JohnWiley & Sons Inc, Taunton, England,1994.
29. R. Conradi, C. Fernström, A.Fuggetta, R. Snowdon: Towards a Reference Framework for Process Concepts. In Lecture Notes in Computer Science 635, Software Process Technology. Proceedings of the second European Workshop EWSPT'92, Trondheim, Norway, September 1992, pp. 3-20, J.C. Derniame (Ed.), Springer Verlag, 1992.

Modeling a Support Framework for Dynamic Organizations as a Process Pattern Using UML

Jin Sa[1], Brian Warboys[2], R. Mark Greenwood[2], and Ian Robertson[2]

[1] Faculty of Computer Studies and Mathematics, University of the West of England, Bristol
BS16 1QY, UK.
[2] Department of Computer Science, The University of Manchester, Manchester M13 9PL,
UK.

Abstract. This paper describes the motivation of modeling processes as process patterns. The work presented here extends UML modeling into the domain of (meta-) process modeling. It shows, through an example, how (meta-) processes can be modeled as process patterns using collaborations in UML. The structural aspects of a process pattern are modeled using class diagrams and the behavioral aspects are modeled using sequence diagrams. The benefits and shortcomings of modeling processes using patterns are discussed.

1 Aims and Structure

The aim of the paper is to describe the results from an exercise on modeling meta-processes as patterns using UML and to explain the benefits we see in such an approach. An example is used to illustrate the approach. The paper is organized as follows: section 2 describes the background and the motivation of the research; section 3 briefly outlines the example, called the Product Evolution Tower (Peltower), used for illustrating our approach; section 4 presents the model of Peltower as a process pattern using UML; section 5 expresses the benefits of our approach; section 6 draws the conclusion and considers the future work.

2 Backgrounds and Motivation

Research in process modeling has produced many notations for modeling processes, for example, [7,12,13,14,15,16,17,20,21]. Most of these approaches model behavior in terms of fine-grained activities. This makes it expensive to construct process models.

Some recent work on process modeling has been influenced by the research in the area of using design patterns in object-oriented software development. The principal idea behind the design pattern approach [8] is that there are many common problems in designing and constructing software systems; often these common problems have

V. Ambriola (Ed.): EWSPT 2001, LNCS 2077, pp. 203–216, 2001.
© Springer-Verlag Berlin Heidelberg 2001

common solutions. Experiences have proved the merits of some of these solutions and hence much work has been done in documenting these common solutions. Many examples can be found in [8,18]. Some of these patterns are described in natural language such as English, and some are described in notations such as UML. Following the thoughts behind using patterns for developing object-oriented software systems, some researchers have applied these ideas to both software process and business process modeling. Examples on modeling processes as patterns can be found in [1,2,6,11].

In the domain of process modeling, there are two kinds of process: "subject" process and meta-process. A subject process of an organization refers to what is happening in that organization, i.e. who is doing what by when. For example, in a software development process, we may have a designer performing a design activity, followed by a programmer performing an implementation activity. A meta-process often employed as a control process for the purpose of defining, monitoring and evolving a process. For example, we can define a meta-process that can produce a process for developing software and it can also be used to evolve that software development process.

Independently developed from the process pattern research, work in the process modeling community on meta-processes, particularly process evolution, has produced some common solutions to some common problems [4,5,9,10,19,22,23]. These solutions although not explicitly described in terms of process patterns as recognized in the pattern's community, they could be easily viewed and applied as process patterns.

Existing work on process patterns based on the idea in object-oriented software development has been largely applied to subject processes in the areas of software processes and business processes, and not focused on meta-processes such as processes for evolution. In this paper, we model one of those meta-processes, a support framework for dynamic organizations, the Product Evolution Tower (Peltower) [10], as a process pattern using UML. Peltower provides a means of creating new processes and for modifying existing processes. The motivation of this research is that

- Peltower is a fairly well developed and understood meta-process for process evolution;
- UML is widely used in industry, modeling Peltower in UML makes the dissemination of our approach easier;
- UML provides a development route from design to implementation;
- A UML description can be easily translated into an Object-oriented language such as Java which is also widely available;
- UML provides a way of modeling patterns that can be naturally mapped to the concepts in Peltower.

3   A Brief Description of Peltower

Peltower [10] is based on the work in [9,22,23]. It is a framework intended to provide an infrastructure for the delivery of support for business processes – including design processes and software development processes. The approach is based on the concept of structuring software development processes in particular, and business processes in general, in a manner that is analogous to the way in which systems (software systems and others) are designed and implemented in the real world. It aims to support and exploit the diversity and richness of the different methods used by organizations to achieve their goals, yet be able to accommodate the dynamic nature of such organizations.

At the top level of a Peltower, there is one node, called the root node, which contains information about the system and information about the process for developing the system. At the next level down, the node is decomposed into a number of nodes, and the system is decomposed accordingly. Each node can be further decomposed in the subsequent levels. Figure 1 shows a hierarchy of a software development process for a retail system.

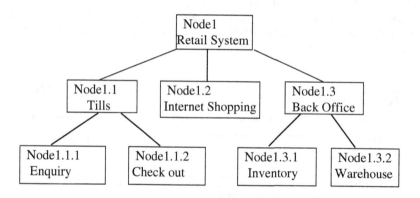

Fig. 1. A Peltower Structure

Different nodes may adopt different specification and development methodologies for constructing the component specifications and products. Each node contains a number of attributes:
- a specification document stating the properties of the node;
- a product that satisfies the specification;
- a methodology description for the operations that can be performed on the node.

A methodology description refers to a collection of methods in a particular context, for example, we may have the specify method allowing users to specify the pre- and the post-conditions in VDM style; the verify method following the verification rules in VDM.

Each node has the following operations:
- specify: creates a specification document for the node using a certain specification method, e.g. a method based on VDM;
- develop: creates a product that satisfies the specification document using a certain method, for example, the method may be Java if the product is a piece of code;
- decompose: creates a number of new nodes for the next level down;
- compose (build): combines the specifications of all the nodes in the next level down;
- verify: checks that the result of any change to the specification document is consistent with the parent specification document and the child specification documents;
- evolve: changes the characteristics of an operation.

In order to evolve the characteristics of an operation in a node, a user invokes the evolve operation which interacts with another process, called P2E as shown in figure 2. P2E is a process for process evolution. It consists of a Managing component, a Realizing component and a Technology component. When a node requires to evolve, the Managing component receives the request for change; it passes the request to Realizing; Realizing then consults Technology to find a suitable methodology for the requested change and passes it back to Realizing. Realizing then sends the solution to the node. The precise detail of P2E is not within the scope of this paper, and this detail can be found in [10,23].

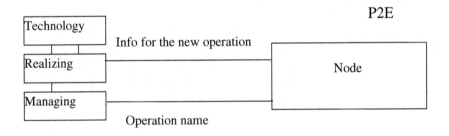

Fig. 2. Interaction between Peltower and P2E

4 A UML Model of Peltower as a Process Pattern

Broadly speaking, a pattern is a common solution to a common problem in a given context. The term is so widely used that sometimes it is used with slightly different meanings. In addition, different approaches may represent patterns in different ways. In this paper, we use the definition and the notation given in UML [3].

In [3], there are two kinds of pattern: a mechanism that is a design pattern and a framework that is an architectural pattern. (Note that the use of the term "framework" here is different from the use of the term in the rest of the paper. The term framework used in this paper refers to the structure of Peltower. The term used here has a precise UML meaning.) A design pattern specifies the structure and behavior of a group of classes. An architectural pattern specifies the structure and behavior of an entire system. An architectural pattern may encompass a set of design patterns. In this paper we have chosen to use the design pattern mechanism to model Peltower because it can be deployed either on its own or as a component embedded in a larger system as in the PIE project [10].

In UML, design patterns are modeled as collaborations, which is a group of classes. The structural aspect is modeled using class diagrams and the behavioral aspect is modeled using sequence diagrams (or interaction diagrams more generally).

Peltower is modeled as a collaboration as shown in Figures 3 to 7.

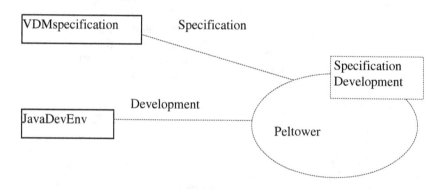

Fig. 3. The Peltower Pattern as a Collaboration

Figure 3 shows the outside view of the process pattern. It states that the name of the pattern is Peltower. Peltower contains a number of classes. Figures 4 to 7 model the internal view of the Peltower pattern. In UML, a process pattern can be either a plain collaboration or a parameterized collaboration. We have modeled Peltower as a parameterized collaboration because we can abstract the essential structural and behavioral properties of the specification part and the development part from this pattern in a domain-independent way. Specification and Development are the (formal) parameter classes in the Peltower pattern. When we apply this pattern in a particular context, these parameters are bound to more specific information. For example, in figure 3, we replace the formal parameter class, Specification, by the actual parameter class,

VDMspecification; and similarly, we replace the formal parameter class, Development, by the actual parameter class, JavaDevEnv.

4.1 The Structural Aspect of the Peltower Pattern

Figure 4 is the structural aspect of the Peltower pattern. It shows how the structure in figure 2 is mapped to the structural aspect in a pattern in UML. The Peltower pattern contains three classes that deal with evolution: Managing, Realizing and Technology (P2E). It has a node class which keeps the structure of the hierarchy as illustrated in figure 1. Each node has a Specification class and a Development class. The Specification class and the Development class are the parameters of this pattern.

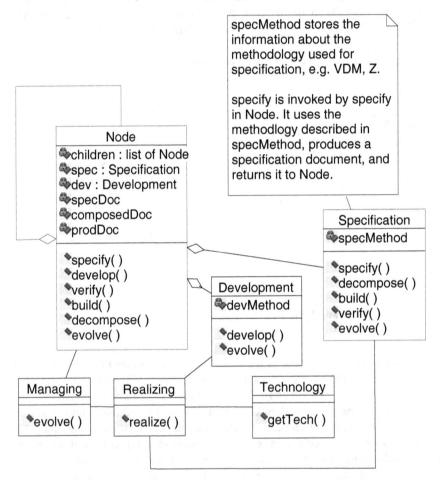

Fig. 4. The Structural aspect of Peltower

Each node has six attributes:

- children: keeps the structure of the hierarchy,
- spec: an instance of the Specification class,
- dev: an instance of the Development class,
- specDoc: the specification documentation of the node,
- composedDoc: the specification documentation of all the children composed together,
- prodDoc: the product documentation of the node.

The methods in each Node act as interfaces to the Specification class and the Development class. They simply call the relevant methods in these two classes. The evolve method will invoke the evolve method in the Specification class, via the P2E components, if the parameter is "specify"; and it will invoke the evolve method in the Development class, again via the P2E components, if the parameter is "develop".

The Specification class has one attribute: specMethod. It contains the methodology specific information, for example, information about VDM or Z. There are five methods in the Specification class: specify, decompose, build, verify and evolve. The first four methods are abstract methods. When we apply the Peltower pattern in a specific context, the Specification class is bound to a concrete specification class. The concrete class provides four concrete methods: specify, decompose, build and verify. These concrete methods will be defined according to the specific specification methodology.

The Development class is similar to the Specification class. It has one attribute, called devMethod which contains the methodology specific information, for example, information about Java or C++.

4.2 The Behavioral Aspect of the Peltower Pattern

The behaboural aspect is modelled by three sequence diagrams as shown in figures 5, 6 and 7.

Figure 5 states that when a user asks a node to perform a specification operation, the node sends the request to the specification component. The specification component uses its information about the specification methodology to produce a specification document and sends it back to the node. When a user chooses to invoke a develop operation, the node sends the request to the development component which contains the information about the development methodology. The development component produces the product document and sends it back to the node.

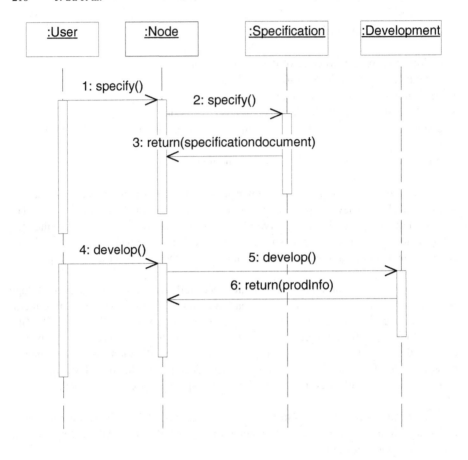

Fig. 5. The Behavioral Aspect of Peltower –1

Figure 6 illustrates the interaction sequences of three operations: decompose, build and verify. When a user asks to decompose a particular node, the node sends a request to the specification component; the specification component then creates the new nodes according to the specific methodology. (Only two are illustrated here.) The list of children is returned back to the node. When a child node is created, it inherits its parent's characteristics, for example, if its parent's specification methodology is VDM, then the child will have VDM as well. However, once created, a node's characteristics may be changed. See figure 7. When a user asks to build a composed specification from all its children, it sends the request to the specification component. The specification component then gets information from all the nodes, and composes them. The composed specification is returned back to the node. When a user asks to verify a node between its specification document and its composed specification document of its children, the node again sends the request to the specification component, the specification component performs the verification and sends the result back to the node. It

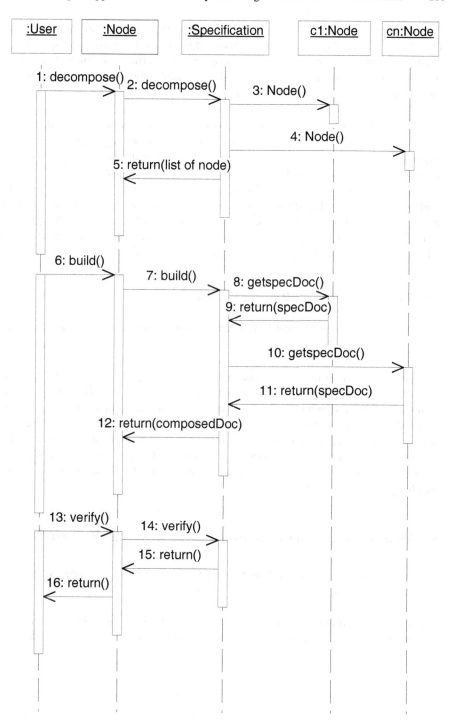

Fig. 6. The Behavioral Aspect of Peltower – 2

may seem to be unnecessary to send the requests to the specification component since the node has both the specification documentation and the composed specification documentation. However the reason is because the specification component contains the information about the specific methodology, whilst the node does not. The node only keeps information about the hierarchy.

Figure 7 states that when a user requests to evolve the specify operation, the node sends the request to the managing component. The managing component sends the request to the realizing component. The realizing component then asks the technology component to find a new methodology. The realizing component sends the new methodology to the specification component. (The specification component will then change its specMethod attribute with information about the new methodology.) The detailed logic behind how the three P2E components find a new methodology is described in [10,23]. The way to evolve the development methodology is similar. Hence, it is not illustrated in figure 7.

4.3   An Application of the Peltower Pattern

Figures 3 to 7 model the Peltower as a pattern. This section presents an application of the Peltower pattern.

Figure 8 shows an instance of the Peltower when applied to the VDM and Java context. For simplicity, figure 8 has omitted the three P2E classes. The hierarchy starts with a node (n1) in which the Specification class and the Development class are bound to VDMSpecification and JavaDevelopment respectively. In the second level, two nodes (n1.1 and n1.2) are created. These two nodes are created with the same characteristics for their parent.   However after performing evolve(specify) and evolve(development) on node 1.1, its specification and development methodologies are changed as shown in figure 9.

5   What Are the Benefits of Modeling Processes as Patterns?

We believe that process patterns can bring the following benefits in process modeling and process analysis.

It creates opportunities for reusing existing models. This can reduce the effort for creating a model from scratch, especially for creating computer-supported models.

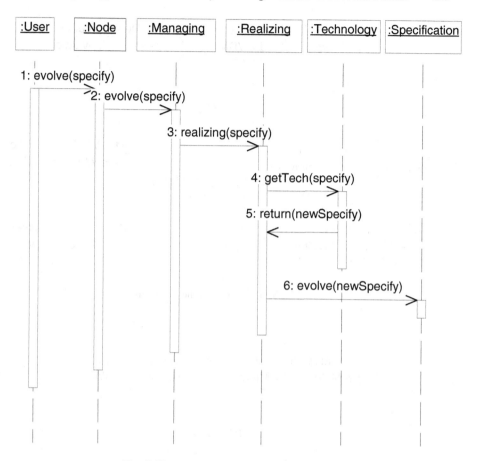

Fig. 7. The Behavioral Aspect of Peltower – 3

Modeling itself is a subjective activity. Given the same process, different modelers may come up with different models. If we have a database of process patterns, a process pattern for a similar process can be used as a reference. This is not saying that the modelers must follow the ideas in the process pattern; it simply provides additional information that may be useful.

Process patterns can also incorporate "standard" process analysis scenarios. This should be useful for novice process modelers and process modelers who have limited knowledge of the business domain.

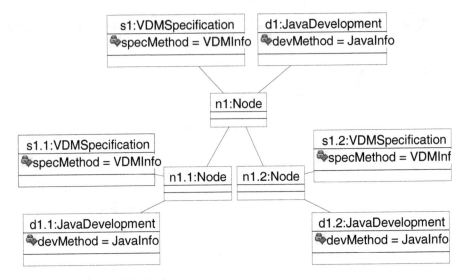

Fig. 8. An instance of the Peltower-1

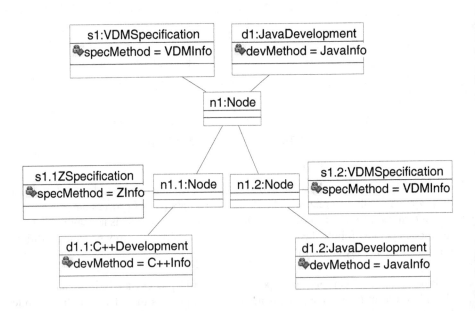

Fig. 9. An instance of the Peltower-2

In addition to the above benefits for modeling processes as patterns in general, the research described in this paper has also brought some specific benefits to work on Peltower. The rigorous application of the UML modeling method has shed some light on the "implied assumptions" in the original Peltower. Many details in the original definition were not obvious to a wider audience. They are now illustrated by the UML model in a way that is familiar by researchers and developers in a much larger community. The particular model defined in this paper has turned out to be slightly different from the original Peltower definition due to different interpretations on the "implied assumptions". For example, the original build operation is used to combine the products of all the child nodes, but the build operation in this paper combines the specifications of all the child nodes. These small differences have caused us to reflect on the design of the Peltower as a meta-process, and on the possibility for Peltower variants leading to a possible hierarchy of patterns.

6 Future Work

The work described in this paper extends UML modeling into the domain of (meta-) process modeling. This paper has shown, through an example, how (meta-) processes can be modeled as UML patterns. It has argued that there are advantages in using UML to express (meta-) processes as patterns. However, compared with notations that are specifically developed for modeling processes such as [23], UML's approach for modeling patterns has deficiencies. For example, the process pattern as defined in this paper does not describe control flows of operations. Activity diagrams in UML can be used to model control flows. However activity diagrams are not as widely used and do not explicitly address interaction which is an important concept in process modeling. It is also not straightforward to map to implementations. Our future work will investigate the possibility of integrating both sequence diagrams and activity diagrams. In general our future work in this area will be to combine the ideas of UML and process modeling approaches to develop a process pattern environment which will be able to store different categories of process patterns, e.g. evolution processes, insurance processes, and university modular system processes; to provide analysis scenarios; to facilitate a computer supported process model for applying process patterns; and to be able to evolve process models at the level of process patterns.

References

1. Amber, S. W., Process Patterns – Building Large-scale Systems Using Object Technology, Cambridge University Press/Sig Books, July 1998, ISBN: 0-521-64568-9.
2. Appleton, B., Patterns for Conducting Process Improvement, In the Proceedings of Pattern Languages of Program Design, 1997.
3. Booch, G., Rumbaugh, J., and Jacobson, I., The Unified Modeling Language User Guide, Addison-wesley, 1999, ISBN: 0-201-57168-4.
4. Conradi R., Hagaseth M., and Liu, C., 1994. Planning Support for Cooperating Transactions in EPOS. In Proc. CAISE'94, Utrecht, June, 1994.
5. Conradi R., Nguyen M. N., and Wang A. I., Planning Support to Software Process Evolution, International Journal of Software Engineering and Knowledge Engineering Vol. 10, No. 1, 31-47, 2000.

6.   Eriksson, H. E., and Penker, M., Business Modelling with UML, Wiley, 1999, ISBN: 0471295515.
7.   Finkelstein, A. et al, Software Process Modelling and Technology, Research Studies Press, 1944, ISBN: 0863801692.
8.   Gamma E., et al., Design Patterns: Elements of Reusable Object-oriented Software, Addison-Wesley, 1997.
9.   Greenwood, M., Warboys, B.C., and Sa, J., Co-operating Evolving Components – a Formal Approach to Evolve Large Software Systems, In the Proceedings of the 18th International Conference on Software Engineering, Berlin, 1996.
10. Greenwood, M., Robertson, I. and Warboys, B., A Support Framework for Dynamic Organisations, In the Proceedings of the 7th European Workshop on Softwre Process Technologies, LNCS 1780, Springer-verlag, Kaprun, Austria, February, 2000.
11. Gzara, L., Rieu, D., and Tollenaere, M., Patterns Approach to Product Information Systems Engineering, Requirement Engineering (2000) 5: 157-179.
12. IDEF0, Integration Definition for Function Modeling (IDEF0), U.S. Department of Commerce, Technology Administration, National Institute of Standards and Technology, Federal Information Processing Standards Publication, Report No. FIPS PUB 183, 1993.
13. Kellner M., Hansen, G., Software Process Modelling, CMU/SEI-88-TR-9, Pittsburgh, PA: Software Engineering Institute, Carnegie Mellon University, 1996.
14. Kovács, G. L., and Mezgár, I., A Process Model and Its Environment to Manage Nonmanufactorying Processes, In the proceedings of IFIP 16th World Computer Congress 2000, August 21-25, 2000, Beijing,China, ISBN 3-901882-05-7
15. Osterweil L., Software Processes Are Software Too, Proceedings of the 9th International Conference on Software Engineering, pp2-12, IEEE, 1987.
16. Osterweil L., Software Processes Are Software Too, Revisited: An Invited Talk on the Most Influential Paper of ICSE9, Proceedings of the 19th International Conference on Software Engineering, pp540-548, IEEE, 1997.
17. Ould, M.A., "Business Processes: Modelling and Analysis For Re-engineering and Improvement", John Wiley & Sons, 1995.
18. Pree W., Design Patterns for Object-oriented Software Development, Addison-wesley 1994, ISBN: 0-201-42294-8.
19. Robertson I., Evolution in Perspective, International Workshop on Principles of Software Evolution at 20th International Conference on Software Engineering, Kyoto, Japan, March 1998.
20. Sa, J., A Formal Specification of a Process Model, In the Proceedings of IEEE International Conference on Systems, Man and Cybernetics, October 12-15, 1999, Tokyo, Japan, ISBN: 0-7803-5734-5.
21. Sa, J., Green, S., Beeson, I. and Sully, A., "Modelling Multiple Software Processes in the Business Context", In the proceedingds of 2nd International Conference on Enterprise Information Systems, Stafford, UK, June 2000, ISBN: 972-98050-1-6.
22. Sa J. and Warboys B.C., A Reflexive Formal Software Process Model, Proceedings of the Fourth European Workshop on Software Process Technology, April 1995, LNCS 913.
23. Warboys B.C., Kawalek P., Robertson T., and Greenwood R.M., Business Information Systems: a Process Approach, McGraw-Hill, Information Systems Series, 1999, ISBN 0-07-709464-6.

A Taxonomy to Compare SPI Frameworks

Christian Printzell Halvorsen[1] and Reidar Conradi[2]

[1] Galaxy Republic AS, Drammensveien 211,
N-0212 Oslo, Norway
christian.p.halvorsen@superoffice.com
[2] Norwegian University of Science and Technology (NTNU),
N-7491 Trondheim, Norway
conradi@idi.ntnu.no

Abstract. The principle behind *software process improvement (SPI)* is that product quality is strongly influenced by the quality of the associated software process for development and maintenance. A number of *SPI frameworks* have evolved from this principle. However, these frameworks are comprehensive and differ in a variety of aspects, making them difficult to compare objectively and to select between for a company. This paper discusses four comparison methods that can be used on SPI frameworks. We have explored one of them further and propose a new SPI framework *taxonomy*. Our taxonomy consists of 25 relevant characteristics, which can be used to point out framework similarities and differences on a high level. An example of how the taxonomy can be applied to six common SPI frameworks is provided.

1 Introduction

More and more people realize that the most critical challenges in software development are not purely technical. As for all engineering work, many problems lie in the interaction between technology and organization. Schedule and budget overruns are common, as are delivered software products with insufficient or unwanted functionality, poor reliability, inefficiency, and so on. These are serious deficiencies related to the development process. Evolution of software needs and requirements as well as an overall unpredictability are major challenges [14][24][25].

Software process improvement (SPI) sprung out as a solution to these process-related difficulties. The assumption behind SPI and the many SPI frameworks is that product quality is influenced by the quality of the process used to develop it. We should therefore focus our improvement efforts on the software process in order to improve software quality. This can explicitly be expressed by the following *causal relation*:

$$\text{Quality}(Process) \Rightarrow \text{Quality}(Product) \tag{1}$$

The words *quality* and *process* are vital to our discussion of SPI. The reader is encouraged to confer with other sources such as [9][14][18][29] for more information:

- *Quality* – Good quality implies happy users. However, Kitchenham states that quality "is hard to define, impossible to measure, easy to recognize" [16].

V. Ambriola (Ed.): EWSPT 2001, LNCS 2077, pp. 217–235, 2001.

- Nevertheless, most SPI frameworks specify a measurable *(process) quality indicator* from which process quality can be inferred.
- *Software process* – "...a set of partially ordered process steps, with sets of related products, human and computerized resources, organizational structures and constraints, intended to produce and maintain the requested software products" [18].

It is interesting to note that many of the differences between SPI frameworks stem from different interpretations of these two words.

1.1 Goals for This Discussion

Many people who work in the SPI domain have chosen one SPI framework as their favorite. This choice is mostly subjective and seldom based on objective evidence of appropriateness. A reason for this is that SPI frameworks are difficult to compare due to their comprehensiveness. The frameworks also differ in basic assumptions such as how the terms *software process* and *software quality* should be interpreted, making the comparison task even harder.

The goal of this paper is to make the comparison of SPI frameworks easier and more objective by presenting a *taxonomy*, which can be used to characterize the various frameworks. We hope it will clarify their similarities and differences, and act as a starting point for further information gathering.

The proposed taxonomy will be related to other comparison methods and we will end the discussion by applying it to the following SPI frameworks:

- Total Quality Management (TQM) [2].
- The Capability Maturity Model (CMM) [14][22][29].
  ISO 9000 [20].
- ISO/IEC 15504 (SPICE) [9][25][29].
- Quality Improvement Paradigm (QIP), Experience Factory (EF), Goal Question Metric (GQM) [4][5].
- SPIQ (Software Process Improvement for better Quality)[1] [26].

1.2 Related Work

There is an increasing amount of literature comparing the major SPI frameworks. Most is written in the last three years and generally covers only a small number of frameworks. A variety of comparison methods have been used, but the method of *framework mapping* seems particularly popular.

In his Ph.D. thesis Sørumgård [24] compared the Capability Maturity Model (CMM), ISO 9000 and the QIP/EIF/GQM approach. He compared the frameworks in pairs using both a textual description and a tabular list of characteristics.

---

[1] Software Process Improvement for better Quality (SPIQ) was a Norwegian R&D project in 1997-99, aiming to increase competitiveness and profitability in Norwegian IT industry through systematic and continuous process improvement. SPIQ proposes a unified, lean and pragmatical SPI framework.

Tingey [28] has dedicated a whole book to the comparison of the CMM, ISO 9000 and the Malcolm Baldridge National Quality Award (MBA). His book presents an in-depth comparison of the three approaches, including a complete mapping between statements and a quantitative analysis of framework focus.

Emam, Drouin and Melo [9] have included a mapping between SPICE and the ISO 9000 standard in their book as well as a textual discussion of their differences.

The Software Engineering Institute (SEI) has published a high-level mapping between aspects of the ISO/IEC 12207 software life cycle, SPICE, the CMM v1.1 and the CMM v2.0 Draft C [23].

Several short articles have also been published about the subject. Haase [11] compares some of the assessment concepts in ISO 9000, SPICE, CMM, Bootstrap, SynQuest and EQA. Bamford and Deibler [3], and Paulk [21] both compare ISO 9000 with CMM. Cattaneo, Fuggetta and Sciuto [6] compare CMM, MBA and ISO 9000. Ares et al. propose the ATAM method to compare assessment frameworks according to six main categories [1]. Lastly, this paper is extended from a position paper at the NASA Software Engineering Workshop in Nov. 1999 [10].

2   Comparing SPI Frameworks

One goal of comparing SPI frameworks is to provide insight into their similarities and differences. However, the kind of insight needed is highly dependent on the context. Tingey [28] discussed two organizational scenarios with different requirements imposed on the comparison method. The essential differences lie in *level of detail* and *point of view*.

First, there are organizations *without* an SPI strategy that would like to learn about different SPI approaches because of competitive pressure or certification requirements. Such organizations usually have only limited general SPI knowledge and even less knowledge about specific frameworks. This requires the comparison to be on a high level with few details.

Secondly, there are organizations *with* an organized and systematic SPI strategy that would like to learn about other frameworks. Many organizations find themselves in a situation where they have to use more than one SPI approach. As an aid in the process of learning about other frameworks one would obviously like to utilize already existent SPI knowledge. A discussion of the lesser-known frameworks from the point of view of the well-known framework could therefore be beneficial.

From our previous discussion we suggest the following four classes of comparison methods:

- Characteristics [1] [6][11] [24]
- Framework mapping (comparing kernel concepts) [9][21][22][23][28]
- Bilateral comparison (comparing textual phrases) [9][21]
- Needs mapping (comparing user needs vs. framework properties)

Each of these will be discussed shortly. It should be clear that it would be neither beneficial nor possible to define disjoint comparison methods. Thus, some overlap is inevitable. Also, differences in *level of detail* and *point of view* should be expected as they satisfy different requirements.

Our new taxonomy presented in this paper is based on the characteristics comparison method, which will be described next.

2.1 Characteristics Comparison Method

We have decided to compare the various frameworks in a taxonomy by defining an extensive list of relevant *characteristics*. Each framework is then described in terms of these characteristics and the results are presented in a tabular format.

This type of comparison is well suited for a general overview of the frameworks and it can be used as a basis for other comparison methods. A lot of information can be inferred from a table listing the characteristics of several frameworks. However, the comparison is on a high level and details must be collected elsewhere. For this purpose one of the other comparison methods can be used.

The characteristics should preferably be *objective*, *measurable* and *comparable*. One can argue what kind of measurement scale should be used, e.g. nominal, ordinal or absolute. Each has its strengths and weaknesses.

2.2 Framework Mapping Comparison Method

Much of the recent comparison work has dealt with *framework mapping*. Each framework, at least the more structured ones, consists of a more or less defined set of statements or requirements dealing with the content and focus of the framework. Framework mapping is the process of creating a map from statements or concepts of one framework to those of another. There are two distinct ways to do this:

- Mapping between existing frameworks.
- Mapping existing frameworks into basis framework established solely for the purpose of comparing. This provides a common point of reference from which the frameworks can be evaluated, compared and contrasted.

In the characteristics approach the goal was to describe key attributes of each SPI framework. However, the purpose of mapping is to identify overlaps and correlations between frameworks and create a map of these statements or correlations. There can exist strong, weak or no correlation as suggested by Tingey [28]. Furthermore, the mapping can be done on either a high or a low level depending on the amount of detail one includes. This also dictates how the mapping results can be displayed, e.g. in a matrix or some kind of visual representations such as a Venn diagram.

Framework mapping is especially useful when an organization employs two or more different SPI frameworks, as corresponding statements can be identified and redundancy reduced. The extra effort needed to employ more than one framework can therefore be minimized.

Framework mapping is definitely a more low-level and detailed comparison method than characteristics. Because mapping goes into the specifics of each framework, it is not very useful for a general overview. However, mapping into a basis framework and supplementing with a quantitative analysis can indicate overall focus and content.

Framework mapping requires that some simplifying assumptions are made. The results are necessarily biased by these assumptions as suggested by Tingey [28].

2.3 Bilateral Comparison Method

In a *bilateral comparison* two frameworks are compared textually, for example the CMM and ISO 9000 [21]. The difference between this comparison method and the two previously described is its textual nature. A bilateral comparison is often a summary or explanation of findings from other the comparison methods.

The bilateral comparison can take on the point of view of one framework and describe the other in terms of that. This is convenient for people with detailed knowledge of one framework, as they can easily get insight into another using familiar terms.

The amount of detail included in a bilateral comparison can vary widely, depending on the purpose for which it is written. Frequently the level of detail is somewhere in between that of characteristics and the mapping approach.

2.4 Needs Mapping Comparison Method

Needs mapping is not a direct comparison between frameworks. Instead, it considers organizational and environmental needs that must be taken into account when selecting which SPI framework to adopt. The requirements imposed by such needs are often highly demanding and can limit the choice of framework severely. Nonetheless, they are of utmost importance and must be considered carefully. Here are some examples:

- Certification requirements, for example to ISO 9000, often imposed on a subcontractor.
- Top-level management requires that the chosen SPI approach should be incorporated in a Total Quality Management (TQM) strategy.
- Financial limitations.

There certainly exist other examples as well, and they can vary substantially from organization to organization, or depend on the business environment. Furthermore, the needs may vary over time as the organization or environment evolves.

3 The Taxonomy

In this paper we propose a *taxonomy* based on the characteristic comparison method described previously. We present a list of 25 characteristics regarded as important for describing SPI frameworks. Sørumgård [24] and Cattaneo et al. [6] have been particularly influential on our work, but we have also tried to capture aspects generally regarded as important in SPI literature (as cited previously).

One could argue that 25 characteristics are too many and that many of them are overlapping. However, the goal is to make a short tabular presentation, which requires each characteristic to have only a short description. More general characteristics would need longer descriptions, which could not easily fit in small table cells. In addition, the overlap between some of the characteristics is important to capture small variations among the frameworks.

A description of each characteristic follows. They have been grouped in five categories to ease readability and comprehension, see Figure 1 below.

General	Process	Organization	Quality	Result
Geographic origin/spread	Assessment	Actors/roles/stakeholders	Quality perspective	Goal
Scientific origin	Assessor	Organization size	Progression	Process artifacts
Development/stability	Proc. improvement	Coherence	Causal relation	Certification
Popularity	method		Comparative	Cost of implementation
Software specifc	Improvement Initiation			Validation
Prescriptive/descriptive	Focus			
Adaptive	Analysis Techniques			

Fig. 1. Categorization of Characteristics in the Proposed Taxonomy

3.1 General Category

This category of characteristics describes general attributes or features of SPI frameworks. Such attributes are often specific to each framework and frequently related to how the framework is constructed or designed.

Geographic Origin/Spread. This characteristic describes where in the world the approach originated as well as where it is commonly used today.

Scientific Origin. The scientific origin of a framework or approach is the philosophical background on which it is based. Some frameworks have originated from purely philosophical principles, while others are based on mathematical or statistical rules. Some frameworks can even be said to originate from previous frameworks, by borrowing heavily from them in terms of concepts, content and focus.

Development/Stability. Another important characteristic is the development and stability of the framework. One should expect that the stability of a framework increases as experience is gained over a number of years. Many frameworks depend on feedback from users to evolve as time goes by, e.g. identification of parts in the framework that are difficult to use or especially useful. Changes in the software engineering discipline may be reflected as well, for example new technologies or the introduction of new SPI frameworks and standards. Naturally, it is desirable to employ a framework that is both evolved and relatively stable.

Popularity. Popularity is also important for an organization selecting to employ a certain process improvement approach. One would like to be sure that support and further development of the framework is continuing in the foreseeable future. Those frameworks with a greater mass of supporters also have a tendency to receive better support.

Software Specific. Whether the framework is software specific or not reveals something about its scope. Some of the approaches are specifically directed towards software development and maintenance, while others are more general. The latter must be adapted to the software development domain and this requires an extra effort.

Prescriptive/Descriptive. A prescriptive framework, as the name suggests, prescribes requirements and processes that are mandatory. In contrast, a descriptive framework does not assign specific actions to be taken by the organization. Instead, it describes a state or certain expectations to be met without stating how they should be accomplished.

Adaptability. The degree of flexibility varies among the process improvement approaches. An adaptive approach has support for tailoring and is customizable for specific uses. A study by Kautz and Larsen [15] indicated that the use of comprehensive SPI approaches is still quite low, partly because of their rigidity. This suggests that adaptability is an important quality of a framework.

3.2 Process Category

The process category concerns characteristics that describe how the SPI framework is used.

Assessment. The improvement work is often initiated by an assessment of the organization's current software process capabilities. Frameworks that include such assessment methods specify techniques for assessing software processes, practices and infrastructure, with the result being an identification of strengths and weaknesses. The assessment often includes recommendations for process improvement and it can therefore be used as an improvement road map.

There are at least two dimensions to assessments, namely *what* is assessed and *who* performs the assessment. The latter part is covered by the next characteristic called assessor.

Our investigation shows substantial differences between the frameworks in what their assessments are meant to cover. For example, some frameworks assess organizational maturity, others process maturity and then again others may assess customer satisfaction.

Assessor. The second dimension of assessments is *who* it is carried out by, i.e. the assessor. Generally, this is the organization itself or an external group depending on the purpose of the assessment. Some studies show that different assessors reach different conclusions when the same organization is assessed. This challenge should be addressed by the frameworks in question and a few initiatives have been made in this direction, e.g. TickIT.

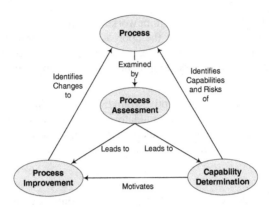

Fig. 2. Software Process Assessment (from [25])

In our taxonomy, assessments are characterized as either "external" or "internal" , or a combination of these.

Process Improvement Method. Some frameworks are purely assessment frameworks, while others include guidelines or process improvement methods used to implement and institutionalize the process improvement. A guideline like this is often called a process improvement life cycle. It "defines the strategy and the process by which improvement is pursued" [6]. This characteristic indicates the type of improvement method included in the framework, if any.

Improvement Initiation. Improvement initiation is related to the previous characteristic and indicates where the improvement work is initiated in the organization. In other words, it is the approach used to achieve improvement. The approach can for example be *top-down* or *bottom-up*. However, other approaches exist as well, e.g. SPICE initiates the improvement work at the level of *process instances*. A combination of these approaches could also have been used.

McGarry and Thomas have written an excellent article [19] comparing the top-down and bottom-up approach. The main difference is between *generality* (universal good practices exist and the organization's processes should be compared with these) and *specificity* (the importance of the local domain should be recognized).

Improvement Focus. Some frameworks focus primarily on experience reuse, whereas others concentrate on management processes or other areas. They differ in improvement focus, i.e. which SPI activities they regard as essential for improvement.

The difference between the focus and the goal characteristic, which will be described later, might not be clear and it deserves some extra attention. Improvement focus is related to activities and deals with the means of achieving the end result. It is therefore placed in the process category. In contrast, the goal characteristic is only concerned with the end result not how it was achieved.

Analysis Techniques. Their use of analysis techniques can also be employed to classify process improvement frameworks. Some frameworks use quantitative techniques, others qualitative and still others might not use any defined techniques at all. Examples of analysis techniques are questionnaires, statistical process control, various measurements etc.

3.3 Organization Category

The characteristics in the organization category are directly related to attributes of the organization and environment in which the SPI framework is used, i.e. who is involved and for what kind of organization is the framework applicable.

Actors/Roles/Stakeholders. Each framework has its own primary actors, which are the people, groups or organizations affected by or taking part in the improvement process. Generally, each such actor or stakeholder has a predefined role in the improvement process.

Organization Size. This characteristic indicates the organization size for which the SPI approach is suitable. Some frameworks are so comprehensive that only large corporations have the resources to use them. Other approaches are easier for smaller companies to employ. However, this relation between organization size and cost-effectiveness is hard to pinpoint and has been heavily debated [6] [8].

Coherence. Coherence is the logical connection between engineering factors and factors related to the business or organization. In an article by Cattaneo et al. [6] this was pointed out as extremely important for a successful SPI implementation, yet still insufficient in many process improvement frameworks. Cattaneo et al. stated that "most software process improvement efforts limit their focus and concern to the technical and engineering aspects of software development [...] They do not consider the relationships between these engineering factors and organizational and market variables."

There are two types of coherence and both should be maximized for the greatest benefits [6]:

- *Internal coherence* – The fit among the different parts of a company, such as organization, technology, human resources, strategy and culture.
- *External coherence* – The fit between the organization and its environment, including market, customers and competitors.

3.4 Quality Category

The quality category deals with characteristics related to the quality dimension by pointing out aspects such as how progression is measured, whose quality perspective is employed and what that means in terms of quality indicators and causal relations.

Quality Perspective. When looking at quality, it is necessary to establish a clear understanding of whose quality perspective the approach adopts. The concept of quality will naturally be different depending on who is asked. For example, the management will have a different quality perspective compared to what a customer might have.

Progression. If the SPI framework is looked upon as a road map, progression along the road can be characterized as "flat" , "staged" or "continuous" as shown in Figure 3. ISO 9000 is a typical flat framework with only one step, namely certification. One cannot be more or less certified. On the other hand, in the CMM there is a discrete ladder of staged maturity levels, each indicating a specific level of process quality. There are also approaches that proclaim a continuous and evolutionary quality progression, e.g. TQM and QIP.

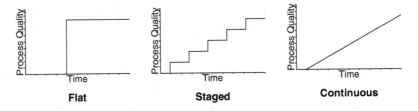

Fig. 3. The Progression Characteristic

Causal Relation. SPI frameworks assume that product quality is affected by the quality of the process used to produce it. However, process quality is difficult to determine and therefore most frameworks measure some *quality indicator* instead (cf. section 1). This suggests the following *causal relation*:

$$F(\textit{Quality indicator}) \Rightarrow \textbf{Quality}(\textit{Process}) \Rightarrow \textbf{Quality}(\textit{Product}) \tag{2}$$

If an improvement can be detected in the quality indicator, the quality of the process is regarded as better and we should expect an improvement in product quality as well.

The quality indicator used differs among the frameworks, but is in all cases based on factors assumed to influence the process and product quality. We have used the functions $F(x)$, $F'(x)$, $F''(x)$ and so on to indicate such relationships. For example, equation (3) shows us that there is a relationship between the SPI framework and the quality indicator used. Furthermore, there is a relationship between this quality indicator and the quality of the process and the product:

$$F''(\textit{SPI framework}) \Rightarrow F'(\textit{Quality indicator}) \Rightarrow \textbf{Quality}(\textit{Process}) \Rightarrow \tag{3}$$
$$\textbf{Quality}(\textit{Product})$$

None of the frameworks explicitly states a causal relation like those above. However, they are implicit and this paper proposes this explicit representation.

Comparative. Some frameworks are comparative in nature, meaning that they can be used to compare certain aspects of different organizational units, either internally or externally. The aspect compared may vary between the frameworks, but it is supposed to represent an objective comparison criterion. For example, two organizations assessed using the CMM can be compared on the basis of their maturity levels, i.e. the one with the higher maturity level is assumed to have the higher process quality as well. In contrast, when using ISO 9000 the only comparison that can be made is whether the organizations are certified, a very coarse characterization.

Frameworks that are not comparative are only used as guidelines within a single project or organization.

3.5 Result Category

This category treats characteristics that describe the results of employing an SPI framework, but also the costs of reaching these results and the methods used to validate them.

Goal. The goal of the framework is its primary objective or end result, i.e. what is achieved by using the framework. As discussed previously it differs from the improvement focus characteristic by only treating the end result, not the means of getting there.

Process Artifacts. Process artifacts are the "things" created as a result of adopting an SPI framework. The process-related artifacts can be tangible, such as documents containing process models, improvement plans, experience data etc. However, the artifacts can also be intangible, e.g. increased knowledge in the organization. In either case, the process artifacts are created in addition to the actual product being produced.

Certification. The International Organization for Standardization (ISO) and a variety of national standard bodies have developed standards to which an organization can be certified. Only conformance with the minimum requirements is measured in the certification process. A standard to which one can be certified is comparative by nature.

Certification is closely related to the flat quality progression previously discussed, indicating that not all SPI approaches lead to certification. There has been some debate on whether a certain CMM level can be regarded as equivalent to ISO 9000 certification.

Implementation Cost. The implementation cost is naturally an important characteristic, because it often dictates whether the approach is financially feasible. There are considerable cost differences among the frameworks, making some impossible for smaller organizations to adopt. Emam et al. [8] state that "the implementation of certain processes or process management practices may not be as cost-effective for small organizations as for large ones" . However, the exact impact of organization size on cost is not obvious.

Because the cost is affected by a number of factors outside the SPI framework, it will be impossible to provide exact numbers in this characteristic. However, rough estimates should be provided where such numbers can be obtained, for example from case studies and other validation efforts. A set of articles on SPI cost/benefits is recently published by Curtis and co-workers in [7]. Some factors that can influence cost estimates are:

- *Organizations specific attributes* – For example organization size.
- *Inconsistent use of cost models* – Different cost models are used, variation in cost/benefit analysis, disagreement on measurement unit, disagreement on which SPI expenses to include in the cost estimates.

Even if the validity of the implementation costs may be questionable, a decision has been made to include it as a characteristic. However, the currently existing cost data is so limited in nature that its inclusion could have given a distorted, biased or even wrong view of reality. The reader will therefore notice that this characteristic is empty for all the frameworks. As more data is collected, some missing data can be included, e.g. as averages or medians, and with standard deviations or min/max values.

Validation. Validation is needed to evaluate whether the improvement efforts have actually worked. Such validation should distinguish between improvements resulting from SPI efforts and improvements resulting from other factors (context). The question we want answered, is whether the same benefits would have been achieved without a comprehensive SPI effort or with an alternative SPI effort. In other words, the difficulty lies in establishing a direct causal relation between the SPI effort and the achieved improvements. Figure 4 shows this problem. For instance, a major success factor may be the actual technology being used, e.g. OO, reuse, inspections etc.

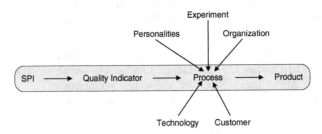

Fig. 4. Multifactor Problem

Some authors have reported that some "improvement" seems to be the outcome, regardless of the activities initiated (Figure 5: a possible "Hawthorne effect"?). Other initial improvements can be attributed to the elimination of obvious process deficiencies ("hot spots") [6][17]. Both these factors illustrate that real, causal benefits are hard to show. Often the actual improvement gains are only seen after 2-3 years ("process refinement"). However, software organizations often experience rapid evolution ("product innovation"), where products become obsolete over that time span -- cf. the term "Internet time" .

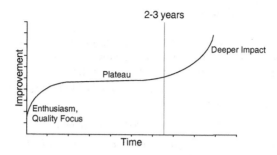

Fig. 5. Immediate vs. Deeper Impact

There have been several attempts to validate the effects of SPI frameworks, e.g. [12][13][15][17]. However, several critical questions can be raised against them:

- *Non-representative* – It is likely that successful organizations are more eager to publish their case studies than unsuccessful organizations [12].
- *Inconclusive* – Often only very vague conclusions are reached, such as "CMM seems to pay off" and "those respondents who reported a better performance tended to be from higher maturity organizations" [12]. Words like "seems" and "tended" reveal that a definitive causal relation between the SPI effort and the achieved improvement is hard to find.
- *Insufficient validation in general* – Many software engineering papers have insufficient or no validation, often based on ad hoc methods [27][30].
- *Less than favorable experiences* – A paper by Herbsleb and Goldenson [12] shows that quite a few people describe SPI as having no or very little effect (26%), or even being counterproductive (4%). To another question 49% answered that they were disillusioned over the lack of results.

However, the scope of this paper is merely to characterize and provide guidance for selection of SPI frameworks, not to demonstrate or validate their effectiveness.

4   Concluding Remarks

The proposed taxonomy has been applied to six SPI frameworks: TQM, CMM v1.1, ISO 9000, ISO/IEC 15504 (SPICE), QIP/EF/GQM, and SPIQ – see Table 2.

There are some cases where a characteristic may not be applicable for a given SPI framework. Those cases are indicated by NA for "Not applicable" . Furthermore, the scope of our taxonomy is rather extensive, so some characteristics could not be determined. The reason could be unavailability of information, or the necessity of further exploration and experimentation. In either case, these characteristic are marked with a dash (-). The reader should be aware of this difference between a characteristic that is not relevant and a characteristic that has yet to be determined.

4.1 Taxonomy Contributions

The goal of the taxonomy was stated in the introduction. It has been proposed as an objective method for comparing SPI frameworks and as a starting point for information gathering. Said differently, it is a high-level tool for use in the process of selecting which SPI framework should be employed in an organization. As such it is indirectly influencing product quality:

$$\mathbf{F'''}(Taxonomy) \Rightarrow \mathbf{F''}(SPI\ framework) \Rightarrow \tag{4}$$
$$\mathbf{F'}(Quality\ indicator) \Rightarrow \mathbf{Quality}(Process) \Rightarrow \mathbf{Quality}(Product)$$

The taxonomy in itself does not provide enough information to enable a sound decision in this selection process. However, it points out areas of interest for someone investigating different SPI frameworks. Such a high-level comparison is needed because of the multitude, diversity and comprehensiveness of current SPI frameworks. It is a daunting and costly task to learn about all of them. Clearly it is valuable to quickly get an overview, so that one or a few frameworks can be chosen for further investigation.

A natural question to ask is whether company SPI efforts, that have been only partially successful, have employed the "wrong" SPI framework. To be successful, the framework's quality indicators must represent the relevant quality of the process and product -- cf. the characteristics "coherence" and "validation" . Typical process qualities are development time and cost, while product quality could be reliability, usability, or even fancyness. It is tempting to "over-structure" the process, and rely too much on the process quality indicators. Further, it is difficult to say that one process indicator or SPI framework is better than another, as long as the customer is satisfied. For example, Nokia has largely been assessed to CMM level 1, while its competitor Motorola has many of its departments on CMM level 5. Even so, Nokia hardly appears inferior to a customer.

The causal relation stated first in this section implies that the taxonomy ultimately affects product quality. However, this through-going causal relation is vague, and *validating* the taxonomy in this respect is close to impossible. Much of the vagueness, however, stems from the problematic causal relation between a given SPI framework and product quality, not being the subject of this paper. A validation of our taxonomy should therefore consider it *in its own right* -- whether it is fit for its purpose. We will therefore only consider the first step in the causal relation:

$$\mathbf{F'''}(Taxonomy) \Rightarrow \mathbf{F''}(SPI\ framework) \tag{5}$$

There are two sides of this. First, it should be indicated how the taxonomy leads to the selection of the "right" SPI framework, as suggested by the causal relation between them. Secondly, the relation above implies that there are several ways that SPI frameworks can be objectively compared, i.e. the choice of SPI framework is a function of the comparison method. A validation effort should therefore include evidence that the taxonomy represents an appropriate comparison method.

With respect to *appropriateness*: The proposed taxonomy is based on an in-depth literature study of *commonly used characteristics* to describe and compare SPI frameworks. It is built on previous comparison work [6][24][28]. The taxonomy has been applied to six SPI frameworks, and we believe it can be applied to other as well.

Further, the taxonomy is very *compact* and provides a quick way of acquiring knowledge. Thus the taxonomy represents an appropriate way of pragmatically describing the frameworks on a *high level*.

Up until this point, little has been said about the *objectivity* of the taxonomy. It is possible to determine some of the characteristics objectively, but not e.g. implementation cost. However, the same argument applies to other comparison methods.

Comprehensibility and *usefulness* are the most important aspects of the taxonomy, and should be used in an *empirical validation* to assess *company satisfaction*. A newcomer to SPI should have little trouble using the taxonomy, while an experienced SPI user should be able to infer even more information. It should also be useful for beginner companies that want to start a systematic SPI effort, and for more mature companies that want to combine parts of different SPI frameworks (e.g. ISO 9000 and CMM).

Table 1. SPI framework causal relations. (F' is split into F1' and F2' for three frameworks, and is similar for the last two).

SPI Framework	Causal Relation
TQM	Not applicable
CMM	**F1'**(*Key Process areas*) $\Rightarrow$ **F2'**(*Maturity level*) $\Rightarrow$ **Quality**(*Process*) $\Rightarrow$ **Quality**(*Product*)
ISO 9000	**F1'**(*Quality elements*) $\Rightarrow$ **F2'**(*Certification*) $\Rightarrow$ **Quality**(*Process*) $\Rightarrow$ **Quality**(*Product*)
ISO/IEC 15504 (SPICE)	**F1'**(*Process attributes*) $\Rightarrow$ **F2'**(*Capability level*) $\Rightarrow$ **Quality**(*Process*) $\Rightarrow$ **Quality**(*Product*)
QIP/GQM/EF	**F'**(*Experience reuse*) $\Rightarrow$ **Quality**(*Process*) $\Rightarrow$ **Quality**(*Product*)
SPIQ	**F'**(*Experience reuse*) $\Rightarrow$ **Quality**(*Process*) $\Rightarrow$ **Quality**(*Product*)

5 Further Work

We have seen that the proposed taxonomy seems reasonable from a theoretical standpoint. However, there are many issues that can only be answered through practical use and further investigation:

- *Cost* – An evaluation of the costs/benefits incurred from use of the taxonomy, for example in terms of training and competence building. We also need more cost data on implementation of the various frameworks.
- *Effectiveness* – Which parts of the framework seem to be the most useful, for whom and for what? We may apply the Goal Question Metric (GQM) method on the taxonomy itself, in order to assess its usability to help making right SPI decisions.
- *Ease-of-use* – Which parts or subsets of the taxonomy appear to be the easiest or hardest to use?

- *Taxonomy as basis for mapping* – Investigation on how the taxonomy can be used as a basis for a more detailed mapping approach.

References

1. Ares Juan, Garcia Rafael, Juristo Natalia, López Marta, Moreno Ana M., A more rigorous and comprehensive approach to software process assessment. *Software Process - Improvement and Practice.* Vol. 5, No. 1 (March 2000), pp 3-30.
2. Arthur Lowell J., *Improving Software Quality - An Insider's Guide to TQM.* John Wiley, 1993.
3. Bamford Robert C., Deibler William J. II, Comparing, contrasting ISO 9001 and the SEI capability maturity model, *Computer*, Vol. 26, No. 10, Oct. 1993.
4. Basili Victor R. The Experience Factory and its Relationship to Other Improvement Paradigms. *4th European Software Engineering Conf. (ESEC'93)*, Springer Verlag LNCS 517, 1993, pp 68-83.
5. Basili Victor R., Caldiera Gianluigi, Rombach H.-Dieter, *Goal Question Metric Approach.* Encyclopedia of Software Engineering (John J. Marciniak, Ed.), John Wiley, 1994, Vol. 1, pp. 528-532.
6. Cattaneo F., Fuggetta A. and Sciuto D., Pursuing Coherence in Software Process Assessment and Improvement. Forthcoming in *Software Process - Improvement and Practice*, 2001, 46 p.
7. Curtis, Bill, The Global Pursuit of Process Maturity, IEEE Software, Vol. 17, No. 4 (July/Aug. 2000), p. 76-78 (introduction to special issue on SPI results).
8. Emam Khaled El and Briand Lionel, *Chapter 7 - Costs and Benefits of Software Process Improvement (part of future book).* Fraunhofer IESE, Kaiserslautern, Germany, 1997.
9. Emam Khaled El, Drouin Jean-Normand, Melo Walcélio, *SPICE - The Theory and Practice of Software Process Improvement and Capability dEtermination.* IEEE CS-Press, Nov. 1997, 450 p.
10. Halvorsen Christian P. and Conradi Reidar, A Taxonomy for SPI Frameworks, *24th NASA Software Engineering Workshop*, Greenbelt/Washington, USA, 1--2 Dec.1999, 4 p. See http://sel.gsfc.nasa.gov/website/sew/1999/program.html. Also as NTNU SU-report 19/99.
11. Haase V. H., Software process assessment concepts. *Journal of Systems Architecture*, Vol. 42, Nr. 8, Dec. 1996, pp 621-631.
12. Herbsleb James D. and Goldenson Dennis R., A Systematic Survey of CMM Experience and Results. *18th Int'l Conf. on Software Engineering (ICSE'96)*, Berlin, March1996, IEEE-CS Press, pp 323-330.
13. Herbsleb James, Carleton Anita, Rozum James, Siegel Jane, Zubrow David, Benefits of CMM-Based Software Process Improvement: Initial Results. *Tech. Report CMU/SEI-94-TR-13*, Aug. 1994, 53 p.
14. Humphrey Watts S., *Managing the Software Process.* Addison-Wesley, 1989.
15. Kautz Karlheinz and Larsen Even Åby, *Diffusion and Use of Quality Assurance and Software Process Improvement Approaches in Norway: A Survey-Based Study.* (Report no 906, 25 p. Norwegian Computing Center, Oslo, April 1996. ESPITI project.)
16. Kitchenham B. A., Evaluating Software Engineering Methods and Tools. *ACM SIGSOFT Software Engineering Notes*, 1996.
17. Løken Cecilie B. and Skramstad Torbjørn, ISO 9000 Certification - Experiences from Europe. 11 p. *First World Congress for Software Quality*, San Francisco, June 1995.
18. Lonchamp Jacques, A Structured Conceptual and Terminological Framework for Software Process Engineering. *Second Int'l Conference on the Software Process.* IEEE-CS Press, 1993, pp 41-53.
19. McGarry Frank and Thomas Martyn, Top-Down vs. Bottom-Up Process Improvement. *IEEE Software*, July 1994, pp 12-13.

20. Oskarsson Östen, Glass Robert L., *An ISO 9000 Approach to Building Quality Software*. Prentice Hall. 1996.
21. Paulk Mark C., How ISO 9001 Compares with the CMM, *IEEE Software*, Vol. 12, No. 1 (Jan 1995), pp 74-82.
22. Paulk Mark C., Weber Charles V., Curtis Bill, Chrissis Mary Beth et al., *The Capability Maturity Model: Guidelines for Improving the Software Process*. Addison-Wesley, 1995.
23. Software Engineering Institute, *Top-Level Standards Map - ISO 12207, ISO 15504 (Jan 1998 TR), Software CMM v1.1 and v2 Draft C*. (Internal report Software Engineering Institute, Feb. 28, 1998.)
24. Sørumgård Sivert, Verification of Process Conformance in Empirical Studies of Software Development. IDI doctoral thesis 1997:14, NTNU, 252 p.
25. SPICE 1998, *Software Process Improvement and Capability dEtermination Web Site*. [Online]. Accessible from: http://www.seq.iit.nrc.ca/spice/ [Last accessed: 12.01.2001]
26. Dybå Tore (ed.): *SPIQ - Software Process Improvement for better Quality: Method Handbook (in Norwegian)* (SINTEF/NTNU/UiO), Trondheim/Oslo, ISSN 0802-6394, Jan. 2000, ca. 250 p.
27. Tichy Walter F., Should Computer Scientists Experiment More? *IEEE Computer*, May 1998, pp 32-40.
28. Tingey Michael O., *Comparing ISO 9000, Malcolm Baldridge, and the SEI CMM for software: a reference and selection guide*. Upper Saddle River: Prentice-Hall, 1997.
29. Zahran Sami, *Software Process Improvement - Practical Guidelines for Business Success*. Essex: Addison Wesley Longman, 1998.
30. Zelkowitz Marvin V. and Wallace Dolores, Experimental validation in software engineering. *Information and Software Technology*, Vol. 39, 1997, pp 735-743.

Appendix: The Taxonomy Applied to Six SPI Frameworks

Table 2. The Taxonomy Applied to TQM, CMM v1.1 and ISO 9000

Category	Characteristic	TQM	CMM v1.1	ISO 9000
General	Geographic Origin/ Spread	Japan/World	U.S./World	Europe/World
	Scientific Origin	Quality control	TQM, SPC	[3]
	Development/ Stability	Entire post-war era	Since 1986	Since 1987
	Popularity	High (esp. in Japan)	Top (esp. in U.S.)	High (esp. in Europe)
	Software Specific	No	Yes	No
	Prescriptive/ Descriptive	Descriptive	Both	Both
	Adaptability	Yes	Limited	Limited
Process	Assessment	None	Org. maturity	Process
	Assessor	NA[2]	Internal and external	External
	Process Improvement Method	PDCA	IDEAL	None
	Improvement Initiation	Top-down	Top-down	NA[2]
	Improvement Focus	Management processes	Management processes	Management processes
	Analysis Techniques	7QC, 7MP, SPC, QFD	Assessment questionnaires	ISO guidelines and checklists
Organ- ization	Actors/Roles/ Stakeholders	Customer, employees, management	Management	Customer, supplier
	Organization Size	Large	Large	Large
	Coherence	Internal and external	Internal	Internal and limited external
Quality	Quality Perspective	Customer	Management	Customer
	Progression	Continuous	Staged	Flat
	Causal Relation	NA[2]	**F1'**(*Key process areas*) $\Rightarrow$ **F2'**(*Maturity level*) $\Rightarrow$ **Q**(*Process*) $\Rightarrow$ **Q**(*Product*)	**F1'**(*Quality elements*) $\Rightarrow$ **F2'**(*Certification*) $\Rightarrow$ **Q**(*Process*) $\Rightarrow$ **Q**(*Product*)
	Comparative	No	Yes, maturity level	Yes, certification
Result	Goal	Customer satisfaction	Process improvement, supplier capability determination	Establish core management processes
	Process Artifacts	Plans, diagrams	Process documentation, assessment result	Process documentation, certificate
	Certification	No	No	Yes
	Implementation Cost	[3]	[3]	[3]
	Validation	None	Surveys and case studies	Survey

---

[2] Not applicable.
[3] Not yet determined.

Table 3. The Taxonomy applied to ISO/IEC 15504, QIP/EF/GQM and SPIQ

Category	Characteristic	ISO/IEC 15504	QIP/EF/GQM	SPIQ
General	Geographic Origin/ Spread	World/World	U.S./World	Norway/Norway
	Scientific Origin	CMM, Bootstrap, Trillium, SPQA	Partly TQM	TQM, QIP/EF/GQM, ESSI model
	Development/ Stability	Under development	Since 1976	Under development
	Popularity	Growing	Medium	Norway only
	Software Specific	Yes	Yes	Yes
	Prescriptive/ Descriptive	Both	Descriptive	Descriptive
	Adaptability	Yes	Yes	Yes
Process	Assessment	Process maturity	None	Customer satisfaction
	Assessor	Internal and external	NA[4]	Limited internal
	Process Improvement Method	SPICE Doc. part 7	QIP	Two-level PDCA
	Improvement Initiation	Process instance	Iterative bottom-up	Top-down and iterative, bottom-up
	Improvement Focus	Management processes	Experience reuse	Experience reuse
	Analysis Techniques	Several (manual and automated). Required.	GQM	GQM, QFD, 7QC, 7MP
Organ- ization	Actors/Roles/ Stakeholders	Management	Experience factory, project organization	Customer, experience factory, project org., sponsoring org.
	Organization Size	All	All	All
	Coherence	Internal	Internal	Internal and external
Quality	Quality Perspective	Management	All	Customer, all
	Progression	Continuous (staged at process instance level)	Continuous	Continuous
	Causal Relation	$\mathbf{F1'}$(*Process attributes*) $\Rightarrow$ $\mathbf{F2'}$(*Capability level*) $\Rightarrow$ $\mathbf{Q}$(*Process*) $\Rightarrow$ $\mathbf{Q}$(*Product*)	$\mathbf{F'}$(*Experience reuse*) $\Rightarrow \mathbf{Q}$(*Process*) $\Rightarrow$ $\mathbf{Q}$(*Product*), but feedback loops here	$\mathbf{F'}$(*Experience reuse*) $\Rightarrow \mathbf{Q}$(*Process*) $\Rightarrow$ $\mathbf{Q}$(*Product*)
	Comparative	Yes, maturity profile	No	No
Result	Goal	Process assessment	Organization specific	Increased competitiveness
	Process Artifacts	Process profile, assessment record	Experience packages, GQM models	Experience packages, GQM models
	Certification	No	No	No
	Implementation Cost	_[5]	_[5]	_[5]
	Validation	Document review, trials (case studies and surveys)	Experimental and case studies	Experimental and case studies

---

[4] Not applicable.
[5] Not yet determined.

Configuration Management Culture as the Kernel to Success in Software Process Improvement Efforts

Thomas C. Green and Kenneth M. Anderson

University of Colorado, Boulder {tomg,kena}@cs.colorado.edu

Abstract. For a Software Process Improvement (SPI) effort to succeed, its participants must have a sense of ownership. One practical technique for achieving that sense of ownership is to apply a meta-process based on the principals of configuration management (CM) to the SPI effort. This paper provides insight into issues of ownership surrounding actual SPI efforts and describes the use of a CM-based meta-process that successfully supported one of these efforts.

1   Introduction

Many software organizations have attempted Software Process Improvement (SPI) efforts in order to achieve higher quality products and more efficient development. Few succeed, although some achieve a measurable level of success. Of those that succeed, few are able to hold onto that success. Why do software organizations fail to make beneficial improvements? Why are some organizations unable to hold onto these improvements?

Under the Software Engineering Institute's (SEI) Capability Maturity Model (CMM) there are five levels of maturity [Hu1]. Studies have shown that the median time to move from CMM Level 1 (Initial) to Level 2 (Repeatable) is 25 months of improvement effort. However, it is not unheard of for this transition to take over six years. Another 22 months is the median for movement from Level 2 to Level 3 (Defined), with some organizations requiring over four years. For software groups where data is available, 18.8% remain at the same level or slip back a level at their subsequent assessment [SE1]. The percentage that slip back from Level 2 to Level 1 reported in the study is likely smaller than actual. Data is available only from groups that voluntarily report their data to the SEI. If an organization slips, they may not be inclined to report their results.

Some organizations, however, are able to improve their processes faster than the norm. Furthermore, some organizations never slip back to their old ways. Why is it that some groups are so successful, while others fail?

One key factor is management commitment. If an organization's managers are not committed and supportive of the required software process changes, then the improvements are doomed to failure. Our purpose in writing this paper is to suggest a deeper reason as to why management commitment helps make SPI efforts succeed. That reason is ownership of the SPI effort by all stakeholders:

V. Ambriola (Ed.): EWSPT 2001, LNCS 2077, pp. 236–241, 2001.
© Springer-Verlag Berlin Heidelberg 2001

management and individual contributors (ICs). The ownership by management bolsters their commitment to make the SPI effort successful. The ownership by ICs allows them to accept the changes to the ways they must perform their work. In this paper, we present insight into actual SPI efforts and draw from this experience a process that can help SPI participants gain a sense of ownership and control over the effort, and help increase their chances of success.

2   Background

The first author was personally involved in SEI/CMM-based SPI efforts in several oranizations. He experienced these efforts from a range of possible stakeholders: as an individual contributor, a software group manager, a project manager, and as an SPI consultant. Each organization started their SPI effort with the goal of achieving CMM Level 2. As such, they each began by creating documents to support Requirements Management (RM), Software Project Planning (SPP), Software Project Tracking and Oversight (PTO), Software Configuration Management (SCM), Software Quality Assurance (SQA), and Software Subcontract Management (SM).

These processes are supposed to be documented "as is" (i.e., the current methods being used to develop software at the organization are captured). Unfortunately, what is typically created is something beyond "as is". The process documenters start out intending to document the "as is" process. Yet, as they see the inherent problems, they add text describing what *should* be done. These additions to the process, however, have not been proposed or approved by the rest of the organization. The stakeholders who need to have ownership of these types of changes are excluded, however unintentionally, from the documentation process.

3   Meta-process

In these situations, a "process for the process", or meta-process, is needed. In such a meta-process, a procedure is defined for the constant improvement of the processes of the organization (See Fig. 1). The organization needs to recognize this meta-process to achieve success. As an organization matures, it recognizes the importance of controlling work products via configuration management (CM). Requirements, design, code, and test documents all need to be under CM control. The earlier the organization understands the SPI effort also needs to be under CM control, the faster and more effective the SPI effort will be.

Applying software development techniques (in this case, CM) to software processes is not a novel idea given Osterweil's assertion that "Software Processes are Software Too..." [Os1], and Sutton's suggestion to use CM to support software process [Su2]. However, it is by no means obvious how configuration management techniques can be applied to SPI efforts in a practical fashion. Our experience provides insight into how any organization can incorporate CM techniques into their SPI efforts and how these techniques can instill a sense of ownership in an SPI effort by its stakeholders.

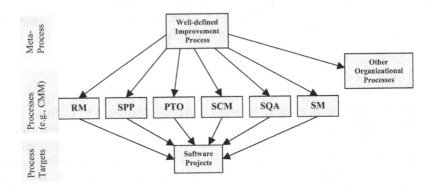

Fig. 1. Relationship of meta-process to regular processes

Processes are not static. Nonetheless, many early SPI efforts start by documenting their processes as if they are. The mere intention of the group to start an SPI effort implies their desire to change. Yet they start the SPI effort without any methods in place to allow change to the processes they are creating.

The first time a change is made to a process document in these organizations, problems start appearing. Not coincidentally, these problems are similar to the difficulties encountered by organizations that do not use CM controls on their software work products! For example, who is authorized to suggest changes to the process documents? Who is authorized to approve a change? Who can decide what the actual changes will be? What are the risks involved in making the change? Once a change is approved, who is authorized to make the change? Where are the new process documents stored? Where are previous versions kept? Who needs to be notified of the change? Will training be involved as a result of the change? When are ICs expected to implement the change?

These are all questions that need to be answered for software documents as part of a mature CM process and, we argue, they also need to be answered for SPI documents. At one of the first author's organizations, process documents were not kept under CM control. Typically the original author of a document made changes at his or her discretion, and then notified *some* people of the changes. Soon, different people in the organization had different versions of the process documents. Since various members of the organization were following different processes, the organization found itself back in the chaos of CMM Level 1!

4   Implementing the Meta-process

In another of the first author's organizations, a change management system for all process documents was instituted. All documents, including checklists, procedure manuals, and the like, were placed into PVCS, a commercially available source management system. With this system in place, all stakeholders who needed to refer to a process document retrieved the latest version of the document from the process document repository. In addition, the latest version of each document was made available on the organizational intranet. This action alone solved the problem of ensuring that all stakeholders had access to the correct version of a process document.

The next step involved ensuring changes to a process document in the repository could not occur without prior authorization. This step was straightforward since PVCS already contained this feature.

Next, the organization needed a method to make change requests (CRs) on the process documents. To handle this task, the organization adapted their existing defect management system. Process documents were treated like any other software artifact, and any stakeholder could enter CRs against any process document. It was also possible to enter a more general request, for example, for a new type of process document.

This organization also implemented a defect review process via a Configuration Control Board (CCB) for their software documents. This system was applied to process documents. Weekly meetings were instituted to review process CRs. In this organization a single meeting was possible for all process documents. Depending on group size and expertise, several different review meetings might be held in other organizations.

The Process Configuration Control Board (PCCB) then reviewed each CR. If additional information was required it was assigned to an accountable person to research and/or retrieve for a future PCCB meeting. Each CR was given a disposition, similar to software document defect dispositions (e.g., rejected, approved, waiting for information, on hold) Representative process users needed to participate on the PCCB to ensure users accepted the change(s).

If the process document was approved for change, someone was assigned to make the change. The change was then inspected, via a peer review process, and given approval for check-in to the process document repository. At this point, if stakeholders always referred to the repository for their tasks, the changes would readily be incorporated into the organization's day-to-day work. Unfortunately, this ideal situation does not occur in practice. Thus, the final step was to notify stakeholders affected by the change, providing details and/or training.

The above meta-process can be easy to implement for any organization already using good CM procedures. It requires the management of an additional set of documents, using existing CM processes, for process changes.

For those organizations not currently following good CM procedures, it is recommended that the CR submission process closely follow the culturally accepted methods for making changes. This makes the new CR procedure more palatable, and it can be improved, over time, with the meta-process.

5 How to Start a Process Improvement Effort

It is our belief that this meta-process is an excellent candidate for being the first process adopted by an organization when starting an SPI effort. In summary, start by creating a source repository for process documents. Place whatever process documents the organization has, if any, into the repository. Then define a meta-process to guide the addition and/or improvement of the process documents, as discussed in the previous section. This improvement process should be monitored with a peer review process (which is defined in a process document, stored in the repository, and improved by the meta-process). It is our contention, that with this simple kernel in place, any software organization can achieve process improvement over time. It is our further contention that this improvement can be accomplished under any improvement model desired (e.g., SEI/CMM, SPICE) and even with no model at all.

Organizational change is not easy. To change, the culture has to change. In large organizations this is difficult, since culture change requires changes by many different people. By making the meta-process the start of a process improvement effort, the cultural change can be smaller. The organization begins by creating a culture that supports change. Then the SPI effort can slowly introduce the changes that are needed to improve the quality of the organization's software development processes. Once an organization has the meta-process in place, then anyone in the organization can make suggestions for improvement. Furthermore, these change requests will have a place to go, will be reviewed, and if changes are made, affected personnel will be notified.

6 Achieving Early Ownership

The first author has developed informal steps for beginning an SPI effort. In particular, each stakeholder is asked to submit at least ten CRs about how the organization's process should change. These CRs should contain a recommended solution, if possible, to help speed the review process. As a manager, the first author found most stakeholders have *at least* ten issues about how poorly their organization is run!

In applying this method, an interesting result occurs. Management is able to say things like "Don't complain, submit a change request!" This helps instill ownership of the process across all stakeholders right from the start. Everyone must take on the ownership and responsibility of how the organization operates and solves its process problems.

Having ten CRs submitted from every member of the organization, managers and individual contributors included, causes an initial avalanche of suggestions. This flood of activity jump-starts the improvement process and sets the stage for a culture change. It also places responsibility on management to take CR submissions seriously. Management must allow for the effort to digest the suggestions as soon as possible or the SPI movement will die. Stakeholders must see changes occurring and suggestions implemented, or their requests will cease.

Once the meta-process is visibly operating, stakeholders submit CRs whenever they notice something did not execute optimally. Managers submit CRs when major defects appear. ICs submit CRs when they do not get the work products they need to perform their jobs. This meta-process, once started and ownership by all stakeholders has been established, is self-correcting. For instance, the meta-process itself receives CRs and is improved. Even with organizations that do not follow any particular process improvement model, the changes implemented over time will move them to higher levels of effectiveness.

A useful meta-process metric is to note the number of CRs submitted per unit time (e.g., week or month). A healthy meta-process will continue to have CRs submitted as the organization matures. If the CRs per month drops significantly, it indicates a drop in ownership.

Another metric to check is the number of CRs implemented to the number of CRs submitted. A low ratio indicates inflexibility or a slow review process.

If an organization attempts to follow a particular process improvement model, the meta-process can help accelerate improvements. With a meta-process established, it is possible to submit CRs like "We need a Software Quality Assurance Procedure (SQAP)", or "We need a template for software requirements documents, draft attached". Following a model like the SEI/CMM, one can submit CRs that will help the organization follow the next step in the model. For SEI/CMM Level 2 that would include requests for documents and procedures that implement RM, SPP, PTO, SQA, SCM, and SM.

7   Conclusion

In this paper, we describe the experience, and lessons learned, of the first author in participating in actual SPI efforts. This experience has provided insights into how to start a practical SPI effort, based on configuration management techniques, that instills a sense of ownership to the overall process. We have argued that this sense of ownership is critical to the success of the effort. We intend to expand on this work in the future by developing a detailed set of heuristics, with accompanying tool support, to study and make software process improvement techniques more practical and easily applied by software organizations.

References

Hu1.   Humphrey, W.S. (1989). *Managing the Software Process*. Addison-Wesley, Reading, MA, USA.

Os1.   Osterweil, Leon J. (1997). Software Processes Are Software Too, Revisited. In *Proceedings of the Nineteenth International Conference on Software Engineering (ICSE 1997)*, pp. 540-548. May 17-23, 1997. Boston, MA, USA.

SE1.   Software Engineering Measurement and Analysis Team. (2000). *Process Maturity Profile of the Software Community, 2000 Mid-Year Update*. Software Engineering Institute.

Su2.   Sutton, Stanley M., Jr. (2000). The Role of Process in A Software Start-up. *IEEE Software July/August 2000* pp. 33-39.

Reporting about the Mod Software Process

Giovanni A. Cignoni

Dipartimento di Informatica, Università di Pisa
Corso Italia, 40 Pisa, Italy
giovanni@di.unipi.it

Abstract. This short paper reports about the software process used for the development of *CFS2 mods*. CFS2 is the latest version of MS Combat Flight Simulator; a mod is a modification of the game that adds new features, fixes existing bugs, or enhances its performance. Mods are not developed by MS; indeed there is a wide community of enthusiastic fans of CFS2 – and smart programmers – that provide free mods through the Internet. This community is a completely anarchic one, but, if we carefully observe it, we discover a repeatable software process. The paper provides an inside report of such process and proposes several discussion issues about the differences between this particular context and the more known industrial one.

1. The Context

Since its early versions, *MS Flight Simulator* was implemented as a very open system. Developing add-ons for the game – many will disagree with this definition – has always been a consistent part of the entertainment. *Aircrafts* can be modified in their look and performance, even created from scratch. The same is for *scenarios* (i.e. terrain representations, airports, and cities) and *situations* (things like landing with a damaged engine in a windy day on a short runway, ice probable).

The more than ten-years history of the game counts 7 major releases of the simulator engine with two intermediate releases, 6.5 and 7.5 devoted respectively to *MS Combat Flight Simulator 1* and *2*, the editions that add the fight experience to the game. The last version, CFS2, has a very impressive number of features that can be modified: besides aircraft and scenarios there are *ships* (CFS2 is specifically dedicated to the Pacific Theatre of Operation in World War II) and *ground vehicles*. Aircrafts and all other objects have *weapon* and *damage* profiles. Situations are replaced by far more complex *missions* and *campaigns*. Finally, there are *effects* used to model smokes, explosions, ship wakes and many other visual issues.

From a technical point of view, developing a mod means writing code and integrating it in a new configuration of the CFS2 system. Many different programming languages are involved; here are just some examples. Object as buildings or vehicles are modelled through a procedural 3D language, sources have to be compiled and integrated so than the simulator engine can execute them to actually draw the objects. Effects are programmed as particle systems defined through sets of declarative statements. The dynamic part of a mission is programmed through a pre/post condition language that uses triggers and actions.

V. Ambriola (Ed.): EWSPT 2001, LNCS 2077, pp. 242–245, 2001.

In some cases there are visual tools that help the development process, as, for instance, the *Mission Builder* bundled with the game or the commercial object designers available by third part companies. However, hacking the source code is a common activity, preferred by developers who want to have access to all system features, in particular to those not documented.

Support from MS is poor: the game was shipped in late October 2000 with many bugs; official documentation about the simulator engine is practically non-existent or released sporadically [1]. On the other side, in three months, the mod developer community fixed several important bugs (just to cite two: the incoherent behaviour of some ships and the ghost payload on add-on aircrafts) and provided many new features (seaplanes and ground troops, as two representative examples). The total number of mods available – as freeware – on the Internet is simply uncountable. In the same time, MS did not release any patch or upgrade. One possible explanation of this decision is that MS do not want to deprive people of such entertainment.

Internet plays a central role in this context. The community of mod developers and the wider community of game players (i.e. mod users) live and communicate on the network. Basically, two fundamental services are needed:

- *public repositories*, where developers publish their new mods and users can download them; repositories are generally controlled and content reviewed to assure the quality of the available mods;
- *forums*, where user have news about ongoing projects and receive support; moreover, dedicated forums are used by developers for technical discussions and information exchange; forums are usually moderated.

Several Web sites provide such services. Two of the most representative examples are [2, 3], but many others exist. Access is generally filtered by some requested membership, that, while offered for free, is used to maintain a little order in the community. Besides these loose control mechanisms, all is left to self-regulation.

Developers are very collaborative. Sharing information and results is a general attitude. In many cases help and specific suggestions are directly provided. Joint projects are common and carried out by developers that co-operate using forums and e-mail as co-ordination means.

2.   The Process

Building CFS2 mods is anything but software development. Users and developers are involved, tools are used, and software products are released. Observing the way mods are ideated, implemented and released, it is possible to figure out a process that generally goes through the following phases:

1. *inception*; have the idea, draw a first draft of the mod requirements;
2. *experimentation*; be sure of the mod feasibility; carry out experiments, discuss technical issues through forums;
3. *design*; define how the mod has to be implemented, which files have to be added or modified, which solutions have to be used;
4. *code*; write down the first version of the mod files; also build the test environment, generally one or more missions to test the mod;

5. ***test & debug***; install the mod on your system, test, rework, test, rework, system crash, test, rework, ... eventually the mod will work;
6. ***test & tune***; same as above, but the goal is to fine tune the look and the behavior of the mod; less system crashes, hopefully;
7. ***packaging***; write the documentation, build the distribution;
8. ***final test***; test the distribution, check that documentation is correct;
9. ***deliver***; upload all, report to the forums, mission accomplished!

The mod software process is a rather classic waterfall with three phases, 2, 5, and 6, that internally are highly cyclic and evolutionary. There is a deep distinction between phases 5 and 6 because exiting phase 5 is the true turning point of a project. The whole process is iterated to build a new release of the mod – a mod of the mod.

There are cases in which the process is truly defined, as it is for the *Assembly Line Process* [4], a process devoted to recreate flight models that have less than 1% tolerance with respect to the real specifications of the aircrafts – far more accurate than the stock aircrafts provided with the game. This Cleanroom-like process absolutely forbids the evolutionary approach and provides spreadsheets to check the correspondence of code to specifications.

More generally, the process is not stated or formalized. Many developers, considering themselves artists or historians more than programmers, if directly asked, will deny their connection with a process. However, the process can be observed and considered as a consolidated praxis. In a CMM-like evaluation it will rate something less than level 2: the necessary self-discipline is in place to repeat the process on similar projects, but schedule and costs are not tracked – well, it's a hobby!

3.   Some Discussion Issues

Observing such a particular context (and analysing it under the software process perspective) points out several discussion issues. All of them relate with differences between the anarchic community of mod developers and the – supposed to be – organised commercial software production. It is worth to note that we are talking of a hobby. The performance of the process is out of the debate: it is not possible to compare people developing for the joy of it with people doing that for work.

The first issue is about process definition. Many experiences report about difficulties in the adoption of defined development processes in the software industry. For instance, a survey on 36 enterprises in Centre Italy [5] showed a dramatic situation: 84% of them do not reach ISO 15504 level 1, and 57% never tried to define their development process, even informally. The close observation of a community of hobby developers shows that a basic software process is in place.

The second issue is about the motivations. Process definition is a way to communicate with the customers. This is a goal stated by many standards: from ISO 9001 to ISO 15504, the process is a way to show how the developers will work, as a quality assurance issue, but also as a way to better reporting about project status. To a certain extent, mod developers and mod users are aware of the underlying development process and use it to communicate about advances in the projects.

The third issue is about configuration management, a classic topic in the software process, a particularly crucial one in a context where hundreds of people modify a system that counts more than five thousands files. While it is difficult to have configuration standards applied in the mod community, the need and the willing to have some control are clearly stated. For instance, almost all developers consistently keep versions of their products. The same need is not perceived in the industry, where often configuration is an obscure or misunderstood term.

It is normal that mod developers put a lot of effort in their hobby: they enjoy it. Such effort justifies their successes: maybe they are not smart programmers, they just do many trials. So we cannot conclude that their results derive from their process. But they use versions, ask for configuration management, have a process and use it to communicate with their users. Compared with the commercial software production, this awareness of best practices is an unexpected result.

Acknowledgements. The community of mod developers and users made possible these considerations. I also bored them in the forums with process related questions. Vincenzo Ambriola suggested writing the paper and helped in reviewing it.

Flight Simulator and Combat Flight Simulator are commercial trademarks of Microsoft Corp.

References

1. *MS Combat Flight Simulator*, official site, http://www.microsoft.com/games/combatfs/.
2. *Combat Flight Center*, public repository and forums, http://www.combatfs.com/.
3. *CFS2 Online!*, public repository and forums, http://cfs2.dogfighter.com/.
4. *Flight Model Research Institute*, Assembly Line Process, http://home.socal.rr.com/flighttest/.
5. G. Bucci, M. Campanai, G.A. Cignoni, "Rapid Assessment to solicit Process Improvement in SMEs", Proc. of the *EuroSPI '2000 Conference*, Copenhagen, November 7-9, 2000.

Author Index

Lecture Notes in Computer Science

For information about Vols. 1–1997
please contact your bookseller or Springer-Verlag